AN INTRODUCTION TO WORLD METHODISM

The world Methodist community now numbers over 75 million people in more than 130 countries. The story of Methodism is fascinating and multifaceted because there are so many distinct traditions within it, some stemming directly from Britain and some arising in the United States. In this book, the authors address the issue of what holds all Methodists together and examine the strengths and diversity of an influential major form of Christian life and witness. They look at the ways in which Methodism has become established throughout the world, examining historical and theological developments, and patterns of worship and spirituality, in their various cultural contexts. The book reflects both the lasting contributions of John and Charles Wesley, and the ongoing contribution of Methodism to the ecumenical movement and interreligious relations. It offers both analysis and abundant resources for further study.

KENNETH CRACKNELL is Professor of Theology and Global Studies at the Brite Divinity School, Fort Worth, Texas, and was previously President of the Cambridge Theological Federation, UK.

SUSAN J. WHITE is Alberta H. and Harold L. Lunger Professor of Spiritual Resources and Disciplines at Brite Divinity School, Fort Worth, Texas. Her special expertise is in liturgy and worship.

AN INTRODUCTION TO
WORLD METHODISM

KENNETH CRACKNELL AND SUSAN J. WHITE

CAMBRIDGE
UNIVERSITY PRESS

CAMBRIDGE UNIVERSITY PRESS
Cambridge, New York, Melbourne, Madrid, Cape Town, Singapore, São Paulo

Cambridge University Press
The Edinburgh Building, Cambridge CB2 2RU, UK

Published in the United States of America by Cambridge University Press, New York

www.cambridge.org
Information on this title: www.cambridge.org/9780521818494

First published 2005

Printed in the United Kingdom at the University Press, Cambridge

A catalogue record for this book is available from the British Library

Library of Congress Cataloguing in Publication data
Cracknell, Kenneth.
An Introduction to World Methodism / Kenneth Cracknell and Susan J. White.
p.   cm. – (Introduction to religion)
Includes bibliographical references (p. 268) and index.
ISBN 0-521-81849-4 – ISBN 0-521-52170-X (pb.)
1. Methodism.   I. White, Susan J., 1949–   II. Title.   III. Series.
BX8231.C73   2005
287′.09 – dc22   2004054646

ISBN-13 978-0-521-81849-0 hardback
ISBN-10 0-521-81849-4 hardback
ISBN-13 978-0-521-52170-3 paperback
ISBN-10 0-521-52170-X paperback

Contents

Illustrations

Preface

It is a genuine pleasure to have the opportunity to contribute this volume to the Cambridge University Press's series of introductions to world religious traditions. The editors determined early on that Christianity has too many variations within itself to be treated in a single volume, and our book will stand alongside introductions to Orthodoxy, Roman Catholicism, Anglicanism, and others. At the time of writing, the Methodist family of churches has over 75 million members and adherents throughout the world, and it exercises a powerful influence in ecumenical Christianity and interfaith relations. An account of the history, culture, and theological trajectories of Methodism intended for both students and general readers seems entirely appropriate for the beginning of the twenty-first century.

But the task of writing about Methodism as a world religious phenomenon is more easily proposed than achieved. One major difficulty is that the Methodist churches of today represent two quite distinct traditions. These traditions, of course, have much in common. Both trace their origins to the British Isles and to the life and work of John Wesley (1703–91) and his younger brother Charles (1707–88). Both traditions look to the Wesleys' pastoral-theological writings and hymns as sources of doctrinal, ethical, spiritual, and liturgical reflection. But even before the death of John Wesley, indeed as early as 1784, a separation of Methodism into a British and an American stream had clearly taken place, and the two streams had begun to flow in decidedly different directions. As a consequence, while many introductory volumes to British Methodism and to American Methodism have been written, rare indeed is a work that holds both traditions together.

Adding to the difficulties is the fact that on both sides of the Atlantic these vibrant traditions have enabled additional religious movements to come into being, each of them "Methodist" in its own way. For example, British Wesleyan Methodism not only gave birth to a variety of Methodist sects but was also the seedbed of the Salvation Army, a movement that remains

Methodist in much of its theology. In the United States the Methodist Episcopal Church was equally fecund in producing Methodist offshoots and also gave birth to the immensely significant Holiness movements and, later, to Pentecostalism, both of which retain theological principles that can be broadly described as "Methodist." An introduction to world Methodism will need to help its readers to understand these connections as well.

From its beginnings, the Methodist movement in all its manifestations showed itself extraordinarily able to adapt to a wide variety of social and cultural circumstances, thus adding to the complexity of the picture that must be drawn here. In Britain and the United States it was able to respond to the masses of people impoverished and dispossessed by the industrial revolutions of the eighteenth and nineteenth centuries, as well as to large segments of the Establishment. This feature of Methodism is particularly obvious in the United States, where there were Methodist slaves and Methodist slaveholders, Methodist factory-workers and Methodist factory-owners, as well as a number of Methodist presidents, legislators, and state governors. Missionaries spread the complexities of Methodism further still, as both the American and British churches planted their particular brand of Methodism in the various mission fields around the globe. In these situations, Methodism adapted itself readily to non-European cultures, finding a home in Oceania, Asia, Africa, Latin America, and the Caribbean. Once again, both indigenous populations and colonizers responded to Methodism as a religious option, and large white Methodist churches have been part of the social fabric of Australia, New Zealand, Canada, and South Africa.

To write on all of these themes demands more skills than any two authors can possess, and we owe an enormous debt to the work of others: historians, sociologists, biographers, journalists, geographers, social scientists, and church administrators. We ourselves bring, in the case of one partner, the tools of the church historian and specialist in liturgy and spirituality, and those of the missiologist and historian of religion in the case of the other. One of us is a Methodist from the United States who has lived for a long time in Britain; the other is a British Methodist who has lived for many years in the USA. We are, therefore, "participant observers," looking from the inside at the traditions that have nurtured us, but seeking at the same time to apply to our subject the scholarly detachment in which we have been trained through our respective disciplines.

Accordingly, we aim to offer a picture of world Methodism that avoids certain tendencies that have shaped much of previous Methodist historiography. It is tempting for those writing from within their own religious tradition to engage in hagiography, and to downplay the sins and errors that are an inevitable part of any human enterprise. Readers of this book should expect that Methodism's failings will become as apparent in the following pages as its successes. Triumphalism in Methodist writings is a prevailing tendency that goes back to the earliest years of the movement, but we hope to avoid any suggestion that Methodism is a normative pattern for all Christians. Methodism's founder John Wesley is all too often portrayed as an ecumenical "man for all seasons," carrying within himself a quasi-magic elixir that can make Calvinists understandable to Catholics, or Pentecostalists happy to be linked to the Orthodox. We shall do our best to assess him more objectively, "warts and all." Nor shall we try to present Methodism itself as a religious bridge between Protestantism and Catholicism, or between Anglicanism and the churches of the Reformation. Many books about Methodism try to offer some real or imagined Wesleyan heritage as the answer either to the current ills of Methodist churches themselves or to the disorder of the ecumenical world, but this seems to us neither accurate nor helpful. We are not crying "Back to Wesley." Nevertheless, it would be disingenuous for us as Methodist Christians not to attempt to show that there are resources in the Wesleys' thought and practice that can make a significant contribution to the theology and spirituality of the whole church.

Other concerns have also shaped the form and content of this book. We have tried to avoid any "single-model" theory of the origins and development of Methodism and will constantly stress that it has been from the beginning a variegated tradition. While some of these many forms that Methodism has taken have been compatible and complementary, others have been in direct conflict with one another. George Whitefield and John Wesley, both claiming the Methodist banner, aimed verbal blows at one another over Calvinism, Northern and Southern Methodists in the United States exchanged bitter words (and finally divided) over slavery, and both British and American traditions of Methodism have had more than their fair share of sectarianism and fissipariousness. It is hard to make bland comments about Methodists in general when they fall out so easily with one another on matters that seem to them to be the life and death of the Gospel, but which seem to the observer essentially irrelevant to their main task.

Like many revival movements, Methodism has sometimes been accused of vulgarity, and some writers seem to be slightly embarrassed by the more disreputable elements in Methodist practice, both early and contemporary. We are more likely to view these as signs of life and spiritual energy. On the other hand, we find it difficult not to be deeply discomforted by

Methodist involvement in wickedness: the compromises related to slavery or to apartheid, or the alliance of Methodist missionary activity with capitalism and imperialism, and it will be difficult not to comment on such matters. Nor will we overlook some tendencies within Methodism that have threatened to undermine the core values of the Gospel: for example, the propensity of the Methodist teaching about holiness to degenerate into personal moralism, and then into sanctimoniousness.

Current understandings within the discipline known as the study of religion have given us a particular perspective on this task. Following Ninian Smart we will pay continual attention to the six elements that he sees as constituting religious traditions: (1) ritual, (2) myth and narrative, (3) experience and emotion, (4) ethics and legal codes, (5) society and culture, and (6) the material dimension. Guided by the insights of Wilfred Cantwell Smith, we will treat world Methodism as a "cumulative religious tradition." By this we mean that Methodism, like every other living religious tradition, is not an abstract set of beliefs and morals or an "essential reality" that is infused into people from the outside. Instead, each individual Methodist not only lives out of the tradition as it is transmitted to him or her, but also modifies it by context and experience. Consequently no two individuals' form of Methodism will be identical, any more than is the Buddhism of any two Buddhists or the Islam of any two Muslims. To be sure, we can state some general propositions, but this will always be done with a certain reserve, and we will try to avoid sentences that begin "Methodists believe . . ." or "The Wesleyan stance is . . ." Toward this end our concern will be, wherever possible, to let individual Methodists speak for themselves, to focus on the "minute particular" within the great movements that have been part of the tradition.

In the end we hope to have given a fair impression of Methodism, both to those inside and those outside the tradition. We hope that Methodists, having read this book, might say, "Ah! Now I see why they do things differently over there!" and that non-Methodists might say, "Ah! So that is what makes Methodists tick." But even if we succeed at the task we have set for ourselves, this book is intended to be no more than an introduction. Working within our limits, we have frequently dealt with matters of great importance in just a few sentences. There is guidance for further study in the Further Reading section and we also offer notes and commentary on the web at http://www.brite.tcu.edu/directory/cracknell.

Acknowledgments

We are in too much debt to friends and colleagues in Methodist and other churches throughout the world ever to offer adequate acknowledgment of all that we owe. All that we have written has its origin in their conversation and in their writings. Where we can still recognize the sources of ideas and insights we indicate our indebtedness in the extended academic references posted on our web page at http://www.brite.tcu.edu/directory/cracknell. For the most part we are no longer conscious of who planted this or that thought in our minds and hearts, but we are grateful to teachers, colleagues, friends, and students who have shared with us in trying to understand the phenomenon called Methodism. We also say thank you to librarians and their libraries: this book would not have been possible without them. First thanks are due to Heather Carson, Curator of the Museum of Methodism at Wesley's Chapel, City Road, London, who provided invaluable assistance in finding resources, especially illustrative material, for this project; to Charles Bellinger, Theological Librarian of the Brite Divinity School, Texas Christian University, for maintaining an excellent Methodist collection; to Valerie Hotchkiss and Page Thomas for their helpfulness in our visits to Texas's outstanding Methodist Collection in the Bridwell Library in the Perkins School of Theology at Southern Methodist University; to Roma Wyatt at the World Methodist Council Museum and Library in Lake Junaluska, North Carolina. We have also received timely assistance from the General Commission on Archives and History of the United Methodist Church in Madison, New Jersey. Jeremy Poynter of Brite Divinity School contributed to our ability to illustrate this book through his digitalization of the photographs and his assistance with the web page. Our greatest debt is to the two great academic institutions in Britain and in the USA where we have taught over the last fifteen years: first the Cambridge Theological Federation, of which Wesley House and Westcott House are constituent parts, where we lived and worshiped ecumenically and came to understand Methodism through other eyes; then our thanks go to Brite Divinity

School, a foundation of the Christian Church (Disciples of Christ) that maintains both academic excellence and ecumenical hospitality. These two Methodist members of its faculty are profoundly grateful. Our last word of thanks goes to our editor Dr Katharina Brett of Cambridge University Press for her patient encouragement and wise guidance.

Abbreviations

AME	African Methodist Episcopal Church
AMEZ	African Methodist Episcopal Church Zion
BCP	Book of Common Prayer
BEM	Baptism, Eucharist and Ministry
CCJ	Council of Christians and Jews
CHPM	Collection of Hymns for the People called Methodists
CMEC	Christian Methodist Episcopal Church (from 1954), formerly the Colored Methodist Church
ECMM	Ethiopian Church of Mangena Mogone
MC	Methodist Church in the USA
MCCA	Methodist Church of the Caribbean and the Americas
MEC	Methodist Episcopal Church
MECS	Methodist Episcopal Church South
MNC	Methodist New Connexion
MPC	Methodist Protestant Church
MSB	Methodist Service Book
MSF	Methodist Sacramental Fellowship
OSL	Order of St. Luke
PM	Primitive Methodist
PMC	Primitive Methodist Church
SS	*Sunday Service of the Methodists in North America*
UMC	United Methodist Church
UMFC	United Methodist Free Churches
WCC	World Council of Churches
WMC	Wesleyan Methodist Church
WMMS	Wesleyan Methodist Missionary Society

Prologue

It is a summer Sunday morning in one of London's oldest streets. On one side of the road is the famous Bunhill Cemetery, where Daniel Defoe and William Blake are buried. On the opposite side, a large company of people flows out of a religious building, which is set back from the street by a wide courtyard and flanked by eighteenth- and nineteenth-century buildings. At the center of the courtyard is a life-size bronze statue of a man in eighteenth-century costume. But the people emerging from the building – men, women, children, and babes-in-arms – are clearly of the twenty-first century. Our first impression of them is of the variety and color of their clothes: many wear the native dress of India and Japan, China and Korea, Africa and the Pacific Islands, the Middle East and South America; others, decked out in the traditional Western "Sunday best," could be from Australia, New Zealand, North America, Europe, or South Africa. It is always considered to be a rather special occasion to be in this place, and the people were in high spirits when they assembled.

Every Sunday of the year this scene is reproduced here, as Methodists from all around the world gather at "Wesley's Chapel," the mother church of world Methodism. Built by John Wesley himself and opened on November 1, 1778, this chapel marked a kind of coming-of-age of his religious movement, and the beginnings of its separation from its religious parent, the Church of England. The people we see today gathered beneath the statue of John Wesley came for a service of Christian worship in the Methodist style, and for a form of Christian fellowship that cuts across national, ethnic, and racial lines. They came to express their common identity as Methodists and to reach back to their common roots as a community of faith. Conscious of themselves as inheritors of a particular history, many have walked out behind the chapel to stand quietly at Wesley's gravesite, marked by a stone obelisk. In immaculate eighteenth-century prose (Wesley died in 1791), the inscription declares:

1. Wesley's Chapel, City Road, London, serves as the "mother church" of world Methodism. Here Dr. Leslie Griffiths, the minister, greets members of the international congregation.

This great light arose by the singular providence of God, to enlighten these nations, and to revive, enforce and defend the pure apostolic doctrines and practices of the primitive Church, which he continued to do by his writings and his labours for more than half a century; and to his inexpressible joy not only beheld their influence extending, and their efficacy witness, in the hearts and lives of many thousands, as well in the Western world as in these kingdoms; but also, far above all human power and expectation, lived to see provision made, by the singular grace of God, for their continuance and establishment, to the joy of future generations. Readers, if thou art constrained to bless the instrument, give God the glory.

All those Methodists who gather around Wesley's grave can claim the key words in this inscription as part of their own religious identity: "providence," "apostolic doctrines," "joy," "witness," "grace."

But if this picture of harmony and union were the only story to be told about the religious tradition called Methodism, we would have a very brief and simple task ahead of us here. As it happens, the journey of Methodism through the better part of three centuries and across six continents, from a founding vision, through a spiritual revival within a national church, to an independent ecclesial body and a worldwide communion of independent churches, has made any complete description of the particularities of Methodist identity a very difficult undertaking.

If we leave Wesley's Chapel in London's City Road and travel six thousand miles southwest across the Atlantic Ocean and back in time, another aspect of Methodism's complicated story begins to reveal itself.

It is the year 1996, and 3,000 Methodists from around the globe have come together in Rio de Janeiro, hosted by the vigorous Methodist Church in Brazil, for the quinquennial meeting of the World Methodist Council and Conference. The opening communion service is a spectacular pageant, with the flags of more than seventy independent Methodist bodies carried in procession, and with worship-leaders from Indonesia, Australia, Liberia, Cuba, Argentina, Western Samoa, Nigeria, Russia, Sierra Leone, Zimbabwe, Angola, Bolivia, India, Ghana, Taiwan, Puerto Rico, Fiji, Canada, Kenya, South Africa, the Philippines, Malaysia, Slovakia, Pakistan, Italy, Finland, Mexico, Portugal, Germany, Spain, Sri Lanka, and Switzerland, as well as from the USA and the United Kingdom. The members of this congregation represent both national churches and subdivisions of those churches, as well as amalgamated ecclesial bodies within which Methodists are an integral part, such as the United Church of Canada, the Church of South India, and the Church of Pakistan. In the days which follow, the Conference participants, joined for this occasion by members of the World Federation of Methodist Women, hear speeches and are led in Bible study by prominent Methodists, as well as by eminent visitors from other denominations, such as General Eva Burrows of the Salvation Army, who reminds those gathered of the words of the founder of that movement, William Booth: "I valued everything that bore the name Methodist. To me there was one God, and John Wesley was his prophet."

By and large, the proceedings take place in the same atmosphere of cordiality and mutual respect that was so evident in our visit to Wesley's Chapel. But on the last day of the Rio Conference, Bishop Peter Storey of the Methodist Church in Southern Africa gives an address entitled "Good News to the Poor" in which he declares unequivocally that "the gospel, as given in scripture and experienced in our Wesleyan heritage, is good news to the poor." He identifies what he calls "a struggle for the soul of world Methodism":

There is a prosperous Methodism in the developed world, and Methodism with the poor in the rest of the world, with some places like South Africa, where both exist in glaring contrast to each other. The question is: what model will become the true sign of what we are? The prosperity model of success is very seductive, and it is sad to see how anxious are many of poorer congregations to emulate it. But the gospel of Jesus – who was rich, yet for our sakes became poor – surely calls for the opposite to happen. Prosperous Methodism must do something about its manna pile. How this is to happen is, I believe, a crucial question for the World Methodist Council.

As Bishop Storey becomes more impassioned and eloquent about his South African experiences, presenting serious challenges to the values of the rich ("God's warning to prosperous Methodism is: find ways of engaging face to face with the poor: your soul depends upon it"), it is noticeable that many in the audience are listening to him with increasing hostility as well as with serious discomfort. When he finishes, half of his Methodist audience rises up in standing ovation; the other half sits silently in their seats.

How can the people gathered at Wesley's Chapel from around the world all describe themselves as "Methodists"? And how can those who describe themselves as Methodists at the World Methodist Conference be so deeply divided? In this book we shall look at some of the factors that have resulted in both the deep unity among Methodist people and institutions, and the significant cleavages that exist between them. We will see how the various branches of the Methodist family have been affected by their different histories, cultural expressions, and sociological contexts, and how these factors have shaped their values and attitudes. We will investigate both the common theological and institutional "core values" which hold all these Methodists together, and the theological and social questions which drive them apart. In the end, we hope that we will have drawn a picture that will help readers understand something about the complex religious tradition called Methodism.

CHAPTER I

The beginning of world Methodism: John Wesley and his movement

Just as the core identity of a human family is defined by a relationship to common progenitors, so too is the core identity of the religious family of Methodists defined by a relationship with the person credited as the movement's founder. The central place of John Wesley in the Methodist story is undisputed. But for his present-day spiritual descendants, debates over Wesley's place in Methodist life, controversies about the meaning of his own life and work, and serious divisions of opinion on the content of his theology and its contemporary application are all central to understanding world Methodism. It is not surprising, then, that we begin our study of Methodism with John Wesley, his life, his world, and his religious program, as we attempt to discover the various ways in which the contemporary multiethnic, multiracial expression of Methodism relates to its English roots in the eighteenth century.

If anyone could be said to be a "man of his age," it was John Wesley; his lifetime came close to spanning the eighteenth century. Indeed, to understand Wesley and to understand his period are deeply interconnected enterprises. Most scholars speak of this as the era that was decisively and pervasively marked by Enlightenment rationalism. The rise of scientific empiricism, combined with increased social mobility, fostered an emphasis on personal autonomy and freedom from the older constraints. But in the British Isles it was also a time of recovery from a long period of religious and civil instability. Just less than a half-century before Wesley was born, the monarchy had been restored after a bitterly fought Civil War. As a result parliament had established new Acts of Uniformity, which imposed the liturgy of the 1662 Book of Common Prayer and demanded allegiance to the new king as head of the Church of England. Presbyterians, Independents, and Baptists were now "nonconformists" (those who failed to adhere to the Act of Uniformity), and many Anglicans sympathetic to their views were physically ejected from their parishes and formally silenced in the affairs of state. These Dissenters had to find a place for themselves in this new religious situation and we shall see how the extended Wesley family was deeply implicated in this religious change. In his own person John Wesley represented so many of the hopes and fears of his time. In adulthood, he would come to play a major role in the passionate public debates over the proper form and substance of piety, the political meaning of religion, and the obligation of Christians to their neighbors in the new social situation created by the beginnings of the Industrial Revolution.

JOHN WESLEY'S METHODISM

Methodists disagree about many things, but none of them doubts that Methodism owes its existence to two men: John Wesley and his younger brother Charles. They were both born in rural Lincolnshire, the second and third sons respectively of a learned but impecunious clergyman and his pious and resourceful wife. Their father, Samuel Wesley (1662–1735), was rector of the Church of England parish of Epworth, where he had a reputation for being both zealous and opinionated. He also demonstrated a general lack of interest in practical matters that eventually resulted in a stint in Lincoln jail for debt. Samuel's own father had been among those clergymen who had been deprived of their parishes for refusing to assent to the 1662 Act of Uniformity. But although Samuel Wesley had been intended to follow in his father's footsteps, he took a different theological path, and at the age of twenty-two he became a High Churchman, enrolling himself at Exeter College, Oxford. After leaving university and taking up his duties at Epworth (under Tory patronage), Samuel Wesley spent much of his time writing rather mediocre epic poems and compiling a massive Latin commentary on the Book of Job. His seeming indifference to the pastoral needs of his flock made him a less than popular parish priest.

The mother of the Wesley brothers had also been affected by the religious instability that followed the restoration of the monarchy. Like her husband, Susanna Wesley (1669–1742) was also the daughter of a nonconformist, Dr. Samuel Annesley (1620–96). Though he opposed the execution of Charles I, Annesley had generally supported the Parliamentary cause and was ejected from his parish in 1662 for failure to subscribe to the Act of Uniformity. He continued to minister to fellow Dissenters in Spitalfields in East London where the young Susanna was brought up. While still in her early teens, Susanna proved herself to be as independently minded as her future husband by turning her back on her family's religious allegiances and becoming a member of the Church of England. Following her marriage to Samuel Wesley in 1688, Susanna gave birth to nineteen children, only ten of

2. The Reverend John Wesley painted by Frank O. Salisbury, 1932.

3. The Reverend Charles Wesley, artist unknown, painted from life sometime around 1735.

whom survived to adulthood; from the beginning she took on responsibility for her children's education and was perhaps the most persistent religious influence in the lives of the Wesley brothers. It was she, for example, who advised her son John to undertake the study of "practical divinity."

There is no doubt that John Wesley's mind was indelibly marked by these two curious, creative, and scholarly parents. Certainly it was they who taught him to trust in reason, which we shall see manifested in his constant appeal to logical argument and his abhorrence of anything that he regarded as "namby pambical." Like many other Anglicans, from the time of Richard Hooker onwards, he could conceive of elements in revelation that were *above* reason; but there would never be anything in the divine economy which would be *contrary to* reason. As a result of his intellectual upbringing, John Wesley would also be the first church reformer equipped to reckon with the Enlightenment, and in particular with its philosophical problems with the divine–human relationship. At the same time, he was also poised to comprehend and respond to the challenges attending the birth of empirical science. He would certainly have known that Deists like John Ray and William Durham were making pioneering observations in botany and astronomy, and that Isaac Newton and John Locke had already made their distinctive contributions to physics and natural philosophy. This sense that the results of science had to be included in any valid explanation of the world led Wesley to reject obscurity or mystery (for example, the appeal to dreams or visions) as a source of religious knowledge, and his own scientific interests, exemplified by his medical experiments with the "electrical machine" (a kind of electro-shock therapy), were fully incorporated into his pastoral responsibilities for "cure of souls."

At the same time there was a particular kind of piety that was transmitted in the Wesley brothers' Christian nurture. Susanna Wesley took responsibility not only for their intellectual development, but for their spiritual development as well, and in the letters of counsel she wrote to them throughout her life she emphasized personal faithfulness, the quest to understand the will and providence of God, and pious attention to prayer and good works. She also provided an example of the importance of mutual care in the religious life. When Samuel was away in London attending the Convocation of the Church of England, the care of the Epworth parish's religious life was taken up by Susanna, and evening meetings in her kitchen rivaled the services in church. Samuel's temporary curate wrote to him in London complaining about the situation and Samuel immediately sent a letter rebuking his wife. A sense of her strong-mindedness can be felt in some of the words of her reply:

As I am a woman, so I am also mistress of a large family. And though the superior charge of the souls contained in it lies upon you as head of the family, and as their minister, yet in your absence I cannot but look upon every soul you leave under my care as a talent committed to me under a trust by the great Lord of all the families of heaven and earth.

For Susanna Wesley, holiness was clearly something to be pursued in shared common life, and not simply passively received, and this too would become a major theme of the Wesley brothers' lives and work.

JOHN WESLEY'S FIRST CONVERSION

After schooling in London and then undergraduate work at Christ Church, Oxford, from 1721 to 1724, John Wesley's mind turned to his ordination. Although the clerical vocation was almost a foregone conclusion in the circles in which he was brought up, it became the catalyst for Wesley's first quest to find real holiness, and he began by seeking out models and guides from the Christian past. He read Thomas à Kempis's influential treatise on the *Imitation of Christ* (*c.* 1418) and Jeremy Taylor's *Rules and Exercise of Holy Living* (1650) and of *Holy Dying* (1651). Wesley says that in this reading he was "exceedingly affected" by those passages in particular which referred to "purity of intention": "Instantly I resolved to dedicate all my life to God, all my thoughts and words and actions, being thoroughly convinced there was no medium but that every part of my life (not some only) must either be a sacrifice to God or to myself, that is in effect to the devil." From this resolve came Wesley's commitment to an ordered life: to fasting, to good works, to journal- and diary-keeping. For many historians of Methodism, this counts as his first conversion, and was an experience as real and as powerful as the more famous conversion in Aldersgate Street thirteen years later in 1738. Nowhere in his writings does Wesley ever repudiate or discount this first turning to God.

But even this profound re-dedication to a more intentional form of Christian living was not the beginning of Methodism. This came a few years later when, according to John, he and his younger brother Charles both saw that they could not be saved without "holiness." In 1727 Charles had followed his elder brother to Oxford where, with some other junior members of the university, he had organized occasional meetings for study, prayer, and religious conversation. John had been ordained deacon in 1725 (priest in 1728). In 1726 he went to assist his father as curate in the parish of Epworth. In November 1729 he returned to Oxford to take up residence as a Fellow of Lincoln College, to which he had been elected before his return

to Epworth. Once there, his natural gifts for leadership asserted themselves
and he took over Charles's meetings.

In the following year these gatherings became distinctively a "Holy
Club." One of their number, William Morgan (1712–32), suggested they
should visit the inmates of the Oxford Castle prison and the poor of
the Oxford slums. This charitable work increased as they did, in Charles
Wesley's words, "what good we could to the bodies and souls of men."
Such actions, along with other habits that outsiders found irritating, such
as rigorous fasting and rising at four or five in the morning for prayer and
Bible reading, led eventually to notoriety for the members of the "Holy
Club" among their fellows at Oxford. They were taunted with various
nicknames: "Bible moths," and "Supererogation men" and members of the
"Godly club." The term "Methodists" was first applied to the group in
1732, when John Bingham of Christ Church observed that "a new set of
Methodists . . . has sprung up amongst us." A total of some forty persons
were involved in Oxford Methodist groups in the six years that Charles
Wesley superintended it. Wesley himself thought later that this Oxford
"Holy Club," with its meditative piety, was the beginning of Methodism,
and represented the first manifestation of God's purpose "to spread scriptural holiness over the Land."

But even this rigorous program of asceticism and good works was not
to bring about the "holiness" that John Wesley had in mind, and when an
opportunity occurred in 1735 to become a missionary overseas, and thus
to "withdraw even more entirely from the world," he seized upon it. This
missionary activity was to be undertaken under the auspices of the Society
for the Propagation of the Gospel, and would involve ministering to the
settlers of the newly established American colony of Georgia. So, with fellow Oxford Methodists Charles Wesley, Charles Delamotte (1714–86), and
Benjamin Ingham (1712–72), John Wesley set off on his missionary venture.
Although he surely had the religious needs of the colonial inhabitants in
mind, other forces were propelling him to Savannah: "My chief motive,"
he wrote at the time, "is the hope of saving my own soul."

Wesley arrived in Georgia on February 6, 1736 and with his colleagues
he set about replicating Oxford Methodism in North America. At first he
met with some success. By late in 1737 attendance at the parish church in
Savannah had grown to between sixty and seventy, and Wesley had even
managed to persuade two or three dozen people to come regularly for
prayers at five o'clock in the morning. One undoubtedly attractive feature
of these services was the use of hymns collected by the Wesley brothers

and published in the first English hymn-book in America as *A Collection of Psalms and Hymns*. Many of the hymns in this collection were freshly translated from German by John Wesley. But, by and large, the stringent Holy Club-style disciplines that Wesley imposed on himself and on the inhabitants of the Georgia colony, including his own clerical celibacy and an insistence on baptism by immersion, were met with hostile resistance, and the pastoral strategy he had set for himself was clearly headed for failure. Wesley persevered, however, making plans for the education of children and for special ministries among both the First Nations and the black inhabitants of his 200-mile-long parish.

But in 1737, before these plans could be implemented, trouble arose. Wesley had been teaching a young woman named Sophy Hopkey, and although he had grown very fond of her, she did not return his affections and contracted a hasty marriage to another man. In his role as parish priest, Wesley considered this action to be ecclesiastically improper; in his role as thwarted lover, he considered it a painful betrayal. As a result, John barred the couple from communion in the parish church. The local chief magistrate (who happened to be Miss Hopkey's guardian) convened a grand jury and a set of ten bills of indictment was drawn up against John Wesley. Thinking that he was likely to be found guilty of the offenses with which he was charged (perhaps especially since, as with his father before him, his popularity among his parishioners was not high), Wesley deemed it expedient to abandon his missionary post. In December 1737 he sailed from Georgia, and by February 1 he was back in England. "I shook off the dust of my feet and left Georgia, after having preached the Gospel there, not as I ought, but as I was able," and he reflected in his *Journal:* "It is now two years and almost four months since I left my native country in order to teach the Georgian Indians the nature of Christianity. But what have I learned myself in the meantime? Why (what I least of all expected) that I who went to America to convert others, was never myself converted to God."

TOWARD A SECOND CONVERSION

Although not a great missionary success, Wesley's trip to Georgia would have at least one significant and lasting impact on the future of Methodism. On the voyage outward from England in 1735, the small ship in which Wesley traveled had been caught in a sudden violent storm. As it happened, the storm had come up just at the time that a group of fellow voyagers,

Moravian missionaries, were beginning their evening service. John Wesley records the scene:

In the midst of the psalm wherewith their service had begun the sea broke over, split the mainsail in pieces, covered the ship, and poured in between the decks, as if the great deep had already swallowed us up. A terrible screaming began among the English. The Germans calmly sang on. I asked one of them afterward, "was you not afraid to die. He answered, I thank God, no." I asked, "But were not your women and children afraid?" He replied mildly, "No; our women and children are not afraid to die."

Witnessing the confidence and the faith of these Moravians was a pivotal experience for Wesley: clearly these pious German people possessed something that he lacked. In Savannah, as he translated Moravian hymns for his parishioners, he began to find poetic expressions for his own struggle toward holiness, including a couplet written by their leader Count Nicholas von Zinzendorf, which beseeches the God of love:

> O shine upon my frozen breast
> With sacred warmth my heart inspire.

As soon as John Wesley returned to London from Georgia, he resumed his spiritual searching. Rather to his surprise, the renewal of religious experience that had been represented by Holy Club Methodism had been flourishing in his absence. George Whitefield (1714–70), a convert to Oxford Methodism after Wesley had left for Georgia, had begun to preach with spectacular success among the various religious societies in London, Bristol, and other parts of England. Whitefield's eloquent preaching of the Methodist principles that he had learned in the Oxford Holy Club kept the revival alive. Moreover, Moravian influence was increasing in England, with a vigorous Moravian-inspired group which met in London's Fetter Lane. As Charles Wesley, who had returned from Georgia after only a year's service, wrote to his brother, "We see all around us in an amazing ferment. Surely Christianity is once more lifting up it head."

This excitement was rather disconcerting to John Wesley, who continued to agonize over the weakness of his faith and the failure of his progress toward holiness. Always conscious of his experience of the storm at sea, he decided to turn to the Moravians for guidance, seeking out Peter Böhler, a Moravian minister who was staying temporarily in London to prepare for his own voyage to the Georgia Moravian mission. Böhler was blunt with Wesley, stating plainly that in his opinion the problem was not that his faith was weak, but rather that he did not have any kind of faith at all.

Persuaded by this analysis of his condition, Wesley determined to give up preaching altogether. But Böhler reproved him, and his words to the thirty-five-year-old John Wesley have rung down through the generations of his Methodist descendants: "Preach faith till you have it, and then because you have it you will preach faith."

At the same time, Charles Wesley was also feeling the influence of the Moravian promise of assurance of faith, a result of being with Peter Böhler and attending the religious meetings in Fetter Lane. On Pentecost Sunday, May 21, 1738, Charles Wesley wrote that he felt a "strange palpitation of heart," and found himself able to cry out, "I believe, I believe." In his *Journal* he records: "I now found myself at peace with God, and rejoiced in the hope of loving Christ. Under his protection I waked the next morning, and rejoiced in reading the 107th Psalm." That day he wrote what he referred to as a "hymn on my conversion." In fact, this hymn, number 29 in the 1780 *Collection of Hymns for the Use of the People Called Methodists* (hereafter *CHPM*), is always known as Charles Wesley's Conversion Hymn. It remains the classic summary statement of Methodist religious experience. He begins with the plaintive cry of the redeemed sinner who feels wholly inadequate to praise the God who has saved him:

> Where shall my wond'ring soul begin?
> How shall I all to heaven aspire?
> A slave redeemed from death and sin
> A brand plucked from eternal fire.
> How shall I equal triumphs raise,
> Or sing my great Deliverer's praise?

Charles signaled the significance of this personal experience of salvation by affirming in almost the same breath the universality of this message:

> Outcasts of men, to you I call
> Harlots, and publicans, and thieves!
> He spreads his arms to embrace you all;
> Sinners alone His grace receives:
> No need of him the righteous have;
> He came the lost to seek and save.

With his younger brother now speaking so vividly of an experience of assurance of salvation, John Wesley was even more troubled about the state of his own soul. He sets the stage for the resolution to his perplexity in his *Journal* entry for May 24, 1738, telling us that on that day he had attended St. Paul's Cathedral where he had heard the penitential Psalm 130 (which

4. Plaque commemorating John Wesley's 'Aldersgate experience' erected in London by American Methodists.

begins "Out of the depths, shall I cry unto thee"). The words of the whole psalm touched him intensely. What follow in the *Journal* are among the most famous words of the whole of Methodism:

In the evening I went very unwillingly to a Society in Aldersgate Street, where one was reading Luther's Preface to the Epistle to the Romans. About a quarter before nine, while he was describing the change which God works in the heart through faith in Christ, I felt my heart strangely warmed. I felt I did trust in Christ, Christ alone for salvation, and an assurance was given me, that he had taken away *my* sins, even *mine*, and saved *me* from the law of sin and death (emphasis in original).

This is not conversion from wickedness as though he had been a heathen or a hypocrite; the earlier conversion of 1725 was too real for that. But Wesley was indeed changed, experiencing a different kind of conversion that moved him from a lack of deep faith to a full assurance of a new standing with God. He passed from formal religion to the religion of the heart, and from being what he later called an "almost Christian" to someone who had entered into the full Christian reality. "What Christianity considered as a doctrine promised is accomplished in my soul," Wesley wrote. "I am now assured that these things are so; I experienced them in my breast." The universal love of God in which he had believed as a proposition was now lodged within him as an experience.

But within this seemingly straightforward description of a decisive renewal of heart and mind lies a persistent puzzle. If this conversion was indeed the pivotal moment in Wesley's religious life (and therefore, by extension, was intended to be seen as the pattern of conversion for all true Methodist Christians), why did Wesley himself make so little of it in his teaching and preaching in the remaining fifty years of his life? Except for a mention of it in a letter to his brother Samuel Wesley Jr. just six months later, there is no other reference in any of his copious writings to what has come to be called the "Aldersgate experience." Throughout the rest of his life, whenever Wesley wanted to identify the real beginning of his disciple-ship, he emphasized the commitment he made to holiness in 1725 rather than the "strange warming" of his heart at Aldersgate Street in 1738. One answer to this puzzle is that in subsequent years the Moravian ideas that had led him to the assurance of faith he experienced at Aldersgate caused him a great deal of confusion, and he was forced as a result to turn back to his own Anglican resources to interpret his religious life history.

THE METHODIST REVIVALIST MOVEMENT

The next step in the journey of Methodism, from a scattering of religious societies whose members wished to live more intentional Christian lives to a worldwide religious phenomenon, was taken with the help of George Whitefield. After the Wesleys' return from Georgia, Whitefield, by this time a Church of England clergyman, continued preaching in his exuberant way to large congregations in London and Bristol. Crossing the Atlantic at the beginning of 1738, he made the first of seven visits to North America where he became a key figure in what is called the First Great Awakening. But this kind of traveling preaching was not without certain very serious institutional difficulties.

Under the parochial system in England and Wales, the country was divided into semi-autonomous ecclesiastical units (parishes), each watched over by a parish priest who had the power to decide who might be allowed to preach in the parish church. On his return to England in 1739, George Whitefield found that many Anglican clergymen were refusing to open their pulpits to his "Methodist" preaching. Whitefield would not be deterred, however, and viewed this exclusion as an excuse to preach in the streets, the town squares, and the marketplaces, following the example of those who had taken Methodism to Wales. There, Griffith Jones (1683–1761) and

Howell Harris (1714–73) were already using fields and meadows, barn steps and market crosses to spread the message of renewal. If entrepreneurship in its modern economic sense had its beginning in this period, Whitefield must be counted as the first great religious entrepreneur. Supremely gifted with the skill of the self-promoter and the talent of an accomplished actor, Whitefield thrived on the attention of large audiences. By treating preaching as a theatrical performance, he competed with the traders and merchants who cried their wares in the rapidly growing cities of eighteenth-century England. With Whitefield, Evangelical Christianity entered the market-place and indeed he can be counted as the spiritual ancestor of all modern television evangelists.

However stimulating it might have been, this method of spreading the Gospel was not immediately welcomed by John and Charles Wesley. In March 1739, Whitefield entreated John Wesley to come to Bristol, where he had been preaching regularly in the open air since February. "I wish you would be here at the latter end of next week," Whitefield wrote, adding with characteristic presumptuousness that, "It is advertised in this day's journal [that you will preach]." When Wesley discovered that Whitefield had been preaching outdoors he was truly shocked, writing in his *Journal* that he could scarcely reconcile himself to "this strange way of preaching in the fields." But he went to Bristol nevertheless, and he reports that on the first occasion he observed, Whitefield had preached on Rose Green to "about thirty thousand people" (an unlikely estimate, since Bristol had at that time only 50,000 inhabitants). It was this obvious success that finally convinced Wesley, and on the next day, April 2, 1739 (a date reckoned by many interpreters to be as important as the date of the Aldersgate experience), John Wesley "submitted to be more vile, and proclaimed in the highways the glad tidings of salvation." His first open-air sermons were delivered first to about 3,000 people "on a little piece of rising ground" just outside Bristol, and then in the days that followed at several other open-air locations in both Bristol and Bath.

By thus indicating that parochial boundaries were no longer to constrain his work, and that indeed (as he put it) "the world is my parish," Wesley had taken a radical step not only toward an independent Methodism but also toward his own future as a religious leader. Jonathan Edwards (1703–58), whose striking account of the Great Awakening in New England he had read while walking to Bristol, had shown John Wesley that the Word of God rightly proclaimed would bear visible fruit. Here before Wesley's own eyes was a great ingathering of people professing faith as a result of his own open-air preaching. His faith, which had been so tenuous and uncertain just a year before, was confirmed by the faith of so many. From April 1739 Wesley becomes a man with an unwavering and unalterable mission; beginning in these spring days in Bristol, and then continuing on through the next fifty years, Wesley's confidence in himself and his message never failed. The utterly unanticipated action of preaching in the open air in Bristol properly begins the Methodist missionary movement that is the subject of this book.

When he returned to London in June, John Wesley gathered large crowds on Blackheath and Kennington Common. On June 24, Charles Wesley joined his brother in the open air, preaching to an estimated 10,000 people in Moorfields, and by September the Wesleys and George Whitefield were attracting very large crowds throughout London. Charles Wesley wrote a hymn to celebrate what was to them an astonishing turn of events. This is the first hymn in *CHPM* and is still in the Methodist hymn-books of the world, often as Hymn number 1. It begins:

> O for a thousand tongues to sing:
> My dear redeemer's praise!
> The glories of my God and King,
> The triumphs of his grace!

The hymn continues with the affirmation of what he and his brother experienced as they preached to the crowds.

> Jesus! The name that charms our fears,
> That bids our sorrows cease –
> 'Tis music in the sinner's ears,
> 'Tis life, and health, and peace.

The Gospel message was now reaching the urban poor gathered on the common lands of London. In Charles's highly charged metaphors the "blind" could now "see" and the "deaf" "hear"; the "dumb" were now using their "loosened tongues" to praise Jesus. These signs of new life set a seal upon both John's and Charles's ministries. There were other manifestations of overwhelming spiritual renewal that both the brothers noted during this period. In his *Journal* John Wesley speaks of people being "thunderstruck," "wounded by the sword of the Spirit," "seized with strong pain," "cut to the heart," and "sunk to the earth." Outsiders also reported seeing the hearers of the Wesleys' message falling into strange fits.

In the eyes of the bishops and clergy of the Church of England, however, these manifestations of religious zeal were an indication of the vice of "enthusiasm" that threatened to undermine the rational basis of true religion. At the beginning of the Methodists' field preaching work in 1739, the Bishop of Bristol, Joseph Butler (1692–1752), told John Wesley that "the pretending to extraordinary revelations and gifts of the Holy Ghost is a horrid thing, a very horrid thing." But such experiences have continued in the life of Methodism and in its pentecostalist and charismatic offshoots to the present day. They continue to present problems to the religiously fastidious and remain the subject of much discussion and debate throughout world Methodism. But enthusiasm and field preaching were not the only innovations that offended the Wesleys' own Oxford High Church sensibilities, nor were they the practices perceived by the Established Church as the greatest threat to its stability. It was the matter of who would be authorized to preach the Gospel that presented the most profound and disquieting challenge. Some of the Wesleys' earliest followers insisted that they had received a call to preach even though they had not been ordained within the Church of England. At first this notion had so disturbed the Wesley brothers' High Church principles that they condemned lay preaching as a violation of good order. But John Wesley's intensely pragmatic spirit led him very soon to reconsider this position, and to recognize that plain men and women might indeed have received the gifts and graces for preaching. Susanna Wesley's advice was critical in this change of heart. Reflecting on the case of the layman Thomas Maxwell, who began preaching in 1740, she told her son, "Take care what you do with respect to that young man, for he is as surely called of God to preach as you are. Examine what have been the fruits of his preaching, and hear him also yourself." John followed his mother's advice and changed his mind, and lay preaching has been an integral part of Methodism ever since.

Very early in the life of the new movement there were difficulties associated with the provision of pastoral care for the large numbers of new converts responding to Methodist preaching. When the numbers were still small, they were comfortably accommodated within the existing "band meetings" of the various religious societies in London and in Bristol, which usually met in private dwellings with between fifteen and twenty people attending. But with the rapid proliferation of converts, serious problems of both meeting space and leadership arose. In Bristol, where field preaching had begun, two existing religious societies joined together in 1739 to form the "United Society." They almost immediately began to build the "New Room" in Bristol's Horsefair to accommodate their meetings, and this building remains a significant Methodist landmark. At the same time, tensions between the Wesley brothers and the Moravians in London were increasing, and a year before John Wesley had severed his connection with

5. The New Room, Bristol, the first Methodist preaching hall opened by
John Wesley in 1739.

the Fetter Lane society. The year before Wesley had acquired the lease on a
disused cannonball factory and arsenal known as the Foundery (Methodism
has always retained the antiquated spelling). This lay a short distance away
from Fetter Lane on the other side of the City Road. With extensive repairs
and renovations the Foundery soon became Wesley's London headquarters. It had a preaching hall that could accommodate about 1,500 people as
well as schoolrooms and accommodation for himself, his mother, and the
travelling preachers. (It was here that Susanna Wesley died in 1742.) In 1778
the Foundery was replaced by his purpose-built New Chapel in the City
Road, the building now familiar as the "cathedral church" of international
Methodism.

The expense involved in building the New Room in Bristol and of
acquiring the Foundery was a huge financial burden for the new religious
movement, and in 1742 Wesley met with the leaders of the United Society
in Bristol to find ways of clearing the accumulated debts. A retired sea-
man, known to us only as "Captain Foy," proposed dividing the United
Society into groups of twelve "little companies or classes" (from the Latin
classis, meaning "division"), with a leader appointed for each class. The

class leader would meet the individual members of the society every week and collect one penny from each of them. Foy himself volunteered to have the poorest members of the society in his class, offering to make up out of his own pocket what they were unable to pay. Wesley immediately saw the potential benefits of the newly proposed system, not only for financing the Methodist enterprise, but also for the pastoral oversight of members. He quickly accepted Foy's suggestion and the Methodist class system was born. In order to avoid any suggestion that John and Charles Wesley were making themselves rich at the expense of their poorer followers, an additional lay leader (designated the "steward") was appointed for each society whose job it was to receive the weekly twelve pennies. Membership of a class was required of everyone wishing to be part of a Methodist United Society, and almost immediately tickets of membership came to be used. By 1744 the classes meeting in various homes had become a permanent fixture in Methodism, and were deemed "a providential means of grace by the first Conference of Wesley and his preachers."

Further innovations would mark the early Methodist years. The spiritual power of hymn singing had been something John Wesley had learned from the Moravians, and he was convinced that the message of Methodism would be carried forward on hymnody. New hymns and songs were needed for the Methodist societies and John Wesley began with the publication of *Hymns and Sacred Poems* in 1740. This collection included the earliest of what would become Charles Wesley's vast output of hymns. Two years later a *Collection of Tunes* to accompany these hymns was published. At the same time, older liturgical practices of the church were revived, such as the watch-night services that were held in Bristol and in London. The disciplines that had been established in the days of the Oxford Holy Club were also encouraged, especially ministries to the poor, the hungry, and the sick. Both John and Charles were themselves constant in prison visiting, and were famous for riding with condemned prisoners to the gallows.

Before long, however, issues of discipline arose among the new converts. As early as 1739, rules of membership for all the Methodist societies had been codified. These were published in 1743 as *The Nature, Design, and General Rules of our United Societies*. The *General Rules* are set out in full on pp. 122–3. On a visit to Newcastle in 1743, John Wesley was shocked to discover breaches of discipline in the society meeting there. He read the *General Rules* aloud to those gathered and some sixty-four persons were expelled from the society, judged guilty of such vices as swearing, brawling, quarreling, drunkenness, idleness, and carelessness.

In this same period (the early 1740s), Methodists also had their first taste of violent opposition. These were dangerous times not only for Methodists, but for all those who in any way drew attention to themselves on the public thoroughfares. England was undergoing a severe economic crisis: inflation was rife, foodstuffs were in short supply, and as a result the poor could not afford the cost of most staple goods. The pervasive discontent that resulted from this situation meant that the rate of crime was high and that mob hysteria could be ignited at a moment's notice. Within this generalized threat of public disorder, Methodists were thrown under the added suspicion that they were fomenting political instability in their "clandestine" society meetings. They were regularly accused of being either sectaries or papists, this latter amounting to a charge of treason or Jacobinism (1745 was the year the Young Pretender, Bonny Prince Charlie, landed in Scotland). These allegations incited further violence against Methodists, and there are many reports of men and women being pelted with rocks, rotten food, and animal dung as they left their society meetings. In 1743, to counter the allegations of inciting political unrest directed at his followers, John Wesley wrote a "plain account" of the movement, *An Earnest Appeal to Men of Reason and Religion.* He followed this with a letter to King George II, entitled "The humble address of the Societies in England and Wales, in derision called Methodists," in which he affirmed that he was prepared to obey the king "to the uttermost" in all things that he conceived to be agreeable to the word of God.

Political controversy was not the only challenge to Methodism; theological controversy was also shaping the movement in decisive ways. On the one hand there was the dispute with the Moravians over the nature of sanctity and justification, and on the other hand there were passionate debates with those Methodists who owed more to Puritanism (and therefore to Calvinism) in their understanding of God's relationship with humanity. Chief among Wesley's associates who relied on Calvinism as a theological resource was George Whitefield, and in 1740 Wesley was forced to part company from him on doctrinal grounds, taking his stand on universal grace and the freedom of the human will in his sermon on "Free Grace" preached in August of that year.

But despite all these difficulties, Wesleyan Methodism flourished, and by June 1744 John Wesley and his company of preachers had established societies in the West Country as far as Cornwall, in Ireland and Wales, in the Midlands, in Yorkshire, and as far north as Newcastle. An intricate network of lay associates and sympathetic clergy had also come into being.

For John Wesley the time had come to lay down the parameters of Methodist theology and discipline in a properly constituted legislative Conference.

By this time, the Methodist societies in England and Ireland had been organized into a number of "circuits": regional rounds through which the itinerant preachers traveled. Increasing numbers of young men were coming forward to serve as full-time preachers, and John Wesley was concerned that some provision should be made for their theological education. First, they needed instruction in Methodist doctrines, and Wesley responded with his *Sermons on Several Occasions* (1746 onwards) designed, as he said, to "contain the substance of what I have been teaching for between eight and nine years last past." A further major educational effort for his new preachers was *The Christian Library*, which was begun in 1749. In this fifty-volume *Library*, Wesley proposed to provide selections from the works of Christian thinkers from all traditions, to show the "genuine religion of Jesus Christ." A few years later, in 1754, Wesley added his *Explanatory Notes upon the New Testament* to the Methodist preachers' doctrinal armory.

By 1750 much of the Methodist system was firmly in place, and nearly 10,000 people were calling themselves Methodists. There were annual Conferences, a pattern of circuits and societies, a rigorously regulated and disciplined membership, distinctive forms of hymnody supported by specially published Methodist hymnals, and a wide range of educational and social-service projects. Despite all of John Wesley's efforts and protestations that he was a loyal clergyman of the Church of England, and that his connexion (a word already in use to describe how existing religious societies were linked together) of societies was simply intended as a renewal movement within the church, Methodism was taking on many of the distinguishing features of a denomination.

This was in part because many of those attracted to Methodism had no other active and immediate church affiliation. They were new converts to an intentional Christian life. Others lived in the rapidly expanding industrial areas where there were no parish churches. And then there were those who were no longer welcome in their parish churches because of their Methodist sympathies. The question of where many of these 10,000 Methodist members were to receive holy communion was now a major issue. As the 1750s began, instances of Methodist preachers taking it upon themselves to offer the bread and wine of communion were increasing, much to Wesley's dismay.

Some of these preachers who were administering the Lord's Supper to Methodists in their circuits advocated a clean and decisive break with the Church of England. In response to these calls, Wesley presented a treatise to the 1755 Conference entitled "Ought we to separate from the Church of England?" Here he outlined his various arguments against separation. But many doubted his ability to hold the line on this issue. Among these was Charles Wesley, who sensed, quite correctly, that the course of Methodism was already set for separation. To emphasize his strong feelings on the matter of remaining within the church, Charles walked out of the 1755 Conference, and withdrew from the inner counsels of Methodism, attending Conference only irregularly in the years that followed. He made his last preaching tour in 1756, and then settled first in Bristol (where his house is kept as a place of pilgrimage), and then in London from 1771. For the remainder of his life, Charles Wesley continued to resist any movement toward a break with the Church of England, characteristically putting his opposition into verse:

> When first sent forth to minister the word,
> Say did we preach ourselves or Christ the Lord?
> Was it our aim disciples to collect
> To raise a party, or found a sect?

For many years Charles Wesley's unrelenting pressure kept his brother firm in his resolution to stay within the Church of England. At the Bristol Conference in 1760, John Wesley specifically refused to ordain Methodist preachers, and his strong stand at that time ended any clamor for special ministerial status for the next two decades. Three years later the *Large Minutes* (1763) incorporated the following instructions that further clarified Wesley's understanding of the relationship between Methodism and the Church of England:

(1) Let all our Preachers go to Church. (2) Let all our people go constantly. (3) Receive the sacrament at every opportunity. (4) Warn all against niceness in hearing, a great and prevailing evil. (5) Warn them likewise against despising the prayers of the Church. (6) Against calling our Society a Church, or the Church. (7) Against calling our Preachers, Minister, our houses meeting house, call them plain preaching house. (Do not license them as such).

The 1760s saw not only signs of the widespread growth of Methodism, but also signs of the routinization of charisma and that increase in internal controversy which can often be detected when religious movements lose their first flush of spiritual excitement. Over the years, John Wesley himself had gradually felt the need to give his organizational efforts some standing in law, and the 1763 "Model Deed" became the vehicle for ensuring the continued availability of Methodist property to the societies and preachers by transferring ownership to local trustees. The Model Deed insisted that only John Wesley "and such other persons as he shall from time to time appoint, at all times, and during his natural life, and no other persons could have and enjoy the free use of the said premises." The trustees appointed by Wesley were charged with overseeing Methodist property and with designating those persons authorized to use it.

Years of controversy between the Wesleys and George Whitefield over Whitefield's Calvinist convictions had eventually split the Methodist movement into two distinct theological camps, giving rise to the Countess of Huntingdon's Connexion and the Welsh Calvinistic Methodists. But when Whitefield died in Massachusetts on September 3, 1770, it was John Wesley who preached the funeral oration in Whitefield's London Tabernacle. Rather than softening the lines of division between the two factions, however, this sermon only served to sharpen them. On this highly symbolic occasion, Wesley insisted that George Whitefield had preached essentially the same "grand doctrines" that he himself had been preaching, that is, "the new birth and justification by faith." But there was no reference in the oration to Whitefield's theology of the covenant, nor to his emphasis on absolute predestination. These significant omissions deeply offended many of Whitefield's Calvinist friends, who unleashed a ferocious barrage of criticism against Wesley, carried in the pages of popular religious journals such as *The Spiritual Magazine* and *The Gospel Magazine*. Wesley, as fully convinced as ever that Calvinism "was the direct antidote to Methodism," countered these assaults in his own new journal, *The Arminian Magazine*, first published in 1778 and intended, he said, "to proclaim conditional salvation within the universal redemption wrought by Christ." In its first issue, the magazine carried a sketch of the life and work of Dutch theologian Jacobus Arminius (1560–1609), whose name is recalled whenever Wesleyan Methodism is described as "Evangelical Arminianism." But however divisive it may have been, this conflict with the Calvinists was soon to be overshadowed by other significant events of the 1770s. The American Revolutionary War was on the near horizon, and the break between Britain and America would prove to be the catalyst for a major bifurcation of the Methodist movement that continues to affect all of Wesley's spiritual descendants to this day.

At first Wesley was sympathetic to the cause of the colonists: "I do not defend the measures which have been taken with regard to America: I doubt whether any man can defend them, either on the foot of law, equity or prejudice," he wrote in his *Free Thoughts on the Present State of Public Affairs* (1768). Elsewhere he spoke of the inhabitants of America as an oppressed people, asking for nothing more than their legal rights, and doing so in "the most modest and inoffensive manner that the nature of the things would allow." Even after the battles of Lexington and Concord in 1775, Wesley counseled against the use of military force, writing to the Secretary of the Colonies as well as to the Prime Minister to express his opinion on the matter.

By this time there was a considerable Methodist community in America, which had grown up as a response to the preaching of lay people, especially Irish émigrés like Philip Embury (1728–73) and Barbara Heck (1734–1804) in New York and Robert Strawbridge (1732–81) in Maryland. Another layman, Captain Thomas Webb (1724–96), had organized the first Methodists in Philadelphia in 1767 and two years later British Methodist preachers began to be appointed by the Conference specifically for work in the American colonies. Among them was Francis Asbury (1745–1816), considered the founder of American Methodism, who arrived in 1771, and who was the most significant voice in the first Methodist Conference in America in 1773.

But when the cry for justice in the colonies turned into a cry for independence and rebellion against the crown, Wesley's High Toryism asserted itself, and he changed his mind almost overnight about the situation in America. The demand for independence, he argued, could hold no prospect for genuine liberty. Between 1775 and 1780 Wesley published thirteen royalist or anti-colonist tracts, leading Francis Asbury to remark: "there is not a man in the whole world so obnoxious to the American politicians as our dear old Daddy; but no matter we must treat him with all the respect we can and that is due to him." Wesley's tracts were, not surprisingly, ineffectual in stemming the tide of revolution, and when the Declaration of Independence was issued on July 4, 1776, American Methodists felt they had to dissociate themselves from John Wesley. All but two of the British preachers who had been appointed by the Conference returned to their homeland; the solitary exception was Francis Asbury.

Even before the war, the most significant religious difficulty for these New World Methodists was that their regular participation in the sacramental life was so uncertain. Those who were members of the Church of England could usually still attend their parish churches in America, but those who had been newly converted as Methodists and who had no other religious affiliation may never have been able to receive communion at all. This pastoral situation was significantly exacerbated by the British military defeat. The colonial Anglican Church was in disarray since, when the outcome of the war became clear, most of its clergy had either returned to England or had fled across the border into Canada. Because of his staunch resistance to a decisive separation from the church that had given his movement its birth, John Wesley had refused to take it upon himself to ordain Methodist clergy to administer the sacraments. Although in England baptism and the

Lord's Supper were being regularly celebrated in Methodist chapels (including his own chapel in the City Road), such services were always presided over by priests who had been validly ordained in the Church of England. But Methodist Christians in America had no such resources to rely upon, especially after the war, and the provision for their sacramental needs had become an urgent pastoral matter.

On the advice of Francis Asbury, who knew first-hand the situation on the ground in America, John Wesley became more forceful in asking the bishops of the Church of England to ordain men for the Methodists of America. But it soon became clear that there was no help forthcoming from the Church of England, and Wesley evolved his own plan of action. He had been convinced as early as 1745 that in the New Testament church those persons designated the *presbyteroi* ("elders") were the spiritual and functional equivalent to the *episcopoi* ("bishops"). He was also certain that nowhere could it be proved that there was any special grace placed upon bishops through an "apostolic succession" of episcopal ordinations. So, as an ordained presbyter of the Church of England, Wesley now believed himself to be a genuinely "apostolic man," fully equipped with the authority of a bishop to ordain.

He determined, therefore, to confer upon his chief assistant in London, Dr. Thomas Coke (1747–1814), the power of ordaining and consecrating (this was not strictly necessary since Coke as an Anglican clergyman was as much an ordained presbyter/bishop as Wesley). Coke was given authority to set apart Francis Asbury as the other "superintendent" (Wesley's translation of the Greek word *episcopos*) for America. John Wesley himself would ordain two English volunteers as "elders" and these would travel with Thomas Coke to America. On September 1, 1784, John Wesley laid hands on Thomas Vasey (*c.* 1746–1826) and Richard Whatcoat (1736–1806), ordaining them first as deacons, and shortly afterwards as elders. Coke was set apart as superintendent; though since he was already ordained a presbyter in the Church of England, according to Wesley's understanding he needed no further commissioning to ordain preachers for America.

Charles Wesley was not consulted about these radical departures from the Anglican order, and was clearly horrified by what had taken place. He used his poetic skills to satirize the ordinations:

> So easily are Bishops made,
> By man's, or woman's whim?
> W...... his hands on C...... has laid
> But who laid hands on him?

6. Wesley's Chapel, City Road, London, anonymous engraving, *c.* 1820. Opened by John Wesley in 1778, City Road Chapel was designed to accommodate worship in the Methodist style.

Coke, Vasey, and Whatcoat sailed for America a few days later, bearing with them a letter from John Wesley acknowledging that the American Methodists were now disentangled from the state and the English hierarchy. They were now, he said, "at full liberty to follow the Scriptures and the Primitive Church." But this belongs to another part of our story.

Wesley had turned seventy-seven in 1780 and in the next few years he began to make more serious preparations for the continuation of Methodism after his death. In 1778 he opened his "New Chapel" in City Road, London, with a layout that proclaimed a fully fledged "church" rather than a meeting house for a religious society. It was equipped with both a communion table and a baptismal font, announcing that the sacraments were to be celebrated there as well as the ministry of preaching (although only those Methodist preachers who were also ordained priests of the Church of England were allowed to preside, Charles Wesley being among them). The "New Chapel" was also a center of fellowship and social service and the headquarters for British Methodism's very extensive publishing enterprises. John Wesley had his living quarters in a house built next door to the "New Chapel," directly across the street from Bunhill Field burial ground where the body of his mother Susanna lay. Two years after the "New Chapel" opened, the largest *CHPM* was published, with 539 hymns arranged "according to the experience of real Christians." This hymn-book was intended to establish Methodist patterns of spirituality that would exist long after the deaths of the Wesley brothers. As John suggested in the preface to the *CHPM*, it was designed to give a "distinct and full account of Scriptural Christianity" and a compendium of "practical divinity." Compiled for a people who were more inclined to sing their theology than to recite it in creeds, this hymn-book and its successors shaped and determined the faith of British Methodists for more than 200 years.

In these years Wesley also took legal steps to ensure the continuity and stability of his movement. He and Thomas Coke, assisted by Methodist lawyer William Clulow, prepared a Deed of Declaration in 1784 that affirmed the identity, constitution, and powers "of the Conference of the People Called Methodists." After Wesley's death the Conference was to consist, for the purposes of the law, of at least 100 preachers (including eleven who were based in Ireland), a body known as "the Legal Hundred." A system of regulations for the Conference was laid down more formally, including procedures for the keeping of records, for the appointment of officers, and for the timing of Conference business. There were then some 300 Methodist chapels founded upon the provisions of the Model Deed. As a connexion (the British tradition always spells this word with an "x"), the societies operated very much like churches within a denomination, notwithstanding all Wesley's protestations to the contrary.

Charles Wesley died in March 1788 and intimations of mortality began to press more earnestly on his eighty-five-year-old elder brother. Charles's loyalty to the Church of England had been unshakeable to the end, and his always forceful words to John about the nature of Methodism as a movement within the church had given shape and direction to their common task for half a century. After 1788 John was on his own to address the pastoral needs which continued to press on the Methodist societies. At the Conference in 1788, John Wesley not only ordained more preachers for missionary service overseas, but also laid hands on Alexander Mather (1733–1800) in order to provide a continuity of ordained Methodist ministry in England after his death. The 1788 Conference also set up a committee to manage Wesley's accounts and to superintend the publishing enterprise which had been such a significant part of his life's work. Between them Coke and Mather took over the duties of leadership from the increasingly infirm leader, presiding over Wesley's last Conferences in his stead.

On New Year's Day, 1791, John Wesley described himself as an old man "decayed from head to foot." "However," he continued, "blessed be God, I do not slack my labours. I can preach and write still." On February 22 he preached for the last time in his "New Chapel," and on March 2 he died, leaving the Wesleyan Methodist movement to make what it could of itself on both sides of the Atlantic.

CHAPTER 2

The British Methodist tradition after John Wesley

Perhaps to their surprise, Wesley's British heirs found themselves fully equipped to ensure both the stability and the growth of the movement after the death of their leader. They had inherited a unified understanding of the Methodist message, a result of both John's and Charles's considerable efforts to give them a deposit of faith and a set of doctrinal criteria embodied in the *Standard Sermons*, the *Explanatory Notes on the New Testament*, and the various hymn-books. The *Arminian Magazine*, renamed in 1798 the *Methodist Magazine*, and from 1822 the *Wesleyan Methodist Magazine*, was a significant resource in shaping a theological as well as a religious culture, not least by lifting up the "ideal Methodist" life-pattern in the biographies and autobiographies of both itinerant and local preachers, class leaders, and other laypeople. Furthermore, the Wesleyan movement had gathered to itself a number of intelligent and theologically sophisticated pastors, many of them, like Adam Clarke (1760–1832) and (a generation later) Richard Watson (1781–1833) and Thomas Jackson (1783–1883), considerable scholars in their own right. Equally central to this religious inheritance was a widespread commitment to the pursuit of holiness by both preachers and members alike. Although the original Methodist bands were beginning to fade away, the class meetings, with their apparatus of class leaders, disciplines, and class tickets, were fully intact at the time of John Wesley's death in 1791. Obituaries in the *Arminian Magazine* and the *Methodist Magazine*, however stereotyped, communicated a sense of the urgent need for scriptural holiness.

On a more institutional level, there was a well-integrated Conference and connexional framework, established on a firm legal foundation with functional continuity provided by the Legal Hundred. There were also at all levels vigorous leaders who had been close to John Wesley and who had absorbed both his spirit and his organizational vision. While Methodists constituted only a fraction of 1 percent of the total population of the British Isles, they numbered 53,691 in 1791 and were confident of a further growth in numbers. Then, as now, alongside those whose names appeared on the rolls as full members, were people who lived and died within the more general Methodist framework, and who would confidently describe themselves in public as Methodist. In addition, many people were known to have been deeply affected by Methodist preaching; they needed only to be brought to a higher level of commitment.

To all of these strengths may be added what scholars of religion call the "mythic" or "narrative dimension" of religious experience. We have alluded to the power of mythic narrative in the Methodist tradition when we indicated the role of the Aldersgate conversion story. Even though John Wesley himself appears not to have put much emphasis on his Aldersgate experience, many Methodists know this story by heart. In addition, the Methodist narrative includes heroic tales of the persecution of Methodists in the 1740s, including physical attacks on Wesley himself, even though by the time of his death he was a widely respected figure in British society. Methodists then as now have been convinced of their providential origins and destiny, and that they were raised up by God "to spread scriptural holiness throughout the land." This providential identity is reinforced in other mythic narratives, such as the story of the six-year-old John Wesley's rescue from the disastrous fire at the rectory in Epworth in 1709. The description of John at that time as "a brand plucked from the burning" (recalling Zechariah 3:2) carries the sense that God's hand was present from the beginning of Wesley's life, preserving him miraculously in order to raise up the Methodist movement.

Such sacred narratives are reinforced with sacred actions and sacred times. Methodists very early began commemorating the Sunday nearest May 24 as Aldersgate Sunday, and have regarded the Wesleys' birthplaces and homes in Epworth, London, and Bristol as important pilgrimage sites. All of this has given Wesleyan Methodists a strong and cohesive identity as a "people": a sense of themselves as occupying a "sacred time" and "sacred space."

So we may speak of Wesleyan Methodism at the turn of the nineteenth century as a community with well-functioning institutional bases, considerable spiritual strength and vitality, and with many of the elements of a full church order. Nevertheless, the awareness that the renewal movement had become a church led to serious internal controversies. While these controversies have their own internal logic, they must also be set against the social and political background of British society at the dawning of the Industrial Age. On the one hand, the social order was undergoing tremendous stress and upheaval as large numbers of people moved from the countryside into

the newly industrialized cities and towns. At the same time, the French
Revolution and the rise of Napoleon Bonaparte (1769–1821), following so
quickly on the heels of the American War of Independence, haunted the
imaginations of the British government and wide sections of the British
public. These "external" factors had lasting effects on the post-1791 period
of the British tradition of Methodism.

These effects may be considered under three headings: (1) the denomi-
nationalization of Wesleyan Methodism itself, leading to its drawing close
to the Dissenting denominations in councils and culture in the later part
of the nineteenth century; (2) the rejection of the particular form of the
Wesleyan denomination by radical Methodists; and (3) the involvement of
Methodists in social reform movements.

THE DENOMINATIONALIZATION OF WESLEYAN METHODISM

The first issue that had to be settled by the Methodists was the matter
of the administration of holy communion by the itinerant preachers, that
is, by those preachers who were not ordained in the Church of England.
Attendant upon this was the question of when and under what conditions
Methodist services of holy communion could take place. Although these
issues had been settled, out of pastoral necessity, for the Methodist situation
in America with the establishment of a Methodist Episcopal Church in
1784, the American experience did not provide a suitable model for British
Methodists. The 1791 Conference was conservative in its overall outlook
and quite resolved to "follow strictly the plan which Mr. Wesley left us."
But in the years that followed, it was recognized that such resolution was
open to a wide variety of interpretations, and by 1795 a fully spelt-out "Plan
of Pacification" had to be developed by the Conference.

If any one document could be said to represent a clear separation of the
Methodists from the Church of England it was the Plan of Pacification,
since it laid down that holy communion might be celebrated in Methodist
chapels where a majority of both trustees and stewards agreed and with the
approval of Conference. Holy communion was to be administered only
by the preachers who were "in full connexion" with the Conference. But,
reflecting a continued desire to follow the spirit of Wesley, the "Plan" also
forbade the celebration of the Lord's Supper at those times when the Church
of England would be celebrating it. The societies only gradually availed
themselves of these stipulations, but eventually holy communion became
an integral part of Wesleyan Methodist worship in each local chapel. This
compromise had a lasting result. The crowded communion services that the

Wesley brothers had known at the height of the revival were no more, and there was no longer any use for Wesley's collection of *Hymns on the Lord's Supper*, which was almost permanently lost to Methodism. A movement that had been at its heart eucharistic as well as evangelical now lost half of its character.

The Methodist itinerant preachers were now well on their way to being clergy in the same way as priests of the Church of England and ministers in the nonconformist denominations, and by 1818 they were referring to each other as "Reverend." This process of clericalization was completed in 1836 when Methodist ministers were first received into full connexion at a Conference session and a few hours later were ordained in Conference services by the "laying on of hands." This practice is still in use in the British Conference. Gradually these ministers began to be placed in settled pastorates, serving one chapel or a group of chapels for a period of years rather than traveling around a wide circuit of pastoral charges. Although preachers were no longer "itinerant" in the strict sense of the word, the language of "traveling" survives to the present time as a description of the work of the Methodist minister.

Consolidation of these early institutional changes was effected in the period of Jabez Bunting (1779–1858), who supplied leadership to Wesleyan Methodism for nearly fifty years. Bunting was first elected secretary of Conference in 1814, and served as its president in 1820, 1828, 1836, and 1844. Bunting was deeply dedicated to the spread of Methodism, and it was during his tenure that the Wesleyan Missionary Society was formed in 1818. Bunting also wanted to see a better prepared ministry, and the older idea of candidates learning as apprentices to more senior preachers gave way to the necessity of a college education. The first Wesleyan theological college of Methodism was established in Hoxton, London, in 1818. In Bunting's first period of service, Methodist membership grew to 200,000. When there was a worrying dip in membership in 1820, Bunting drafted the "Liverpool Resolutions," which urged a renewal of field preaching and public prayer meetings, as well as an end to "the spirit of strife and debate" in Methodist meetings. Interpretations of Jabez Bunting differ. In 1837 he said of his own vision of Methodism, "Ours is, and must be, to all eternity, Wesleyan," and he clearly saw himself as charged with the duty of maintaining that form of Methodism which John Wesley himself had established. In fact, as the first part of the nineteenth century progressed, Wesleyan Methodists increasingly thought of Bunting as the one man who was able to interpret the mind of John Wesley. Neither Wesley nor Bunting believed in democracy in the life of the church, and as Wesley's legitimate successor, Bunting devoted much of his energy to upholding Conference authority, which in his view was rooted in an understanding of the ministry established from above rather than emerging from below. Any suggestion of the lay administration of the sacraments was rejected out of hand and the presence of lay people in the Conference was strongly resisted. In Bunting's view, these measures would ensure that Methodism would stand in the great stream of Christian tradition as "a great church" and "a branch of the visible church of Christ."

As Methodism became a denomination in its own right, and as the primary allegiance of Wesleyans moved from the societies to the chapels, the older discipline expected of class members waned. Class meetings began to decline in significance, as did the influence of the class leader. Wesleyan Methodists now faced the problem of the mixed church, consisting of some who were fervent believers and others who were Wesleyans only by virtue of being born into a Methodist family. One Wesleyan minister of the period put the problem into sharp focus. There was, he averred, a need for "a less personalized and exacting form of religious exercise." At the same time, such middle-class Victorian values as respectability and restraint played their part in shaping Methodist piety, and services of worship moved toward increasing formality.

The peculiar character of Methodism as an evangelistic movement concerned with personal holiness was at this time manifestly giving way to the less demanding model of a "broad church." The Wesleyan concept of sanctity became more generally social and less pietistic in this period. The statistics for church membership demonstrate the appeal of this more permissive form of Methodism; by 1850 the Wesleyan Methodist Church had grown to 370,000 members including 21,000 in Ireland. (According to the 1851 census, the combined membership of all the various Methodist denominations was 534,000, or 3 percent of the adult population of Britain.) The Wesleyan Methodist Church would maintain its steady growth throughout the rest of the century.

One effect of the loss of the original spiritual energy inherent in the membership of small closed societies and bands, and the influence of a wider community of men and women who were Methodist "by birth," was the shaping of a particular and distinctive culture. Wesleyan Methodism became a world turned in upon itself. One of the more perceptive ministers of the period, John Rattenbury (1828–79), declared that "Methodist evangelism was entirely conducted in the chapels," and that it "made no deliberate attack on the outside world." A later historian has observed that this Methodist world contained "thousands of people for whom life was a Wesleyan creation, who saw the world through Wesleyan spectacles, for whom the future of Wesleyan Methodism mattered far more than the fate of secular empires." This self-containment was exemplified in the founding of Methodist schools and colleges, including the Wesleyan Teachers' Training College in Westminster in 1851. Its first principal, James Harrison Rigg (1821–1909), expounded the particular style of Victorian Methodism in his writings, notably in his 1887 *Principles of Church Organization.* Rigg vigorously defended Methodism against Anglican and Congregationalist detractors, attacked the "Christian socialism" of Frederick Denison Maurice, and eventually produced a biography of John Wesley that presented him as the model of a late-Victorian Evangelical. By 1890 the renewal movement that had been Methodism had come to see itself as a Free Church and therefore anti-Anglican and anti-Roman Catholic.

A chief cause of so much of the anti-Anglican feeling was the rise of the Oxford, or Tractarian, Movement in the Established Church. Its emphasis on elaborate ceremonial helped drive Wesleyan Methodists toward the historical Dissenting churches – the Presbyterians, Congregationalists, and Baptists – resulting in Methodists increasingly thinking of themselves as nonconformists. But, perhaps paradoxically, the Oxford Movement had the effect of forcing the Dissenting denominations to think about themselves in new ways. Historians see in this period the rise of a new ecclesial style among Baptists, Congregationalists, and Presbyterians. The outward manifestation of this new self-confidence was in more formal church architecture and modes of worship. In 1869 a veteran Congregationalist, Thomas Binney, spoke of the new buildings of English nonconformity where there were:

spires, towers, architectural elaboration, chancels, transepts, painted windows, and other medieval attributes; and that in many cases, the worship should increase in richness, variety, depth, devotion; while the service of song should expand and rise, taking in chant and anthem, and be distinguished by skill and culture, instead of, as before, being discordant, harsh, somnolent or boisterous, as the case might be.

Wesleyan Methodists, deeply influenced by this cultural shift, modified their styles of worship and archictecture accordingly.

In 1892 the first Free Church Congress took place in which the Wesleyans were thoroughly at home with their Dissenting friends, and "Free Church" became increasingly the term that they used to describe themselves. When the National Council of Evangelical Free Churches was established in 1896, the Methodist leader Hugh Price Hughes (1847–1902) was elected as its first president. Against this background the ecclesial self-consciousness of

Wesleyan Methodism reached its pinacle in 1897, when for the first time the minutes of the Conference used the term "Methodist Church" rather than "Methodist Connexion."

A new form of Methodism was being born, one that would take on new social and ecumenical patterns in the twentieth century. Among Hugh Price Hughes' legacies was a strong sense that Wesleyan Methodism was no longer a relatively impoverished and conservative denomination existing mainly in the North and the Midlands, but was a wealthier and more educated, more liberal and more socially committed church. With its headquarters in London, its impressive London missions, its Methodist members of parliament, and its two national newspapers, Methodism was prepared to play a role center-stage in the life of Britain.

There were nevertheless continuing manifestations of the old Methodist revivalism within Wesleyan Methodism. Thomas Champness (1832–1905) and his wife Eliza began training lay evangelists in their own home in Rochdale in Lancashire in the 1880s. In 1883 they began a weekly paper called *Joyful News*, modeled on the Salvation Army's *War Cry*, which soon reached a circulation of 30,000, and from 1889 Champness was released from circuit work for full-time evangelistic activity. In 1903 this work was taken over by the Wesleyan Home Mission department that established Cliff College (just outside Sheffield) to house the "Joyful News" evangelists. Cliff College would become the center for Holiness teaching in the British Methodist churches in the twentieth century.

THE RISE OF METHODIST RADICAL CHURCHES

The differing views about John Wesley's intentions for the future of Methodism could not always be contained within the structures which he set up. Within a decade of his death there were a number of breakaway movements from the Wesleyan center. Many of these, like the Protestant Methodist Association (1828) and the Wesleyan Association (1836), did not survive into the modern period, and are not therefore part of the living tradition we are looking at in this book. Others brought their particular emphases and experiences into the various schemes of reunion, culminating in the Methodist Union in 1932. (The notable exceptions are the Salvation Army and those Pentecostal churches descended from Methodism. They retain their distinctive identities and, while they exhibit some identifiably Methodist features, are only peripherally part of the Methodist family.)

Some of these groups were established in reaction to Wesley's autocratic structures of authority. In 1797 the Methodist New Connexion (MNC) was born when 5,000 Wesleyan Methodists met in Ebenezer Chapel, Leeds, to demand lay leadership within the Conference. The MNC survived throughout the nineteenth century and brought 40,000 members into the United Methodist Church in Great Britain in 1907. Other groups were keen to carry forward the Wesleys' evangelical zeal. The Bible Christians were formed in the West of England, led by Cornish farmer William O'Bryan (1778–1868), who once said that John Wesley was "ever near him." With fiery and energetic preachers such as "Billy" Bray (1794–1868), by occupation a tin-miner, the Bible Christian message reached parts of Devon and Cornwall that Wesleyan preachers had never penetrated. The "Rules of Society" of the Bible Christians were modeled on Wesley's *Rules* and the vigorous individualistic evangelism of the group led eventually to a Bible Christian membership of some 32,000. They too rejoined the larger Methodist fold as a part of the 1907 merger of the Methodist churches.

The splinter movement with the longest-lasting influence on British Methodism is the Primitive Methodist Church. The title it chose for itself represents the desire to return to the freedom of the first field preaching of 1739, as well as to continue being a church of the poor. In 1800 a small but fervent prayer meeting in Harriseahead in Staffordshire attracted the attention of Lorenzo Dow, a gifted although eccentric (he was known as "Mad Lorenzo") American freelance Methodist preacher from Connecticut who was traveling in England. Dow told the Harriseahead people of the wildfire success of the camp meetings in the USA. Two of his hearers, Hugh Bourne (1772–1852) and William Clowes (1780–1851), both Wesleyan preachers, saw the evangelistic possibilities of this type of meeting in England. On May 31, 1807, the first English camp meeting, and the forerunner of British nineteenth-century revivalism, was held on Mow Cop on the rugged Cheshire–Staffordshire border. Because of their association with the revival and their failure to attend class meetings regularly, Bourne and Clowes were expelled from the Wesleyan Methodists (in 1808 and 1810 respectively), but soon had small groups of like-minded people gathered around each of them. In 1811 the two associations, Bourne's "Camp Meeting Methodists" and the "Clowesites," united as the Primitive Methodists. The first Primitive Methodist chapel was built and class tickets were issued. With Wesleyan Methodism set upon the road to "respectability," the Primitive Methodists could cater to the manifest need for fervent religious expression among its working-class converts. Its camp meetings also offered a religious alternative to the northern English social custom of "wakes weeks," the annual summer holidays when the potteries, factories, and mills were closed, and when workers engaged in noisy revelry and heavy drinking.

Primitive Methodism was peculiarly at home in the large industrial villages of the North and the Midlands, as well as in rural areas like East Anglia and Lincolnshire. London was left untouched. Primitive Methodism had a special appeal to coal miners, factory-workers, North Sea fishermen, and agricultural laborers. Amidst the chronic poverty and economic depression that marked daily life, the Primitive Methodists taught that "hardship, struggle, exhaustion, blisters, were mere by-products of a world in sin: Christ was the Way out and the Way forward." Integral to the spread of this message was music. As one social historian has written of Primitive Methodism, "music spearheaded its mission; it marked out the good life and pointed out the bad; it sang out the dead and sang in the reborn." Recording the death of a Primitive Methodist coal miner named Grieves in County Durham, the same historian writes, "Just before his final breath the chapel brethren visited him and bawled hymns and prayers around his bed. Grieves himself joined in the last two lines of 'Guide me, O Thou great Jehovah!' and demanded them to sing over and over again, 'Songs of praises, songs of praises I will ever give to thee.'" Singing in the chapel was as vital to the "respectable" miner in clarifying his new self-image and celebrating his self-significance as drinking in the public house was to the "unrespectable."

But, like Wesleyan Methodism, the Primitive Methodist Church was also on its way to upward social mobility, even though it took a little longer than its parent denomination. The Primitive Methodists established a theological college in 1881, guided by distinguished teachers such as Arthur S. Peake (1865–1929). They also built highly ornate urban churches, which someone described as "the mahoganification of Primitive Methodism." By 1903 it was calling itself "the Primitive Methodist Church," and in 1912 it established its headquarters in London. Like the Wesleyans, Primitive Methodism had become a denomination, and at the time of British Methodist Union in 1932 there were 222,000 PM members with over 1,000 ministers and 13,000 local preachers.

Three other breakaway movements from Wesleyan Methodism have survived to the present day. The first is the Wesleyan Reform Union, which began as a reaction to the anti-democratic and centralized authority structures enforced by Jabez Bunting and others in the mid-nineteenth century. At a meeting in 1852, this group demanded that "all future deliberations affecting the interests of the church . . . be conducted in the presence of the people, who shall be fully and fairly represented." When hope of change within Wesleyan Methodism faded, the Wesleyan Reform Union drafted a constitution, which upheld the autonomy of the local congregation and provided for its own annual Conferences. Today this strongly evangelical group has over 2,000 members and 115 chapels. They are closely affiliated with the British Evangelical Alliance.

The Independent Methodist Church traces its origins to 1806 as a union of Methodist revivalist groups in the north of England and North Wales, each of which retained its own name: Quaker Methodists, Band Room Methodists, and Christian Revivalists, for example. With its emphasis on local autonomy, there was never a need for annual Conferences, although the Independent Methodist Connexion of Churches established a "committee" to manage the business of the Connexion. Independent Methodists have always maintained a strong revivalist tradition and an equally strong affirmation of the necessity for an unpaid ministry.

The separation of the third group, the Salvation Army, represents the most serious loss to the British Methodist tradition. Founded in London's East End by William Booth (1829–1912), who began his evangelistic work as a Wesleyan Methodist local preacher, the Salvation Army carries on Booth's own strong commitment to work among the poor. When Booth found the scope of his preaching limited within Wesleyan Methodism, he resigned and in 1854 joined and was eventually ordained in the Methodist New Connexion (MNC). But once again he felt constrained by the Methodist structures, and in 1861 heated disagreement with the MNC Conference about where he should be stationed and how he should be used caused him to leave Methodism altogether. His work among the poor in East London led to the founding of the Salvation Army in 1865. Salvationists still retain features of Methodist theology, especially in their holiness teaching, but there are no longer any formal links with either the British or American traditions of Methodism. Just recently Salvationist–Methodist conversations have begun under the auspices of the World Methodist Council and representatives from the Salvation Army are often invited to take part in the gatherings of the World Methodist Council.

THE INVOLVEMENT OF METHODISTS IN SOCIAL REFORM MOVEMENTS

According to his son and biographer, Frederick Denison Maurice (1805–72), the most significant Anglican theologian of the nineteenth century, was often asked the question, "How do you account for the fact that England at the end of the eighteenth-century escaped a revolution like that of France?" Maurice's answer was always the same: "Ah, there is not the least doubt as to that. England escaped a political revolution because she had undergone a religious revolution." When he was further pressed, "You mean that brought about by Wesley and Whitefield?" Maurice would answer,

"Of course." Whether or not they are familiar with Maurice's views on this matter, modern historians and social scientists have given a great deal of attention to the role played by Methodism in influencing social change in Britain in the early period of its existence. Some have thought it highly unlikely that Methodism played a significant role in averting political upheaval because the number of Methodist converts was relatively small (as we have seen, at the time of Wesley's death Methodists represented less than 1 percent of the population). Others have suggested that Methodism would have had to have been much more firmly embedded in the working class of the eighteenth century to have made any contribution to preventing revolution. But, as Maurice clearly perceived, Methodist influence on British society was undoubtedly greater than might be suggested by the numbers of Methodists recorded in the census data. The Methodist movement summoned people to assert a reasoned control over their own lives, while at the same time showing how a system of mutual discipline could provide the vehicle for a new kind of social and ethical consciousness.

So we meet a paradox. Although the Wesleys and their revival movement were phenomena of the eighteenth century, it was in fact the nineteenth century that Methodism would decisively help to mold. This molding of the nineteenth-century social fabric happened in a variety of ways, according to the different emphases of the various Methodist groupings. As we have seen, Wesleyan Methodism's origins lay in the High Church Toryism of its founders, whose protestations of loyalty to the crown were both vigorous and heartfelt to end of their lives. In the year before John Wesley died, the minutes of Conference gave in answer to the question, "What directions shall be given concerning our conduct to the Civil Government?"

None shall, either in writing or conversation, speak lightly of the Government under which he lives: we are to observe that the oracles of God command us to be subject to the higher powers, and that honour to the King is therefore connected with the fear of God.

But the precise relationship between Methodists and politics was left to be worked out in the nineteenth century. The struggle began with an immense civil protest. Against the background of the Napoleonic threat, when all forms of Dissent were feared by those in authority, a bill was formulated in 1811 by Lord Sidmouth, the Home Secretary, that would have severely curtailed Methodist preaching by limiting the number of licenses granted to dissenting preachers. Resistance by Methodist laymen was both immediate and potent, with over 700 petitions with 30,000 signatures, and, as a result, the proposed legislation was dropped. Nevertheless Wesleyan

Methodists had begun to recognize that their continued existence depended upon ever louder assertions of their loyalty to the king. As Thomas Allan (1774–1845), a prominent Methodist lawyer, told the Prime Minister of the day: "In times of scarcity and distress we may safely say that among colliers, miners and mechanics, Methodism has been the grand instrument of preserving subordination." By 1819, the year of the Peterloo Massacre, the statements of official Wesleyanism were repudiating any alliance with radicalism and exercising discipline on those members who transgressed, instructing Methodists to "Fear the Lord and the King: and meddle not with them that are given to change." After the immediate ferment of this period died down, Wesleyan Methodism generally took a neutral political stance. At the Wesleyan Conference in 1831 (the year before the passing of the first Reform Bill in 1832), Methodists were advised "Let not worldly politics engross too much of your time and attention."

But the more Wesleyan Methodism gravitated toward becoming an ecclesiastical establishment, and the more its preachers were perceived to be professional clergy, the more Primitive Methodism and the other groups grew. When the British trades union movement was legalized by the repeal of the Combination Acts in 1825, Primitive Methodism was sufficiently strong among urban artisans to be a major influence in popular politics, and contributed men and women who had learned leadership and public-speaking skills in their chapels and class meetings. A reliable authority has suggested that something like 20 percent of the most politicized members of the adult working class were associated with the chapel communities (he included the Wesleyan working people in this estimate). Among these were such labor leaders as Joseph Arch (1826–1919) among the agricultural workers and, in a later generation, Peter Lee (1864–1935) among the coal miners. Organizationally, the trades union movement clearly appropriated Methodist structures, with its three tiers of annual conferences, district meetings, and local societies. As a religious option, Methodism was sufficiently imbued with radical notions to make its members a potentially disaffected people, but Methodist discipline always exercised a moderating influence, and it was clear that the proper ends of life were not to be achieved by political means. The annual address of the Wesleyan Association said in 1839:

Whatever may be your political opinions, never introduce them into the Church of Christ, nor suffer them to interfere with your religious duties, or unduly to occupy your attention. Never substitute the Newspaper for the Bible, or the company of political partisans for that of the followers of the Lord Jesus Christ, or political meetings for the means of grace.

The reasons for the social disruption that increasingly marked the nineteenth century were made abundantly clear by the first national census in 1851. In the half-century since 1801, the population had almost doubled, from less than 11 million to more than 21 million. The rapid migration of people from rural areas into the industrialized cities and towns had put overwhelming pressure on urban infrastructures, and the majority of the English public who lived in cities had very few social amenities. The foundations of the class structure were also being undermined, and reform movements and welfare societies were plentiful, many concerned directly with the plight of the poor.

This social and political ferment resulted in two, mutually contradictory, effects on Methodism. On the one hand, the greatest disruption of Methodist unity occurred between 1847 and 1852, when more than 100,000 members severed their connection with Wesleyan Methodism. Most of those who left attached themselves to the Wesleyan Methodist Association (another group who had resisted Jabez Bunting's anti-democratic policies). These joined with the Wesleyan Reformers in 1857 to make up the United Methodist Free Churches (UMFC). At the same time, however, this period also marks a new stage in Methodist growth, mirroring similar increases in membership among the Congregationalists, the Baptists, and other Dissenting bodies. In the case of Wesleyan Methodism membership grew from 348,274 in 1849 to 463,224 in 1902, an increase of 33 percent (with similar expansion taking place in the other Methodist connexions). With the rise in numbers came a concomitant increase in political influence, and the question soon arose: "How should our political influence be used?"

The social problems of the period weighed heavily on the conscience of Methodism, and that sensitivity was heightened as the Methodist population increased. Various resources were available to aid Methodists in reflecting on their responsibility for their neighbors. Two years after the publication of Karl Marx's *Communist Manifesto* and the 1848 Paris uprising a group calling themselves: "Christian Socialists" – F. D. Maurice, J. M. F. Ludlow, Charles Kingsley, and Thomas Hughes – began publishing a weekly paper, *The Christian Socialist*. These men, all Anglicans, argued forcefully for a renewed social order in which cooperation would replace conflict. Their views were widely publicized in the popular novels of the day, such as Kingsley's *Alton Locke* and *Yeast*. More secular social thinkers like John Ruskin were widely read among Methodists and Dissenters alike, and in 1883 an anonymous writer (now known to have been a Congregationalist minister) published the influential book *The Bitter Cry of Outcast*

London, further raising the Methodist sense of social responsibility for the urban poor.

Coming to maturity in these years was Hugh Price Hughes, whom we have already met as the first president of the National Council of Evangelical Free Churches. As a London missioner he knew first-hand the terrible condition of the urban poor and was thoroughly aroused by *The Bitter Cry of Outcast London*. Hughes laid down this challenge:

Methodism has reached the parting of the ways. We must either go back into the obscurity of a Class religion, and the impotence of a moribund sect; or we must go forward into the blessed opportunities and far reaching beneficence of a national religion, which preaches the Gospel to the poor.

The Wesleyan response to Hughes' call for action was the "Forward Movement," founded in 1885 as a determined effort to bridge the increasing chasm between Methodists and the poor. This movement led directly to the building of the Methodist Central Halls as centers of social work and popularist worship in the urban areas. But, as in many other cases when churches do good "from the outside," the immense energy given to the Forward Movement was aimed at the symptoms of social deprivation rather than at its causes. In 1885 Hugh Price Hughes became the founder-editor of the *Methodist Times: a Journal of Religious and Social Movement*, which he used as a platform to raise issues of personal morality, including the use of alcohol, gambling, and sexual ethics, as well as broader themes like the rights of women, non-sectarian education, and international and national peace (including Home Rule for Ireland). All these were the burdens of "the Nonconformist conscience."

The commitment of the Forward Movement to political action as a means of solving social problems was usually worked out as broad support for the aims of the Liberal Party. But there were limits. The concern for social morality was focused sharply on temperance and sexual purity in the face of what was seen as aristocratic libertinism. Thus we have Hughes' memorable statement, at the time of the scandal in the divorce case concerning the Irish politician Charles Parnell, "What is morally wrong cannot be politically right," which has given guidance to generations of Methodists in shaping their public lives. Some historians have considered that Hughes overemphasized Charles Parnell's adultery (a micro-ethical issue) and failed to see Parnell's crucial role in bringing about Home Rule for Ireland (a macro-ethical issue).

Happily, alongside Hughes' passionate but often theologically ungrounded eloquence, other gifted Methodists like Samuel E. Keeble

(1853–1946) and John Scott Lidgett (1854–1953) offered a more profound analysis of social change. Described in his Conference obituary as "a major prophet within our church," Keeble was among the first to examine the underlying causes of social evils by using some of the tools supplied by Karl Marx. He once said "a purified socialism is simply an industrially applied Christianity." Both his writings and his organization of study fellowships and working groups, like the Wesleyan Methodist Union for Social Service and the Wesleyan Methodist Peace Fellowship (1916), enabled many British Methodist ministers and laypeople to play a leading part in the Labour Party and in the advocacy of Christian pacifism throughout the twentieth century. But the greatest influence on the shape of early twentieth-century Methodism was undoubtedly John Scott Lidgett, who founded the Bermondsey Settlement in the slums of south London in 1892, where he stayed for sixty years. As Hughes' successor as editor of the *Methodist Times* from 1907–18, as vice-chancellor of the University of London, as leader of the Progressive Party in the London County Council, as president of the Wesleyan Methodist Conference in 1908, and as president of the 1932 Union Conference, Lidgett influenced the way Methodists thought of themselves at many different levels. He was a disciple of F. D. Maurice and was passionately on the side of the working class. His vision of the Fatherhood of God, set out in a major theological work, enabled him to work out his own version of the Social Gospel. Though never a member of the Labour Party, he looked toward a redeemed society in which cooperation rather than competition would be the key to social relations. In the judgment of one historian, Lidgett offered British Methodism a vision of "the total development, spiritual, mental and physical of people, by themselves and in community."

As we conclude this brief survey of nineteenth-century British Methodism, we must make it clear that there were issues that we have not touched on here. They are certainly important for an accurate understanding of religion and society in the nineteenth century, but now form very little part of the cumulative tradition of world Methodism. As the twentieth century began, the changes in theology, common life, worship, spirituality, social ethics, and ecumenical attitudes that were signaled in the work of Hughes, Keeble and Lidgett were the forces shaping the British Methodist denominations. How these worked themselves out we shall see in chapters 5–10.

CHAPTER 3

Methodism in North America

American Methodism has its roots firmly planted in the birth of the new republic. Its rise as a newly independent church paralleled the rise of the newly independent nation, and Methodism both reflected and contributed to the democratic impulses embodied in the Declaration of Independence. The religious situation in which it found itself was a very different one from that of its Methodist parent, largely as a result of the American constitutional doctrine of the separation of church and state, and the resulting lack of any form of Established Church. The class system had indeed been transplanted to the colonies in the early days of settlement, with almost feudal traditions that insisted that individuals should "know their place." The hierarchy also included the university-educated clergy, whether Congregationalist in New England or Anglican in Virginia, who were treated with particular deference.

But after 1776 most forms of this kind of social elitism began to perish, and in the churches mechanisms of patronage and rigid structures of clerical succession were soon abandoned. In many places, especially as Americans began to resettle away from the older cities and towns of the eastern seaboard, the idea of conformity to an imposed ecclesiastical framework was disappearing, and with it much of the respect for educated clergy. The new nation that came to birth in 1776 was bursting with life and energy. The population, which at the time of the Revolution was 2.5 million, rose to 9 million by 1815, and then to 23 million in 1850. At the same time the America of George Washington, John Adams, and Thomas Jefferson had a passion for expansion and a zeal for religious reconstruction, and the great westward migration began with all its turbulence and vitality.

With its own commitment to numerical and geographical extension matched by an eagerness to abandon the old ways of European Christianity, Methodism mirrored the ideals of the young republic. Beginning with a few thousand members at the time of the Christmas Conference of 1784, the Methodist Episcopal Church grew to about a quarter of a million by

1820, then to half a million by 1830 and to over one million by 1843. Like the founders of the republic, the first bishops of American Methodism believed that religion was a purely voluntary matter. Methodist preachers believed their movement should become a rapidly expanding association of freely committed faithful persons. Under Francis Asbury, the Methodists (along with the Baptists and the Disciples who shared the same kind of vision) became self-consciously an expansionist movement, pressing ever westwards as the frontiers were continually enlarged.

But what was this American Methodist Church? We left off our narrative in the first chapter with John Wesley sending Thomas Coke, Richard Whatcoat, and Thomas Vasey across the Atlantic to ensure the continuity of his movement in America. Wesley had acknowledged, however reluctantly, that American Methodists were now totally disentangled from both the British state and the Church of England hierarchy and were "at full liberty to follow the Scriptures and the Primitive Church." But he surely never envisioned just how "full" this liberty would become.

Desperate pastoral need for ordained clergy had precipitated Wesley's radical step of ordaining Vasey and Whatcoat for the work in America, and the need for further ministers would be the first challenge to be faced by American Methodists. The question of authority immediately confronted Francis Asbury, who saw that in a democratic nation any authority he might exercise over the American Methodists had to come from "below" rather than from "above." It would not help him to be seen as having been given his right to exercise authority in American Methodism by John Wesley, by then an extremely unpopular figure in America on account of his views on the War of Independence. It is not surprising, then, that Asbury was dismayed when he met Thomas Coke and Richard Whatcoat for the first time at Barratt's Chapel, Delaware, on November, 14, 1784, and they told him of Mr. Wesley's plan to commission him as superintendent. He wrote in his *Journal* that he was "shocked," but allowed that "it may be of God." Astutely he insisted that the American preachers must elect him as their leader, commenting, "I shall not act in the capacity I have hitherto done by Mr. Wesley's appointment." Asbury won his point, and the group of American preachers with him in Delaware put forward the possibility of an independent Methodist Church overseen by superintendents or "bishops."

A date and place were set for a Conference of all American itinerant preachers: December 24, 1784 in Baltimore. Always referred to as the "Christmas Conference," the nearly sixty preachers who assembled agreed to form themselves, in Asbury's words, "into an Episcopal church, and to have Superintendents, Elders, and Deacons." "When the conference was seated," Asbury recorded in his *Journal*, "Dr. Coke and myself were unanimously elected to the superintendency of the Church, and my ordination followed, after being previously ordained deacon and elder." By 1788, Asbury had dropped the title "superintendent" for one that best suited his position in an "Episcopal Church," and he became Bishop Asbury. John Wesley was outraged. He wrote to Asbury,

How can you, how dare you suffer yourself to be called Bishop? I shudder. I start at the very thought! Men may call me a knave or a fool, a rascal, a scoundrel, and I am content; but they shall never by my consent call me Bishop! For my sake. For God's sake, for Christ's sake put a full end to this.

Charles Wesley had his own way of expressing his anger:

> A Roman Emperor 'tis said
> His favorite horse a consul made;
> But Coke brings greater things to pass
> He makes a bishop of an ass.

In the context of such strong and intractable sentiments, close ties of affection and respect between John Wesley and the Methodists in America could no longer be maintained. From this point Wesley's authority no longer extended to America. By 1792 the Conference had radically altered Wesley's *Sunday Service for the Methodists in North America*, leaving little except a brief section in the *Book of Discipline* called "Sacramental Services." Soon even John Wesley's name was dropped from the *Minutes* of the Methodist Episcopal Church (hereafter MEC). Asbury's power increased and he ruled unchallenged as the Methodist bishop in the new republic (Thomas Coke, the other superintendent ordained at the Christmas Conference, was but an occasional visitor in America and never used the title of bishop.)

Asbury's autocracy was not without its problems; his preachers' ideas of democratic government were at variance with his own notions of one-man rule. In 1792, James O'Kelly (1757–1826) demanded that preachers be allowed to object to the appointments Asbury imposed on them, and denounced him as "tyrannous" and "papistical." Such charges of behaving like a pope left Asbury unmoved: "For my part, I pity those who cannot distinguish between a pope of Rome and an old worn man of about sixty years." In Asbury's view, the duty of the Methodist bishop lay in maintaining the traveling nature of the preachers. Like George Whitefield before him, Francis Asbury was a salesman of the Gospel. America's new settlements were full of potential customers, and it was the task of Methodist preachers to reach them all. He himself traveled ceaselessly, crossing the mountain ranges of eastern America again and again. Repudiating the Catholic doctrine of the historic episcopacy (which he referred to as the "crooked muddy succession"), Asbury reflected on what he called "the true primitive order" of the New Testament, and suggested that bishops should be recognized by their actions. Bishops had no authority simply because of order or hierarchy. They should resemble him and his colleagues. In one of his finer pieces of rhetoric, Asbury asks about the older episcopal churches:

Would their bishops ride five or six thousand miles in nine months for ninety dollars a year, with their traveling expenses less or more, preach daily when opportunity serves, meet a number of camp meetings in a year, make arrangements for stationing seven hundred preachers, ordain a hundred more annually, ride through all kinds of weather, and long roads in the worst state, at our time of life – the one sixty-nine, the other in his fifty-sixth year?

In addition to his own preaching and administrative work, Asbury recruited as many "assistant salesmen" as he could as circuit riders, demanding of them a level of devotion and entrepreneurship equal to his own. He had been raised in humble circumstances (his father had been a gardener), and he saw himself and his preachers as committed to an apostolic order of poverty and itinerancy. Always the traveling preachers were to move from the center to the periphery; they were never to settle in one place, and always they were to act under discipline and strict obedience to the bishop.

The bishop's role was to admit candidates for the ministry, to test them, and then to ordain them. Those who felt called to preach began as class leaders, then became exhorters, and after that local preachers. At this point, if their call to preach was affirmed, they would be licensed as itinerant preachers on probation, receiving a kind of apprenticeship by riding with slightly older preachers. These relentlessly energetic young men became the core group of itinerant preachers (or "circuit riders"). As one early Methodist wrote of himself:

> As full of zeal and pure desire
> As e'er a coal was full of fire,
> I flash'd and blazed by day and night
> A burning and a shining light.

Though they themselves were nearly destitute (their annual salary of $80 was rarely paid in full), these itinerant preachers focused upon the needs of the poor. Asbury insisted that all the trappings of middle-class professionalism should be laid aside: no fine dress, no airs and graces, let alone any financial security. "We must," he said, "suffer *with*, if we labor *for* the poor."

By 1828, some 2,500 itinerant preachers were recruited to this way of life, but as studies indicate, only a minority lasted more than twelve years. Most died before they were forty, and a high proportion of them, before they were thirty. But, despite this, the circuit riders as a group were enormously successful in spreading the Gospel, and it can be said with confidence that hardly a hamlet in early republican America was left unvisited by a Methodist preacher. Bishop Asbury became the most instantly recognized American of his times, and other Methodist leaders like Peter Cartwright (1785–1872) were household names. An early American Methodist song summarized their mission like this:

> God's ministers like flames of fire
> Are passing through the land,
> Their voice is here: "Repent and fear,
> King Jesus is at hand!"

In Asbury's time only traveling preachers or circuit riders were permitted to be members of the Annual Conferences. Those who wished or were forced to "locate" (that is, to stop itinerating, usually because of marriage or a failure of health) became local preachers again, losing their place in the Conference. Primary ministerial identity lay in membership of the Conference where Asbury ruled supreme.

This energetic form of Methodism was contemporary with what is known as the Second Great Awakening, a mass religious movement that had as its primary thrust the need to convert sinners by every possible means. A new instrument invented for this purpose was the camp meeting, the first of which took place in Cane Ridge, Kentucky, in August 1801.

Ever pragmatic, Methodists warmly embraced camp meetings, for they were tailormade for the needs of rural pioneers who gathered after harvest time for three, four, or even more nights to alleviate the isolation and extreme loneliness of frontier life. Unlike the field preaching of George Whitefield or John and Charles Wesley, the focus in the camp meetings was not so much upon the message of the preacher, as upon ensuring the participation of every person present. Camp meetings encouraged personal testimonies, which might include public sharing of private religious experience and overt physical displays of powerful emotional release (the kind of physical manifestations that John Wesley noticed in his early field preaching). In America, those who attended camp meetings were prone to "fainting, shouting, yelling, crying, sobbing and grieving"; a contemporary witness reported leaving off his own preaching at a camp meeting just to watch this phenomenon. This preacher "saw them in every part

7. Camp meeting in the southern United States, engraving by E. W. Clay, published in New York by H. R. Robinson in 1836.

of the congregation with streaming eyes, and groaning for mercy, while others were shouting praises to God for delivering grace." Unlike the earliest Methodist preaching, there was a distinct emphasis on the dangers of hell-fire and songs detailing the miseries of the damned were common:

> Can you sport upon the brink
> Of everlasting woe?
> Hell beneath is gaping wide.
> Vengeance waits the dread command.
> Soon will stop your sport and pride,
> And sink you with the damned.

By such means camp meetings were designed to bring sinners to the point of utter despair. But then, when all seemed hopeless, the preachers' themes became simple and straightforward: repentance, the acceptance of the offer of salvation by faith in Jesus Christ, and the assurance, or witness, of the Holy Spirit.

Francis Asbury described camp meetings as "fishing with a large net." "Camp meetings! Camp Meetings!" he enthused, "The battle ax and weapon of war!" Such gatherings would, he said, "break down walls of wickedness." In May 1806 he reported by letter to his colleague Thomas Coke (still a superintendent of the Methodist Episcopal Church, though increasingly an absentee) that 8,273 new members had been added to American Methodism, chiefly through camp meetings. Asbury reported a four-day camp meeting northeast of New York City and another one of a hundred days and nights in Delaware. By this time Wesleyan Methodism in Britain was concerned about the propriety of this method, and when Asbury's letter was published in England in the *Methodist Magazine*, all the references to these camp meetings were omitted.

But even before Asbury's death in 1816 there were signs of impending change. An American "pilgrimage to respectability" was about to take place that was similar to that already affecting British Methodism. As in the British Isles, part of this was a result of social mobility within an increasingly urban and industrialized landscape, attracting migration from the farms and villages. The cities of the eastern seaboard of the new republic were mushrooming, and roads and canals were being built, making travel from one place to another much easier. These growing cities needed pastors who would remain in one place, and for their part the Methodist preachers themselves increasingly wanted to marry and settle down. In fact all the bishops elected after Francis Asbury and William McKendree (1757–1835) were married men.

Larger buildings were also required to accommodate growing member-
ships in the cities. So, for example, $30,000 was raised in this period to
enlarge St. John Street Church in New York, with another $600 pledged to
build the first Methodist "manse," or preacher's house. Before long other
methods, somewhat more respectable than the camp meeting, would be
found to add members to the church, and Christian nurture and socializa-
tion started to replace revivalism as the main source of new members.

Among the preachers leaving the rural areas to settle in the new cities
was Nathan Bangs (1778–1862). Bangs had started out as a circuit rider
in Upper Canada and Quebec, arriving in New York in 1812. His first
appointment was as "preacher-in-charge" of New York City, superintending
five preaching places with five preachers and some 2,000 members. Though
he was soon transferred to other work, during his lifetime he witnessed the
growth of New York Methodism to sixty churches with 17,000 members.
He soon took over the administration of the Methodist Book Concern,
which under his care became the largest and most prosperous publishing
house in the world, with large-circulation journals including the *Christian
Advocate and Journal* (1828) and the *Methodist Quarterly Review* (1830), as
well as a long list of books in print. Bangs' religious publishing ventures
made him not only a fixture on the New York scene, but also a significant
influence on the whole Methodist connection though his editorial policies.

Nathan Bangs is for American Methodism what Jabez Bunting was for
British Methodism. Firmly opposed to the evangelistic phenomena that
Asbury had so much encouraged, he reversed many of Asburys' frontier policies. Like Bunting in England, he intensely disliked enthusiastic
revivalism with its "spirit of pride, presumption and bigotry, impatience
of scriptural restraint and moderation, clapping of the hands, screaming
and even jumping," claiming that it "marred and disgraced the work of
God." Bangs also worked to reverse what he regarded as Asbury's error in
keeping the preachers poor, and was profoundly concerned to raise both
the intellectual and the economic standards of Methodist preachers. As
we saw with Jabez Bunting and the Theological Institution in England,
the idea of apprenticeship very quickly gave way to seminary training as
the preferred mode of theological education for Methodist preachers. The
New England Conference set up the Newbury Biblical Institute in Vermont
in 1836, which was to be the predecessor of Boston University School of
Theology. Similarly, Bangs used both the Methodist periodicals for which
he was responsible, the *Christian Advocate and Journal* and the *Methodist
Quarterly Review*, to "draw forth the most matured efforts of our best
writers," and thus cultivated literary taste within the Methodist population.

Methodism was on its way to being the great church of bourgeois America, "tempered," as one writer has said, "with the virtues of middle class propriety and urbane collegiality." As a result, American Methodism produced mayors and senators, judges and lawyers, bankers and industrialists, and civic leaders of all kinds. The MEC was beginning to lose its vital concern for the poor just as the Wesleyan Methodist Church of Great Britain had done.

The impulse to divide over matters of doctrine and practice was as strong in American Methodism as it was in Britain, and within a short time of the establishment of the MEC Methodist "side-streams" began to be produced, some of which would diverge from the parent denomination completely, while others would eventually return to contribute to the wholeness of the United Methodist Church when that was formed in 1968.

Some of these secessionist tendencies were the result of precisely the same internal forces that had split Wesleyan Methodism in England. When James O'Kelly's demand for a more democratic governing structure and more autonomy for preachers was defeated by the 1792 Conference, he gathered like-minded followers and established the Republican Methodist Church. Although it registered some success, especially in Virgina where 4,000 Methodists joined it, the Republican Methodist Church failed to thrive and eventually the churches in O'Kelly's connection joined with the Congregationalists. But other Methodist divisions in America had no British parallels and were the direct result of the distinctively new situation in the United States.

Drawn by the promise of land and equal opportunity, immigrants of many nationalities had begun to converge on the new United States of America. In areas of considerable German immigration, notably in Pennsylvania, many German-speaking evangelistic movements sprang up, two of which in particular were closely related in their spiritual and religious life to the Methodists. The first of these, the Church of the United Brethren in Christ, was led by Philip William Otterbein (1726–1813), whose close relationship to English-speaking Methodism was marked by his presence at the Baltimore Christmas Conference in 1784. A second German-speaking group, the Evangelical Association, was led by Jacob Albright (1759–1808), a layman also greatly influenced by Methodist doctrines. By 1803 Albright was able to gather his people in a two-day meeting and eventually in 1807 to constitute a church (and later an association of churches) that was entirely Methodist in practice and discipline. For the first part of its life the work of the Evangelical Association was done exclusively in German. Despite much mutual goodwill between the United Brethren and the Evangelical

Association, these two communities did not unite until 1946, at which time they called themselves the Evangelical United Brethren (EUB). The EUB in its turn joined with the MEC in 1968 to constitute the present-day United Methodist Church (UMC). Although the EUB had existed as an independent entity for only twenty-two years, it was the repository of memories and traditions that dated back to the early years of the republic. The German spiritual style of these Methodist Christians brought a more sectarian frame of mind into the union, a sense of the importance of a deliberate separation from secular pleasures, and a willing acceptance of persecution. Their vision, it has been suggested, was less triumphalistic than that of their more prominent and visible Methodist cousins, and its effects on local congregations of the UMC after the 1968 union have been pervasive and persistent.

Some of the tensions in the Methodist Episcopal Church in this early period mirrored tensions that were at work in the United States more generally. Perhaps the most significant of these challenges for both church and nation was the question of racial discrimination. By the middle of the nineteenth century the question of slavery would divide Northern and Southern Methodists, causing a disruption that in some respects has never been completely healed. But long before this institutional rupture took place, racial issues had begun to divide American Methodists.

In the early republic the message of freedom in Christ resonated powerfully and authentically with slaves, whose company the early Methodist preachers frequently chose to keep as part of their ministry with the poor. Certainly these preachers encouraged a heartfelt response to the proclamation of the good news and patterns of religious expression that were in tune with African-American culture, including forms of communal ecstasy with spontaneous shouting, chanting, and singing. Methodism in this style tapped into the rich heritage of African traditional religious beliefs, worship, and spirituality and it evoked a deep and widespread response within the black population. By 1800 nearly 20,000 African Americans were Methodists. One African-American Methodist leader of this period explained this attraction:

The Methodists were the first people that brought glad tidings to the colored people . . . for all other denominations preached so high-flown that we were not able to comprehend their doctrine. Sure am I that reading sermons will never prove so beneficial to the colored people as spiritual or extempore preaching.

Nevertheless, racial prejudice manifested itself very early within Methodist congregations. In St. George's Methodist church in Philadelphia,

African-American members were confined to a separate part of the church during services of worship. This blatant segregation, together with other forms of discourteous treatment of African Americans, led Richard Allen (1760–1831), himself a freed slave as well as a Methodist local preacher, first to protest and then to lead a group out of the church to form their own congregation. At first they intended only to leave St. George's, and not the whole MEC, and Bishop Asbury himself dedicated their first church building in 1794. But continued friction with the white-dominated Conference and rumors of racism in other American cities led to the establishment of the African Methodist Episcopal Church (AME) in 1816, with Richard Allen as its first bishop. The AME's *Book of Discipline* of 1817 was closely modeled on the *Book of Discipline* of the MEC. The new denomination expanded vigorously, sending missionaries to Haiti in 1821 and reaching the Pacific coast in the 1850s. The AME grew steadily throughout the nineteenth and twentieth centuries, and by the turn of the twenty-first century it reported a membership in the USA of 2 million and had produced a number of influential theologians like James H. Cone and Jacqueline Grant. As a result of its missionary activities, the AME has a total worldwide community of 3.5 million in 8,000 congregations on four continents.

Similar experiences of exclusion in a Methodist congregation in New York led James Varick (*c.* 1750–1827), a shoemaker and local preacher, to form an alternative African-American congregation, and in 1821 a number of other African-American religious societies in Long Island. Connecticut and Philadelphia soon joined to form the African Methodist Episcopal Zion Church (AMEZ), with Varick as its first bishop. They rejected affiliation with both the MEC and the AME. In the early years the AMEZ was confined to the northern states, but as soon as the Civil War ended the denomination expanded into the former Confederacy, becoming particularly strong in North Carolina. In 1876 a North Carolina pastor, Andrew Cartwright, set up a mission in Liberia that later expanded into the Gold Coast (Ghana) and Nigeria. Further missionary activity established AMEZ Conferences in Jamaica, South Africa, India, and England.

Despite the vigor of these black denominations, many other African-American Methodists remained steadfastly within the MEC, albeit often within separate congregations. The oldest of these, still flourishing, is Zoar United Methodist Church in Philadelphia, founded in 1816. As the nineteenth century progressed, a pattern of African-American Conferences began to emerge in the MEC, partly as a result of the first stirrings of what would later be called "black nationalism." By 1895 there were no longer any racially mixed Conferences remaining in the MEC. Although this obviously represents another kind of involuntary segregation, such separation did enable African-American traditions of worship and spirituality to flourish, and the special political and religious interests of black Methodists to be treated seriously.

Another factor in the close allegiance of African Americans to early Methodism was undoubtedly the attitude of John Wesley, who called American slavery "the vilest that ever saw the sun," and of both Thomas Coke and Francis Asbury, who visited President George Washington asking him to emancipate the slaves. From its beginning the leadership of the Methodist Episcopal Church committed itself to anti-slavery and the *Book of Discipline* contained the rule "Every member of our Society who has slaves in his possession, shall, within twelve months after notice given to him, legally execute and record an instrument, whereby he emancipates and sets free every slave in his possession." But, as we shall see, very many Methodists were slaveholders and believed that emancipation should come only gradually. As a result, even though the bishops of the MEC always believed slaveholding to be against the will of God, the rule was dropped.

Although the debates in the wider society over slavery became increasingly polarized, the MEC managed to hold itself together for some decades, maintaining its unity not least by simply hoping the problem would go away. One episcopal address of the period affirmed that the "only safe, scriptural, and prudent way for us, both as ministers and people, to take, is wholly to refrain from the agitating subject." Evincing a similar attitude, the denominational journal of the Church of the United Brethren completely closed its columns to controversy about slavery in the 1840s.

But by the mid-1830s the argument for gradual emancipation had worn thin for reformers like William Lloyd Garrison (1805–1879). In 1833 Garrison founded the American Anti-Slavery Society, together with its journal *The Liberator*, and demanded immediate freedom for all slaves. He began to mobilize the northerners and to polarize the nation around the issue. Within Methodism there began an extended period of rancor, with numerous lawsuits filed which were ostensibly over matters of property and boundaries, but in reality were over slavery. Euphemistically called by one historian "the Years of Disagreement," these were actually years of hostility and resentment, with congregation set against congregation and Methodist set against Methodist, even to the point of fistfights.

Running hand in hand with the anti-slavery controversy was an ongoing pressure for increased democracy within Methodism. A number of breakaway movements resulted from the demand for lay people to have some formal voice in the institutional life of the church. The Methodist

Protestant Church (MPC), constituted in Baltimore in 1830, eliminated bishops and presiding elders (also known as district superintendents) and set up equal representation of ministers and lay people in its Conference. But during the nineteenth century the MPC suffered the same kinds of divisions over race that were being experienced in other parts of Methodism, and by 1900 eight "colored" Conferences had been set up to accommodate the needs of African-American members. The MPC supported missions in Japan, India, and China and eventually rejoined the two larger connections in 1939.

The Wesleyan Methodist Connection, led by Orange Scott (1800–47) of the New England Conference, broke away from the MEC in 1843. Scott was a prominent and vocal abolitionist, to the extent that he was removed from his position as a presiding elder; soon afterwards he became a traveling agent for the American Anti-Slavery Society. Sensing the implacability of the MEC leadership toward any kind of reform, he joined with other leading Methodist abolitionists to form his new connection. The new body declared its opposition to "slavery and episcopacy." With the constitutional abolition of slavery in 1867, many Wesleyan Methodists returned to the main Methodist churches. Others, however, established a new coalition with the Holiness churches, eventually merging with the Pilgrim Holiness Church in 1969 to become the Wesleyan Church. At the turn of the twenty-first century, this church had a worldwide membership of just over a quarter of a million.

Gradually a large majority of the Northern members of the MEC General Conference became committed to seeing that the church formally adopted the abolitionist cause. In 1844 they went to Conference determined to use the case of James O. Andrew (1796–1871) to force their Southern colleagues to renounce slavery. Andrew was a bishop in Georgia who held two slaves whom he had inherited from his first wife, although he had made various attempts to secure their freedom (not easy in Georgia where manumission was illegal). Delegates from the slaveholding states and Conferences protested vehemently against taking any action in the case of Bishop Andrew, claiming that he was not in violation of any existing church law. But the Northerners commanded a majority in the Conference and voted to remove Andrew from his post. Immediately a "Plan of Separation" was drawn up by the Southerners, and by the time the General Conference adjourned on June 11, provision had been made for a Southern section of the MEC. The new Methodist Episcopal Church South (MECS) was formally organized in Louisville, Kentucky, in 1845, when plans were laid for its first General Conference at Petersburg, Virginia, in 1846.

At first the two MEC churches, North and South, went their separate ways in a fairly fraternal manner. But the next MEC General Conference, meeting in New York in 1848, was different in tone and attitude to the one in 1844. Packed with delegates of a staunchly abolitionist frame of mind, it adopted a resolution not to enter into fraternal relations with the MECS and declared the "Plan of Separation" unconstitutional. The bitter dispute over property rights, particularly those that were involved in the immensely prosperous Methodist Book Concern, had to be adjudicated by the US Supreme Court in 1854, which found in favor of the MECS.

The American Civil War (or, as it is often known in the South, "The War between the States") broke out in 1860. A desperate tragedy in itself, it proved an unmitigated disaster for the Methodists living in the war-affected states. The Northern preachers could not work in the South outside the big cities, and Southern preachers were forced to abandon their churches in the face of the advancing Northern armies. The MECS General Conference of 1862 could not assemble, bishops could not reach their annual Conferences, the publishing house at Nashville was commandeered, and church services were dangerous and sparsely attended. During the period from 1860 to 1866 the membership of the MECS declined precipitously, from over 750,000 members at the beginning of the war to less than 500,000 six years later.

For the Christians of this nation, which was less than a hundred years old, the Civil War represented a watershed, destroying any dreams they may have had of a "Christian America." While the United States remained overwhelmingly Protestant, there was now little hope of establishing a unified evangelical "kingdom of God" in America. As one historian has written, for Methodists "the great turning point was past. It was a different country, a new world."

But other massive changes were taking place in the social landscape in this period, not least of which was a spectacular growth in the United States' population. When the Civil War ended 32 million people lived within the boundaries of the continental United States; by 1915 this number had grown to more than 100 million. The pace of industrialization that marked the great cities of the East had increased, with the multiplication of vast steel works, coal mining operations, and manufacturing facilities of every kind. As a direct result of this burgeoning of industry, the United States steadily overtook Britain and then the rest of industrialized Europe in economic power. The exponential growth of the railway system opened the West to mass migration, and the opening of the 394-mile-long Erie Canal in 1825 allowed goods to be easily and cheaply transported between New York and the cities of the Midwest. Such amazingly rapid growth required vast numbers of new laborers, and immigration brought millions of new residents into the United States, not only from Europe, but also from eastern Asian countries like China and Japan. The demographic impact of all this was felt not only as a vast increase in population but also as a massive shift from a rural to an urban America. The world in which the camp meetings flourished was one in which there were fifteen rural inhabitants to every one city-dweller; by 1850 there were just five country people to each urbanite. In 1800, 6,000 people lived in New York City; in 1860 the city had increased by ten times that number, and in 1915 it numbered 4,700,000. Boston, Philadelphia, and Chicago also claimed millions of inhabitants.

The white Methodist churches generally kept pace with this population increase. Between the end of the Civil War in 1865 and 1915 the MEC grew from 1 to 4 million members. After the tremendous losses during the Civil War, the MECS reorganized and recovered so fast that it could claim over 700,000 members in 1872 and 2 million in 1915. The Evangelical Association grew from 60,000 to 185,000 and the United Brethren in Christ from 95,000 to 350,000.

Such an astonishing increase in numbers put serious pressures on the structures of all the white Methodist churches in both North and South. Just as we saw the movement toward the frontier at the beginning of the century leading to a greater emphasis on the camp meeting at the expense of the class meeting, so now the needs of the urban communities led to the need for a different form of Methodist ministry. The traveling preachers no longer traveled. In the large new urban churches they became what are now called the "resident resource persons" responsible for burying the dead, performing marriages, meeting the classes, attending the prayer meetings, and doing pretty much everything in the church. With such pastors taking on themselves the spiritual nurture of the whole congregation, the old offices of the class leader and the local preacher became almost obsolete. The class leader came to be regarded primarily as a sub-pastor and local preachers rarely preached even locally. The efforts of Nathan Bangs in raising the cultural standards of Methodism in New York, as well as pioneering the concept of an educated ministry, had laid the foundations of this profound change.

All these changes had repercussions. Faced Sunday by Sunday by hearers who now had the leisure to read and think, the newly resident ministers needed to prepare well-informed and well-polished sermons. Methodist preachers therefore needed to have a deeper grounding in theological scholarship, and sustained periods of study in seminaries became required for ordination; by 1900 all the Methodist connections had established at least one graduate theological school for the professional education of their ministers. These new, more sophisticated Methodists also required higher education for their children, and the Methodist churches founded scores of new universities and colleges in both the North and the South. In the large churches, purpose-built in Gothic or Romanesque style for upwardly mobile congregations, "ritualized membership" replaced the high-intensity spiritual formation of the old class meeting. Paralleling the decline of the class meeting taking place at the same time in Great Britain, the MEC abandoned attendance at Class Meetings as a requirement for church membership in 1866. Worship styles became much more formal and ministers took to wearing distinctive clerical attire with white ties, and even frockcoats and striped trousers. Complaints about the poor quality of congregational singing led to the establishment of church choirs, the importance of which was later manifested in their prominent placement at the front of the church facing the congregation.

Making new members of the church was now emphatically through the "nurture" provided by new schemes of religious education all taking place on church premises. Just as in the case of Wesleyan Methodism in the UK, field preaching of any kind was a thing of the past. A Methodist moved toward Christian perfection by maturing gradually rather than by any instantaneous action of the Holy Spirit, and discipleship was expressed in new forms of social service, in educational programmes, in attendance at Sunday schools, and in the refined forms of summer camps that bore the generic name of "Chautauquas" (the name of one famous holiday settlement in New York State).

To be sure, these massive changes did not go unchallenged. There were those who longed for the old romantic days of frontier Methodism, with its circuit riders, camp meetings, and fervent evangelistic preaching. Such men as Peter Cartwright lamented the growth of formal theological training, saying Methodists could set things on fire while other clergy were still collecting their degrees. Various revival movements arose in opposition to the new notion of salvation by nurture and education rather than by an immediate infusion of spiritual assurance and grace, protesting against the takeover of Wesley's movement by what one commentator describes as "middling Americans in bland cahoots with bourgeoisification and market culture." One such movement, the Free Methodist Church, was initiated by Benjamin Titus Roberts (1823–93), who offered a satirical description of the "Old School" and the "New School" Methodists: "The latter build stock Churches and furnish them with pews to accommodate a select congregation; and with organs, Melodeons, violins, and professional singers, to execute difficult pieces of music for a fashionable audience. The former favor free Churches, congregational singing and spirituality, simplicity and fervency in worship." "New School" Methodists had, Roberts charged, no interest in "promoting revivals" and in general had "deep distrust of all professions of deep Christian experience." Even worse:

When these desire to raise money for the benefit of the Church they have recourse to the selling of pews to the highest bidder; to parties of pleasure, oyster suppers, fairs, grab bags, festivals, and lotteries. The others appeal to the love they bear to Christ. In short the Old School Methodists rely for the spread of the Gospel upon the agency of the Holy Spirit. The New School Methodists appear to depend upon the patronage of the worldly, the favor of the proud and aspiring; and the various artifices of worldly policy.

But Roberts was not alone. Many within the MEC began to be concerned that the formality and respectability which attended the rising socioeconomic status of its members were undermining the spiritual life of Methodism. As a result, the Free Methodist Church, which had come into being in 1860, had 10,862 members committed to Holiness teaching by 1878. As we shall see, all Holiness movements promised not only the "first blessing" of justification and new birth, but even more importantly an instantaneous "second blessing": an infusion of the Holy Spirit with its power and its gifts. This "second blessing" would actually make the sinner free from sin and thus entirely sanctified, a concept originating with John Wesley and other early Methodists, but greatly simplified in the hands of the Holiness teachers.

Much of the energy behind the Holiness movement was generated by Phoebe Palmer (1807–74), who held Tuesday meetings for "the Promotion of Holiness" in her home in New York to share her own experience of entire sanctification and the "higher Christian life." Later she became a traveling speaker (not a "preacher," she insisted) at Holiness camp meetings and other gatherings. We discuss her theology and spirituality more fully in chapter 7. Palmer's belief in the "second blessing" of immediate sanctification resonated throughout the Methodist churches of the mid-nineteenth century, driven by her "Shorter Way" method of achieving holiness which she promoted in her journal, the *Guide to Holiness*. By 1867 the movement had gained sufficient momentum to form the National Camp Meeting Association for the Promotion of Holiness under the leadership of William B. Osborn, a Methodist presiding elder in Florida, and in 1885 Park Avenue M. E. Church in Chicago was the venue for a General Holiness Assembly. Holiness teaching crossed the Atlantic, leading in the

UK to the organization of the Keswick convention and in Germany to the Gemeineschaftsbewegung, influential in the Evangelical and Reformed churches and the developing German Methodist Church.

The gatherings of seekers after the full experience of sanctification were a continuation of the *ecclesiolae in ecclesia*, the "little churches within the church," that we discuss in chapter 5. The advocates of Holiness believed the marks of being a fully saved Christian (as opposed to a Christian in name only) had to be visible. As a result, Holiness Methodists exempted themselves from tobacco and alcohol, from dancing and theater-going, from jewelry and flamboyant forms of dress especially among women. A presiding elder in the Southwest, sympathetic to Holiness teaching, observed pointedly: "A worldly, card-playing, theatergoing, tobacco-using church never gains converts in any considerable degree."

Holiness meetings were generally held on weekdays, with invited Holiness speakers and a regular ritual of personal testimony. Such methods created an entire "Holiness subculture," producing large numbers of Methodists with a way of thinking, feeling, and acting that was increasingly at odds with the majority. As the Holiness movement grew, the leadership of the MEC, MECS, and other Methodist churches came under mounting pressure to inject Holiness principles into the mainstream of their teaching, and a high point for the Holiness movement came in the General Conference of 1872 when five of the eight new bishops chosen were unabashed friends of the Holiness people. Yet the leadership of both the MEC and the MECS became increasingly concerned about the threat of sectarianism posed by the Holiness groups. This anxiety can be seen in a declaration by the MECS bishops in 1894. After restating Wesley's teaching on perfect love, the bishops said:

But there has sprung up among us a party with holiness as a watchword; they have holiness associations, holiness meetings, holiness preachers, holiness evangelists, and holiness property. Religious experience is represented as if it consists of only two steps, the first step out of condemnation into peace, and the next step into Christian perfection.

The theologians of American Methodism were equally as concerned as the bishops. In his 1887 *Systematic Theology*, Miner Raymond (1811–97), who was teaching at the Garrett Biblical Institute in Chicago, indicated that sanctification was "by a gradual process," although he did concede that it could occasionally be received instantaneously. Unsurprisingly, with these kinds of negative responses to their movement, Holiness men and women saw no future for themselves in the MEC or the MECS.

But if the MEC and the MECS were resistant to the appropriation of Holiness principles, previous breakaway movements, and especially the Wesleyans (from 1843) and the Free Methodists (from 1860), became more firmly entrenched as Holiness churches. They were joined by the Salvation Army, founded in Britain in 1868 and brought to the USA in 1880. But there were also new Holiness churches made up of disaffected Methodists, the most significant of which is probably the Church of the Nazarene, the union of many disparate Holiness congregations coming together throughout the 1880s and 1890s. The Church of the Nazarene views itself as firmly Wesleyan in its doctrine and practice, and keeps the *General Rules* and *Articles of Religion* as part of its Methodist heritage. At the turn of the third millennium there were 1 million members of the Church of the Nazarene worldwide.

Conflicting attitudes arising from the widespread social dislocations after the Civil War marked all the various streams of American Methodism. Differences in social class certainly played some part in the growth of the Holiness churches. Small shopkeepers and self-employed artisans were losing their recognized niches in the towns as larger companies and corporations grew, and as rural Americans migrated to the cities. Such people were scrambling both for an economic foothold and a sense of personal value. When they looked to the MEC or the MECS for solace they found only Methodists who were much more economically secure and much better educated than they were, and whose way of life seemed to embody the social stratification that was causing their discomfort. The Holiness movements, with their intense communal feeling and freedom of expression, offered the socially and economically depressed a place to feel at home.

The African-American churches were naturally profoundly affected by the Civil War. Slaves made up a high percentage of the membership in both North and South when the disruption between the MEC and the MECS took place in 1844. As the war progressed and the slaves were beginning to be freed in the South, the AME and the AMEZ churches claimed many of them as members. But even so many African-American Methodists remained loyally within the MECS, although the numbers had dropped from over 200,000 in 1860 to just under 80,000 by the end of the war. But those who remained indicated their dissatisfaction with their second-class status in the MECS, and it became clear that new arrangements needed to be made.

Thus, according to the wishes of the black membership, and with much white help, the Colored Methodist Episcopal Church (CME) was formed in 1870 (it was renamed in 1954 as the Christian Methodist Episcopal Church). Two African-American bishops, including the outstanding figure of Isaac

Lane (1834–1937), were ordained by the MECS, property was transferred to the new denomination, and much financial support was poured into their work. Education was a major enterprise, and the CME established schools and colleges all over the South. At the same time, the AME and AMEZ churches were extending their work into the South and West, and as a result were experiencing a phenomenal growth of membership, from about 20,000 in 1860 to 400,000 in 1880. AME- and AMEZ-founded schools and colleges contributed to the raising of educational standards for black Americans in the South and throughout the country, and the *AME Review* is the oldest magazine published by black people in the world. Despite their different histories, all three of the African-American Methodist churches have much in common. They keep the Methodist standards of doctrine and the *General Rules*; they maintain excellent relations with one another and organic unity has often been discussed. Representatives from each of the three African-American Methodist churches were present in the first Methodist Ecumenical Conference in 1881 and they remain active in leadership roles in the World Methodist Council. As we write, Thomas C. Hoyt, Jr., a CME bishop, is president of the National Council of Churches in the USA.

Other ethnic groups within Methodism developed their own leadership and Conference styles. Work with Native Americans required the establishment of an Indian Mission Annual Conference in 1844; work among Spanish speakers began in Texas and led eventually to the formation of the Rio Grande Conference in 1885. Membership of the MEC grew among German immigrants, and by 1915 ten German Annual Conferences had been organized. Somewhat surprisingly, Methodism was also attractive to the million and more Swedish immigrants, many of whom settled around Chicago and in Minnesota and the northern plains. A Northwest Swedish Conference was organized in 1877. Parallel work went on among the Danes and the Norwegians. In the next century work began on the West Coast among the Chinese and the Japanese. The first Japanese pastor, Kanichi Miyama, was ordained in 1887.

By the time the twentieth century dawned, American Methodism had become entirely at home in its context, so much so that it had become almost the established religion. Bishop Matthew Simpson (1811–84) perfectly illustrates this development. Without a formal education, Simpson became a traveling preacher in Ohio and Pennsylvania. A highly talented orator, he came to the attention of many outside Methodism through his patriotic address, "The Future of our Country." Through this speech he became a close friend and adviser of Abraham Lincoln, and was chosen to preach Lincoln's funeral oration in May 1865. After Simpson's time, Methodist bishops were increasingly seen as part of the mainstream life of the nation.

A modest prosperity and obvious social status marked all the Methodist, United Brethren, and Evangelical Association churches at the end of the nineteenth century. Huge cathedral-style buildings in the cities, imposing church buildings on the main streets of smaller towns, and more modest chapels with their neat white spires nestling in the countryside could be found throughout the USA. The Methodist academies had grown into some of North America's leading universities, providing a steady stream of well-educated church leaders and ministers, as well as laypeople for all the professions. Critics of this evolution have described Methodism in the United States as faith tradition that accommodated itself (and in their view it still continues to do so) uncritically to American culture, mixing piety with patriotism into an unassailable form of civil religion and seeing upward social mobility in soteriological terms.

Yet, as is the case of British Methodist traditions, changes in theology, common life, worship, spirituality, social ethics, and ecumenical attitudes were in place at the end of the nineteenth century. Thus the rise of the Social Gospel movement paralleled the Forward Movement in British Methodism and set the tone for the other changes to be discussed in chapters 5–10.

CHAPTER 4

World Methodism at the beginning of the twenty-first century

The people we described in the Prologue, who are part of the congregation at Wesley's Chapel and who participate in the World Methodist Council gatherings, represent the millions of Methodists living in some 135 countries around the globe, including, of course, another great cluster of Methodist people who are too poor ever to think of leaving their own countries, yet cherish their sense of belonging to the worldwide Methodist family. Not without reason these churches that are set in troubled parts of the world are seeing rapid growth in membership. An eyewitness reports the recent baptism of 200 people in a Methodist church in Cuba, and another describes the baptism of 2,000 new Methodists on one occasion in Indonesia. At the turn of the twenty-first century, new churches were being established at a rapid rate in what may seem to be unlikely places like Senegal, Cambodia, and Nepal, and older missionary activity was being reinvigorated in, for example, Russia and Bulgaria. At the same time links were being forged across the boundaries of the two traditions we have been describing, with Methodist churches that claim an inheritance from Britain and those that claim an inheritance from America making new connections with one another.

All of this is but the latest chapter in a notable story of the spread and growth of Methodism around the world, which is itself a result of the ways in which the descendants of John and Charles Wesley have understood the whole world to be their parish. The particularities of the two great traditions of Methodism have manifested themselves as quite different patterns in the various places where they have exerted their influence. On one level the most noticeable difference lies in the institutional organization of the Methodist communities in various parts of the world. The churches of the British tradition have become autonomous almost everywhere, with independent Conferences and total freedom to structure their internal lives as they have seen fit. In contrast, the outreach of the various forms of American Methodism has planted mission colonies around the world. With some notable exceptions, the areas in the world where Methodists of the American tradition have established churches function as episcopal areas within the General Conference of the United Methodist Church. They keep to the pattern of Annual Conferences and send participants every four years to the General Conference meeting somewhere in the United States. (The exceptions to this rule are Korea, Mexico, and Brazil, which are independent Methodist Churches.) This pattern of strong organizational ties to the parent body is the direct result of the robust episcopal tradition in the American churches. In the case of the United Methodist Church, its financial power and its sense of authority as one of the two largest Protestant churches in the USA deeply affect its relations with its constituent conferences overseas.

Much of the expansion of Methodism has taken place through individual initiatives, and betrays little sense of cohesive planning. This is a persistent fact of all missionary activity, since the first "missionary" in the more technical sense has rarely been the first Christian to speak about his or her faith in any given situation; there were always traders or market women who "gossiped the Gospel" to their neighbors and friends. In the case of Methodism, with its wide appeal among those serving in the military, the first Methodist society was often founded by a soldier or a sea captain, often times well in advance of the formally appointed missionary to a particular place. As we try to tell this story, it has seemed good to begin at the very beginning, with the early planting of the Methodist Church in Ireland and, under the direction of Thomas Coke, in the Caribbean, Canada, and Sierra Leone, and then to tell the story continent by continent.

IRELAND

Chronologically the first area of overseas expansion for the young Methodist movement was in Ireland, where today there is still a vigorous and independent Methodist Church. John Wesley visited Ireland no fewer than twenty-one times, and spent, when all the years and months of his visits are added up, a total of nine years there. In Wesley's day Ireland had a population of over 2 million, of whom 1.75 million were Roman Catholic. By 1747 there were two preachers and two preaching stations in Ireland, and in the next year open-air preaching began; reports of its success led the Wesley brothers to spend time in Dublin and the south. But, as was the case on the mainland throughout the 1740s, Irish Methodists were subject to intense persecution, and there were many riots stirred against the new preachers. In Cork, for example, a Grand Jury found Charles Wesley "to be a person of ill-fame, a vagabond and a disturber of the peace, and we pray that he may be transported." One of the Irish preachers observed, "No one is fit to be a preacher here who is not ready to die at any moment."

But soon the strength of Irish Methodism manifested itself, and its influence on the wider missionary expansion of the Methodist movement began to be felt. In 1752 John Wesley preached in County Limerick, and among his hearers was Philip Embury (1728–73), the son of Palatine German migrants, who became a highly effective class leader and a local preacher. At the same time Barbara Heck (1734–1804) joined the Methodist Society that had been established in Ballingrane. Both Embury and Heck were part of a group of linen workers who traveled to New York in 1766 seeking economic opportunities, and soon after their arrival they founded a Methodist Society there. Another Irishman, Robert Strawbridge (c. 1732–81) from County Leitrim, became the first Methodist preacher in Maryland, and his fellow Irish Methodists introduced Methodism into Virginia and Newfoundland. (During the course of the nineteenth century more than 200 Irish ministers served the Methodist communities of Canada.) But Irish Methodists were destined to take Methodism even further afield, and James Lynch (1775–1858) was the leader of the first missionary party to land in Asia (in Sri Lanka in 1813). If there is any branch of Methodism that can claim to have been at the beginning of world Methodism it is the contemporary Irish Methodist Church.

By the time of Wesley's death in 1791 there were six districts in Ireland, with twenty-nine circuits, with a membership of 15,018 served by seventy-two preachers. The growth of Irish Methodism had taken place at first largely in southern cities and market towns, but later caught fire in the "linen triangle," an industrial district of Ulster. Although John Wesley had initially directed his preaching to the revival of Ireland's "slumbering" Protestants, as many as 700 of the first Irish converts to Methodism were former Roman Catholics. By 1816, Irish Methodism had splintered into various Methodist sects, but unity was restored in 1878 when the Methodist Church in Ireland was formed. This church is still united, despite the division of Ireland in 1922, and three of its districts are partly in Northern Ireland and partly in the Republic. This unique position has allowed Methodism to have a distinctive voice in Irish politics, and Methodist leaders have been in the forefront in the peacemaking process in Ireland.

At the turn of the twenty-first century, members of the Methodist Church in Ireland number about 18,000, with 60,000 in the wider Methodist community. The filial relationship between the Irish Methodist Church and the British Methodist Conference is symbolized by the presence of the British president of Conference in the chair at Irish Conference meetings, while the Irish president sits to his or her right as vice-president. This practice is now felt by many Irish Methodists to be anachronistic and, by some, deeply offensive. Another, more practical, manifestation of the relationship is Irish Methodism's extensive overseas work (there is still a very vital Missionary Society, with many active overseas workers), which is channeled though the London offices of the British Methodist Church.

THE CARIBBEAN

If the work in Ireland were to be considered as simply a natural extension of the Methodist movement in the British Isles, then the first official overseas work of Methodism might be dated from 1786, when Methodism was planted in the Caribbean. This development was, at least in part, something of an accident. In 1783 John Wesley's right-hand man Thomas Coke had published *A Plan of the Society for the Establishment of Missions amongst the Heathens*. Oddly, given his own early missionary zeal, Coke's plea for Wesleyan foreign missions displeased Wesley, who did not welcome another claim on the limited resources of his movement. Much more urgent, in Wesley's view, were the needs of the Methodists in America who had been so recently cut off from his direct oversight by the War of Independence. And of course, as we have seen, Wesley had his own plans for Thomas Coke in the new republic that kept him occupied in 1784 and 1785.

But eventually Coke had his way in the matter of Methodist missions. In 1786 he had made another effort to attract British Methodists to his viewpoint in *An Address to the Pious and Benevolent, proposing an annual subscription for Missionaries in the Highlands and adjacent Islands of Scotland, the Isles of Jersey, Guernsey, and Newfoundland, the West Indies and the provinces of Nova Scotia and Quebec*. Coke's powers of persuasion were effective this time, and later in that same year he was able to set sail for Newfoundland, along with a number of preachers destined for Canada. But violent storms in the Atlantic forced the captain of the ship to turn south and, on Christmas morning 1786, Coke and his party landed in Antigua. Much to their surprise, they found that there were Methodists already there. A West Indian planter, Nathaniel Gilbert (1721–74), had heard Wesley preach in London, and upon his return to the Caribbean he had preached what he had heard to his own slaves and established a Methodist society. After Gilbert's death his work had been continued by his sister-in-law Mary Gilbert and by John Baxter, a government shipwright who had arrived in Antigua in 1778. By the time Coke arrived on the island, there were already 1,500 Methodists, only three of whom were white, and it was to this congregation that Coke (at Baxter's invitation) preached a now-famous Christmas sermon. In January 1787 Coke and his colleagues visited the neighboring West Indian islands, and as a result of these experiences the religious situation became clear to Coke: "It is impossible to have any doubt concerning the will of God," he wrote. "All is as clear as it was written by a sunbeam." The men who had been intended for the missionary work in Canada were immediately stationed in St. Vincent and St. Kitts. The next year, 1788, the British Conference stationed missionaries in Dominica, Barbados, Nevis, Tortola, and Jamaica. Five years later in 1803 the Methodist mission in the Caribbean was extended to the Bahamas and, in 1809, to Trinidad. Although Methodist preaching aroused strong opposition from plantation owners, who persecuted both the preachers and their hearers, by 1814, the year in which Coke died, there were twelve Caribbean circuits with 17,000 members.

The quest for freedom from slavery is a vital part of the historical imagination of all Caribbean Methodists. In the early nineteenth century, Methodist chapels throughout the islands were full of slaves and former slaves, and on an August night in 1834 they heard the words of the Act of Emancipation read by their own preachers in their own chapels. Rapid growth in Methodist membership followed emancipation and today there is a vigorous Methodist Church of the Caribbean and Americas (MCCA), established as a self-governing body in 1967. This church comprises work in the Bahamas, the Turks and Caicos Islands, the Leeward and Windward Islands, Jamaica, Haiti, Belize, Honduras, Panama and Costa Rica, Trinidad and Tobago, and Guyana. A hymn by Hugh Sherlock, the first president of the MCCA Conference, celebrates Methodism's autonomy in these islands:

> Gone the days of cruel scourging
> Gone the tyrant's blood-stained chains:
> Now for us the Spirit's urging.
> Now the love of Christ constrains.
> Shout we then in acclamation.
> Gladly we our chorus raise.
> Mainland join our celebration.
> Islands join in loudest praise!

As Caribbean Methodism moved into its third century, the MCCA had a total membership of 189,295 and an extended community estimated at nearly half a million. Caribbean Methodists have had excellent leadership and have provided leaders both for the World Methodist Conference and for the wider ecumenical movement. Philip Potter from Dominica served as one of the six general secretaries of the World Council of Churches (WCC).

CANADA

In the early years of Methodism, this vast country, with terrain if anything more difficult than that traversed by Asbury's preachers in the United States, was more often the scene of colonial settlement than of missionary work in the narrower sense, and therefore records of Methodism's place in Canada's pioneering days are a little confused. It is, however, clear that Methodist work in the Maritime Provinces had begun as early as 1760, with an Irish Methodist preacher and Anglican clergyman named Lawrence Coughlan (d. 1784) forming Methodist classes in Newfoundland. With the outbreak of the American War of Independence and the loyalist migrations to Canada, Englishman William Black (1760–1834), who had been caught up in a revival in 1779, traveled through the whole of Nova Scotia to organize Methodist classes there. In 1784 Black went to Baltimore to participate in the first meeting of the MEC, the Christmas Conference, where he pleaded for more preachers for work in Canada, and two were sent to Nova Scotia, including Freeborn Garrettson. Black himself was ordained by Coke and Asbury in 1789. But the link he formed between the Canadian Methodists and the MEC was severed in 1800, by which time he had returned to Britain to ask for help for the work in Canada from the British Conference, which responded by assigning four men to the Canadian mission. Officers and men from the British regiments stationed in Canada were among early Methodist local preachers. Tensions increased between the two North American branches of Methodism as anti-American feelings were aggravated by the War of 1812.

Despite the immense geographical difficulties, Methodism made its home in Canada, linking tiny and isolated settlements with the new cities then beginning to grow. As elsewhere, the early Canadian Methodists lived hard lives, facing long hours of labor, the rigors of disease and disaster, and fearful winters. The Methodist preachers brought light and warmth and hope to their souls. In 1855 the British Wesleyan Methodist Church established an autonomous Conference in eastern Canada. Various other British Methodist bodies, particularly the Primitive Methodists, the Bible Christians, and the Methodist New Connexion, arrived in Canada during the first half of the nineteenth century, but all of them found themselves able to unite with the Wesleyans in 1884, making a church with

170,000 members. Serious mission work among the Indian peoples of Manitoba, Alberta, and British Columbia began in this period, and the first Canadian missionaries sailed for Japan and western China. In 1925, after a period of continuous expansion throughout Canada, 418,000 Methodists joined with Congregationalists and many Presbyterians to form the United Church of Canada. (Dislike of Methodist Arminianism and Methodist enthusiasm for temperance and the Social Gospel surfaced, particularly among Presbyterians of Scottish background, who remained as the Presbyterian Church of Canada.) The United Church of Canada is the most successful of the attempts at union among North American churches, and today is about 2 million members strong. It keeps its links with, and representation in, the World Methodist Council. There is also the Free Methodist Church in Canada, a movement going back to the 1860s. These Methodists sought, as they said, to be free from slavery, free in the simplicity of their worship, and free from pew rentals and vows of secrecy.

AFRICA

The *Methodist Magazine* for December 1808 told its readers of a letter sent to Adam Clarke by Mingo Jordan, "a Preacher of Colour in Sierra Leone," a place only just being settled by a few white adventurers, some African Americans from Nova Scotia, and the men and women freed from the slave ships by the British navy. This letter contained a number of requests: "Dear Fathers and Brethren in the Gospel of the Lord Jesus Christ. Write to us at the first opportunity, and for a token of love, please to send us some Hymn Books, and the Preachers will be thankful for any wearing apparel suitable for the work."

The first missionary appointed by the British Conference for work in West Africa was George Warren in 1811. But, as one missiologist has noted (and as we already have seen in these pages), "the first was never the first," and Methodist laypeople were already active in Sierra Leone when he arrived. But within eight months Warren was dead, and indeed the premature deaths of missionaries was a pattern that repeated itself throughout West Africa. A bit of doggerel entitled "The White Man's Grave" described the problem:

> Take heed and beware of the Bight of Benin.
> For few come out, though many go in.

Nevertheless, a ready succession of volunteers for West Africa followed Warren. These early missionaries, many of whom were trained at Richmond

College, London (the successor to the Hoxton Institution), were truly the equivalents in Africa of the circuit riders in pioneering America, except that their average life expectancy in West Africa was approximately two years. Each of these Wesleyan missionaries would have echoed the sentiments of their contemporary, the Fijian missionary James Calvert (1813–92), who, when asked "Were you not afraid that you would die?", replied "We died before we went." Calvert made it home to England from the South Seas. Great numbers of missionaries to West Africa never did.

These early deaths, as well as early retirements for health reasons, made it difficult to implement consistent missionary policies and strategies in tropical Africa. Nevertheless the Methodist Church grew in Sierra Leone and throughout the neighboring countries of West Africa, with some remarkable successes. In 1838 Thomas Birch Freeman (1806–90) arrived and served in Cape Coast as a Wesleyan missionary. The son of an African father (a freed slave, hence the surname Freeman) and an English mother, Freeman was perfectly at home in West African society. Africans often said with genuine delight, "He understands our customs." Freeman is counted as the founder of Methodism in Ghana, Benin, Dahomey, Togo, and western Nigeria. In southeastern Nigeria the Primitive Methodist Church began a very successful enterprise in 1893, deeply affecting the life of the Efik and Igbo peoples not least through its educational work. In 1962 the Methodist Church of Nigeria was founded in Lagos, bringing together the former Wesleyan Methodist districts of western Nigeria and the former Primitive Methodist districts of eastern Nigeria. Since then the Methodist Church of Nigeria has grown exponentially with a total of 3.5 million, which includes both official members and the wider Methodist community. Nigeria also has a steadily expanding Methodist community arising from the work of the EUB in Bauchi province, and there are now nearly 3,000 members related to the UMC.

The oldest republic in Africa is Liberia, established in 1822 as a homeland for freed slaves. In the very next year, the first MEC missionary arrived, and missionaries from the AMEZ and the AME came in 1876 and 1891 respectively. Until 1897, the Liberia Conference of the MEC had oversight of all the MEC work in Africa, and William Taylor (1821–1902) was appointed bishop in 1884, having had previous experience in South Africa. Taylor was perhaps the greatest missionary thinker produced by American Methodism. Working to a theory that he called "Pauline missions," he conceived new churches as being independent, self-directing, and entrepreneurial in spirit, and therefore as generally beyond the control of the home church. Moreover, his African experiences in the 1860s had led him to believe that

African culture was comparable to his own and he made no effort to reformulate it, trusting Africans to be able to express the Christian faith in their own ways. In Taylor's view, the missionary had nothing to do but plant "the pure gospel seed," and he objected to the notion that mission boards could make decisions for clergy and laity from 10,000 miles away. He also experimented with these methods in India between 1870 and 1875 and in Latin America between 1878 and 1884. So it was that he set the patterns for Methodist expansion between 1884 and 1896, initiating work in Angola, the Congo, and in what were then called the Zambezi Districts.

Taylor ensured the growth of MEC work in the neighboring countries of West Africa, particularly in Sierra Leone. Today the Liberian and Sierra Leonean Methodist churches are rebuilding themselves after the privations of the civil wars; they offer care to the neediest in the community, among them large numbers of orphaned and homeless "child soldiers" released from the factional armies. Nearly all West African countries have a Methodist presence, and the most recently established among these is in Senegal, where in 2003 there were reported to be eleven new churches founded by Senegalese men and women returning to their homeland from other parts of West Africa.

Southern Africa

The story of the planting of Methodism in Southern Africa begins, once again, with the arrival of Methodist soldiers in the early nineteenth century. In an 1806 letter to a friend in England, one of these soldiers, George Middlemiss, described attending love-feasts and regular class and band meetings. "But," he wrote, "we are short of books. We would thank you to send us some Hymn-books, Bibles and Mr. Wesley's works for our Instruction. We have collected a small sum of money for that purpose." It was not until 1816, however, that the first Methodist missionaries in Southern Africa, Barnabas Shaw (1788–1857), and his wife Jane arrived at Cape Town. Clearly people of adventurous and pioneering spirit, the Shaws almost immediately set off into the interior by ox-wagon. He vividly describes the pioneering missionary life: "In travelling, heat, cold, hunger, thirst; sleeping in wagons, in Hottentot huts, or on the ground. On arriving at his station – no bread, till he sows corn and reaps it; no vegetables, till he has made gardens; no house to live in, till it is built by the missionary's own hand." Despite all hardships, Jane and Barnabas Shaw persisted. Their work in Namaqualand enabled the people to learn practical arts as well as the

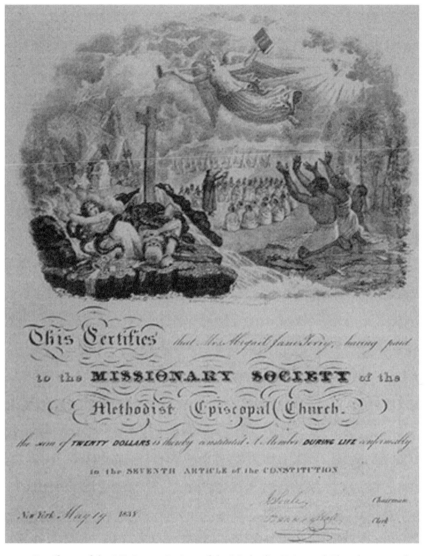

8. Certificate of the Missionary Society of the Methodist Episcopal Church engraved by Nathaniel Currier in New York, *c.* 1838.

Christian story, and laid the foundation for many other missionaries to move northwards. Shaw trained the first indigenous candidate for Methodist ministry, Jacob Links, whose name was recorded as an "assistant missionary" in 1822. Jacob Links was martyred just a few years later.

The second Methodist missionary in southern Africa was William Shaw (1798–1872; no relation to Barnabas), who joined a large party of ex-soldiers from Britain intending to settle in the Eastern Cape in 1824. William Shaw discovered in Grahams Town a small Methodist community that was being led by two Methodist sergeant-majors. From Grahams Town, Shaw moved further inland with the intention of establishing a series of mission stations among the Xhosas. Shaw's success was such that even now the main strength of South African Methodism lies along the route of the chain of stations that he envisioned and helped to found. From these beginnings, Methodism spread throughout the regions that make up the present-day South Africa, Botswana, Lesotho, Namibia, and Swaziland, and by 1883 there were enough Methodists in the region to set up a Southern African Conference, although entirely under white leadership. Today, Methodists in these countries belong to the Methodist Church of Southern Africa.

The success of Methodism in Southern Africa among indigenous peoples, as well as white discrimination, also led to the formation of Wesleyan-inspired African independent churches like the Ethiopian Church of Mangena Mogone (ECMM). Mangena Mogone (1851–1931) himself had been a Wesleyan minister before founding his independent church. Although American Methodism is not generally present in South Africa, the ECMM was formally adopted by the AME after a visit from AME bishop Henry M. Turner (1834–1915) in 1898. There are several other independent churches that have Methodist roots and hold themselves close to Methodist tradition, singing from the same Xhosa or Sotho hymn-books and feeling themselves to be part of the Methodist family.

In the Republic of South Africa, dominated as it was by the ideology of apartheid, the Methodist Conference took a courageous stand in 1958 when it declared that the Methodist Church was "one and undivided." Nevertheless, the leadership of Methodism in South Africa remained almost wholly in the hands of the white minority, and many ministers and members were deeply compromised by apartheid. Although the Methodist Church in Southern Africa elected its first black president in 1963, the balance of power in Methodism remained with the white leadership until the 1980s, when Mmutlanyane Stanley Mogoba was appointed the first black secretary of the Conference. Today, black South Africans hold many of the leadership roles in the Conference, and the former presiding bishop, Mvume Dandala, is currently serving as the general secretary of the All-Africa Council of Churches (AACC). The Methodist community in South Africa numbers just over 2 million.

If there is one supremely significant South African Methodist, it is Nelson Mandela (b. 1918). Although among the first to deny that he is a theologian ("I am just an ordinary person trying make sense of the mysteries of life"), Nelson Mandela makes it known that he is a Christian, owing his education almost entirely to the Methodist Church. Mandela was cared for by the Methodist Church throughout the long years of exile on Robben Island, receiving holy communion regularly from visiting Methodist ministers. A mark of his Methodist heritage is seen in his openness to other forms of faith, and at his inauguration as President the world faith communities in South Africa were given a prominent part in the celebration.

East and central Africa

In 1858 David Livingstone gave an influential speech in the Senate House at Cambridge University that ended, "I beg you to direct your attention to Africa." A Methodist response to Livingstone's appeal was particular attention to missionary work in east and central Africa; it would not, however, be the Wesleyan Methodists that would be the first to respond, but rather the United Methodist Free Church. Thomas Wakefield (1836–1901) arrived in Ribe, not far from Mombassa, in 1861 and stayed for twenty-seven years, and J. B. Griffith began the Methodist work in Meru in 1895. Despite the labors of Wakefield and Griffith and their colleagues, by 1907 there were only 4,040 members in the East Africa District. (One hundred years later, however, a different story can be told; the autonomous Kenyan Methodist Church counts a community of 1,200,000 and is still growing.) The Primitive Methodists began work in south central Africa in 1889 and offered, as they had in southeastern Nigeria, a Gospel to the whole person through churches, workshops, schools, and clinics. This mission expanded into northwestern Rhodesia where it was served by, among others, the great Africanist Edwin W. Smith, known to the Ila-speaking people as "Chituta-mano," "the quiet wise spirit." Significantly a Roman Catholic historian of African Christianity calls the period 1925–1950 "The Age of Edwin Smith." Smith said of African missionary work: "our aim must be to make of the Africans not European Christians but Christians . . . and allow them to organize their faith in a manner suited to their traditions and environment." Wesleyan missionaries finally joined the Primitive Methodists in central Africa in 1891. They too engaged in high-quality educational work, producing future leaders for the developing African nation-states of Zambia and Zimbabwe.

American Methodist interest in east and central Africa continued, and in 1896 a new Congo Mission Conference was authorized by the General Conference, which elected Joseph Crane Hartzell (1842–1928) as bishop. Hartzell arrived in Zimbabwe the following year and a chain of mission Conferences came into being in central Africa. These Conferences have grown over the past hundred years into significant Methodist churches like that in Zimbabwe, where its first African bishop Abel T. Muzorewa (b. 1925), an ardent critic of colonialism, became for a short time the first black Prime Minister of Zimbabwe. Part of the continuing Zimbabwean Methodist contribution to nation-building was the opening of Africa University at Old Mutare in 1992. The UMC is also present in neighboring Mozambique, another country which has suffered from the upheaval of civil war.

SRI LANKA (CEYLON)

Thomas Coke had dreamed in 1783 of a Methodist mission to India, and in 1814 it seemed that this dream might be fulfilled; he had gathered a group of willing volunteers and had set sail for the subcontinent. But when that first band of Methodist missionaries arrived in Ceylon later that year, Coke was not with them, having died at sea en route. But the leaderless and dispirited group was welcomed by a Methodist former soldier, Andrew Armour, who had arrived in Ceylon a few years before and who served there as the court interpreter. Ceylon was mainly Theravada Buddhist, with Hindu Tamils in the northern section, and Armour helped his new friends find ways into the complexities of Sri Lankan life. Methodism pinned its hopes for missionary advance on education, and primary schools, high schools, and other forms of training were established. The Methodist Church in Sri Lanka, which became autonomous in 1964, has produced notable world church leaders like D. T. Niles (1908–70) and S. Wesley Ariarajah. Energetic in establishing programmes of evangelism, with ninety full-time evangelists and two colleges of evangelism, the Methodist Church today is on the point of becoming Sri Lanka's largest Protestant denomination.

INDIA AND PAKISTAN

Until the renewal of its charter in 1813, the East India Company was hostile to missionary activity. Its chaplains were in India solely to minister to the Company's employees and were neither authorized nor anxious to preach

9. Methodist church, Columbo, Sri Lanka.

to the Indian people. There was no law, however, forbidding soldiers from offering Christian witness. Andrew Armour, whom we have just met in Sri Lanka, had previously been in the British army in Madras, where he had formed a Methodist society that was still meeting for prayer and fellowship in 1816. Hearing of the arrival of Coke's team of missionaries in Ceylon, members of this society asked that one of them might be spared to come to India, and in 1817 they welcomed the first British Methodist missionary in India, James Lynch, the Irish preacher.

Because of the deeply entrenched Hindu culture and the complex caste system, India has never been easily receptive to the Christian message, and Methodism took root only slowly. American Methodists arrived in the mid-nineteenth century. They were the first to see that their mission could most fruitfully be directed to the Dalit community (then called "untouchables") and some significant mass movements took place among these peoples. By 1908 there were 200,000 Indian Methodists associated with the MEC; by 1939 this figure had risen to more than half a million. The British also saw times of rapid expansion, with large numbers of conversions to Christianity in the 1880s among the Telegu-speaking Dalit peoples, then in Hyderabad in the early 1900s. Such mass movements continued in south India for the next thirty years.

It is perhaps in India that the institutional differences in the approach to mission churches between British and American Methodism can be seen most clearly. The British-related Methodist community was still growing in 1947 when India's southern province entered into union with Congregationalists, Presbyterians, and Anglicans to form the Church of South India. British Methodists were participants in another ecumenical breakthough when the Church of North India was formed in 1970. But the Methodists of the American traditions have generally kept themselves aloof from both schemes, placing a higher value on their links with the USA than on local ecumenical unity. In Pakistan the Methodists became part of the united Church of Pakistan in 1970.

SOUTH ASIA: MYANMAR (BURMA), MALAYSIA, SINGAPORE, AND INDONESIA

The linguistic, religious, and sociopolitical complexity of South Asia has made the story of Methodist missionary progress an uneven one. Christian mission began in Burma, for example, in the late nineteenth century, at a time when Burma had been annexed to the British Empire because of the Burmese wars of 1852–85. In the south, Rangoon became the center for American activity from 1873, and in 1887 British missionaries in Mandalay, in the north, began work. But the strength of Burmese Buddhism meant that neither British nor American missionaries made significant progress numerically. To the north of Mandalay were the tribes of the Shan Hills and the Lushais of the Chindwin Valley, and there the mission did take hold. The Methodists in both Rangoon and Mandalay became self-governing in 1965. Today, shut off by the current regime in Myanmar from any possibility of traveling outside Burma, Burmese Methodists cherish any links they can have with the wider Methodist family.

From Burma, Methodism in its American form spread southward into Malaysia and Singapore, and then to Indonesia. Malaysia also received Methodist missionaries from Australia and the British Isles. Schooling has been a prominent part of the Methodist mission in Southeast Asia, and over 300 churches have been established in a country where often unwritten governmental policies make it difficult for Christians to acquire property. The Methodist Church in Malaysia has been autonomous since 1968. In both Malaysia and Singapore Methodist Christians come chiefly from the Chinese and Tamil communities and in Singapore, for example, these demographics are embodied in the three Methodist Annual Conferences: the Trinity Annual Conference (English-speaking), the Chinese Annual Conference and the Emmanuel Tamil Conference. Indonesia has had Methodist work since 1904 and today has two Annual Conferences.

THE FAR EAST: CHINA, KOREA, JAPAN, AND THE PHILIPPINES

When Methodism began its worldwide expansion, China thought of itself as "the Middle Kingdom": the repository of an ancient culture and civilization. It was impregnably closed to "foreigners," especially to what were perceived to be the ruthless European imperialists of the mid-nineteenth century. The two "opium wars" of 1839–44 and 1856–60, which were such disgraceful episodes in British history, led first to the forcible cession of Hong Kong and, in the aftermath of the first opium war in 1844, the opening of the five Treaty Ports. These "unequal treaties" were a source of deep resentment among Chinese people, and were a very real hindrance to communicating the story of Jesus Christ for British missionaries. The reputation of Americans was less negative, and MEC and MECS missionaries began work in China in the years 1847 and 1848. The MECS started work in Foochow and Shanghai, while the Northerners moved into the interior. In 1851 the British Wesleyan Methodists arrived in Hong Kong, followed by colleagues from the various other British Methodist groups – the Methodist New Connexion, the Bible Christians, the United Methodist Free Church, and the Primitive Methodists – all of whom had missions in China by the end of the nineteenth century. Sizeable mass movements among the Miao people occurred in southwest China, where the key figure was the linguist Samuel Pollard (1864–1915) of the Bible Christians.

In the twentieth century, two great disruptions of missionary activity took place: the Sino-Japanese War (1937–45) and the Chinese civil war that broke out immediately after the capitulation of Japan in 1946. The victory of the Communists in China resulted in the severing of all Western missionary links and the withdrawal of all missionary workers. But the seeds of Methodism had been firmly planted in China, and in 1950 there were 21,000 Methodists and a wider community of 57,000 in the China districts of the British Methodist Church, with another 190,000 in American-based Methodism. At the behest of the Communist government in 1951 the Methodists in China had to break all ties with the West and become "the three-church: self-governing, self-supporting, and self-propagating." Between 1950 and 1978, Christians in China had no contacts with the West but survived the Cultural Revolution and added very considerably to their numbers. More recently, with the renewal of freedom of religion, over 10,000 Protestant churches have been opened in China: Chinese Christians delight to tell the rest of the world that six new churches open every day in their country. Although no mission work by foreigners is permitted in China today, Methodist churches around the world are in close touch with the increasingly effective and growing Christian church in China.

Both the MEC and the MECS began work in Korea in 1884 and, as in other Asian countries, American Methodist missionaries put much emphasis on education, responding to the aspirations of Koreans themselves for "Suh-Hak," or "Western learning." Some of Korea's great universities, such as Ewha Women's University, are Methodist foundations, and Methodism has produced some of Korea's outstanding educators like Helen Kim (1899–1970). By the end of the First World War there were 25,000 members of the Methodist Church in Korea, and in 1930 the Korean Methodist Church became self-governing. All Christian churches in Korea grew during the period of Japanese hegemony, and at the turn of the twenty-first century there are nearly 1.5 million Korean Methodists, who support more than a hundred lay missionaries in forty-three countries, including Russia, Sri Lanka, the Philippines, and Malaysia. We may also note that the class meeting is alive and well in all the Korean Protestant churches, and Korean Christians all over the country meet in their classes on Friday evenings.

Only after 1853 was Japan open to any kind of Western influence, and it would be another twenty years before Methodist missionaries would arrive there, with a group from the Evangelical Association in 1873, followed by the United Brethren in 1895. Here is another instance where only American and Canadian Methodists were active, and only a small Methodist community took root as a result of their preaching. But Japanese Methodists have had outstanding leaders, among them Yoitsu Honda, the first Japanese bishop of the MEC. In 1941 the greater part of the Japanese Methodist community united with other Protestant churches in Japan in the Koran, or United Church of Christ in Japan in 1940.

After a slow start (the American Methodist missionary presence did not begin until after the Spanish-American War in 1898), the Philippines today has a variety of Methodist churches, and the Methodist community numbers approximately 1 million. All of these Methodist Churches participate in the Asian Methodist Council, which was set up in Seoul in 2001.

AUSTRALIA

The population of Australia in the early years was made up of free settlers and deported convicts, who were served by a few British chaplains and teachers. Two of these teachers were Methodists, and they wrote to London pleading for a Wesleyan missionary. Their plea was heard, and Samuel Leigh (1782–1852) arrived in Sydney in 1815; the ground had been well prepared for him, through the initiatives of Methodist laypeople in establishing class meetings. Samuel Leigh formed the first Methodist circuit in Sydney, and Methodist work expanded from there into Tasmania in 1820, to Melbourne in 1836, to Adelaide in 1837, and to Perth in 1840. All of these places were merely canvas townships and Methodism grew with them into well-organized communities. Very early on there were deeply committed Methodist laymen who assumed responsibility for what was called the protection of Aborigines. By 1855 it was possible to form the Australasian Methodist Conference, which immediately assumed responsibility for mission work in the South Pacific. Because of the vastness of Australia, it seemed wise to follow the American pattern of Conferences with a General Conference (meeting every three years) and Annual Conferences in New South Wales, Victoria, Queensland, South Australia, Western Australia, and Tasmania, as well as one in New Zealand. In 1881 the Australian census recorded that 241,968 persons called themselves Methodists. In 1902–4, all the Australian Methodists, including the UMFC, the Primitives, and the Bible Christians, united to form the Methodist Church of Australasia. In 1977 Australian Methodists united with Congregationalists and Presbyterians to make up the Uniting Church in Australia, which retains its membership in the World Methodist Council. At the beginning of the twenty-first century the Uniting Church has a community of over 1 million and is deeply committed to new styles of ministry alongside the Aboriginal and Islander peoples and multicultural and interfaith ministries.

NEW ZEALAND AND OCEANIA

In 1818 Samuel Leigh visited New Zealand accompanied by an Anglican missionary, Samuel Marsden. When he returned to England on leave, Leigh launched a special appeal for work in those islands and in 1821 he himself was appointed to oversee the missionary work in New Zealand. Missionary history in New Zealand follows two streams: along New Zealand's east coast Christianity spread through the efforts of Anglicans, and along the west coast it spread through the efforts of Methodists. These years during which Methodist missions were becoming established coincided with the beginning of the colonization of New Zealand, and both the Church Missionary Society and the Wesleyan Methodist Missionary Society protested colonial expansion. A few sentences from an address by John Hardy, the chairman of the Wesleyan Methodist Missionary Society (WMMS), in 1838 shows the deep disquiet that Methodists felt about the linking of mission and colonization:

To evangelize is one thing; to colonize another. The colonist goes "with arms of mortal temper in his hands; with the musket, the bayonet, and the gunpowder"; but your Missionaries go "with the sword of the Spirit, which is the word of God." I trust that they will be permitted to go unmolested. Nothing can be greater than their disinterestedness in that cause. They cannot be suspected of any objects of ambition: they go poor and defenceless, to make many rich; whereas colonists generally go to make many poor, in order to enrich a few.

This statement is typical of missionary attitudes in this period of British imperial expansion, not only in New Zealand but also in many other countries, such as South Africa, where the inhabitants owe much to the missionary protest against the power of empire. As another part of this protest, British Methodists and Anglicans were involved in the negotiations that led to the Treaty of Waitangi in 1840, ensuring some measure of protection of the rights of the Maori people. In terms of organization, New Zealand Methodism began as part of the Australian Methodist Church, becoming an autonomous Methodist church in 1913. Today the Methodist Church in New Zealand is known by the Maori name Te Haahi Weteriana O Aotearoa (The Methodist Church of New Zealand) and has many intercultural initiatives.

The islands of Tonga, Vava'u, and Ha'atafu (once known as the "Friendly Islands") lie in the Pacific Ocean east of Australia. Methodist missionaries from Britain were present in the islands from 1822, but work was hindered by the hostility of the inhabitants. The turning point for Methodist work there took place in 1830 with the baptism of Taufa'ahau of Ha'apai, a man exemplifying the doctrine of prevenient grace by possessing both godliness and morality before he had ever heard the name of Jesus Christ. He became a Methodist local preacher and in 1845 was enthroned as the first Methodist king anywhere in the world. As King George Tupou I, he founded a dynasty of Methodist rulers, among whom was Queen Salote

Tupou III, who made a deep impression upon the British at the time of the coronation of Queen Elizabeth II. With a population of 100,000, Tonga is a Methodist stronghold. The Free Wesleyan Church ("free" that is from the Australian Methodist Church) reports a membership of more than 30,000 and an extended community of 70,000, and it may fairly be said that in Tonga Methodism is the "established religion."

Following the lead of local Christians from the other islands and British Methodist missionaries William Cross (1797–1842) and David (1809–43) and Margaret Cargill (1804–40) crossed to Fiji in 1835. They arrived to find a cannibal feast in progress. But they and their colleagues, with the aid of many local people, found their way around the Fijian islands, establishing schools and baptizing community leaders. Gradually cannibalism declined, and Fiji came under British rule in 1874. As a part of the British Empire, the islands experienced an influx of indentured laborers from India, and British Methodists launched an Indian Mission on Fiji in 1892. The autonomous Methodist Conference of Fiji and Rotuma came into being in 1964, and has been marked by a deep commitment to being a multiracial, multicultural church. Of its 215,000 membership nearly 3,000 are Indo-Fijian.

In 1857, the newly constituted Australian Conference entered Samoa, and although not large (there are many other denominations at work in Samoa), the Methodist Church became autonomous in 1964. There are just over 35,000 Samoan Methodist members, with another 40,000 in its community. Like many other Methodist conferences we have mentioned, Samoa takes responsibility for its own people in congregations in New Zealand, Australia, and the USA. Of their 182 parishes, 77 are overseas.

SOUTH, CENTRAL, AND LATIN AMERICA

In South America the advance of Methodism faced the twin difficulties of the long domination of the Roman Catholic Church and the extraordinary diversity of political systems operating on the continent. Methodist missionary activity here has chiefly been in the hands of the various American Methodist churches, although some work begun by the British remains active in the heartland of Brazil. The Methodist Church of Brazil dates from 1835, receiving a great deal of support when large numbers of Southern Methodists fleeing the effects of the Civil War settled there after 1865. The MECS formally established a mission there in 1867. Today the Methodist Church of Brazil is self-governing, with a community of half a million divided into six ecclesiastical regions, one missionary region in northeast Brazil and a national mission field in the north and northwest. Most of these are Pentecostalist in their style of worship and practice, though the church cherishes its ecumenical connections and was the first church in Latin America to become a member of the WCC.

Methodists from both the MEC and MECS came to Mexico from 1872 onwards after a visit by Bishop Gilbert Haven to the President of Mexico. Assured of religious freedom, Methodism was formally inaugurated at a service led by Alejo Hernandez, the Mexican preacher from the Texas Conference of the MECS, and in the presence of a MECS bishop. Large numbers of missionaries, including representatives of the Women's Foreign Missionary Society, arrived in the next decades. The work of the two missions, Northern and Southern, was combined in 1930 when a self-governing Methodist Church of Mexico was organized. At the time of its organization, the Methodist Church of Mexico had 10,000 members, and by the end of twentieth century nearly half a million Mexicans called themselves Methodists, meeting in 400 churches with two seminaries and a university. Their social service to both the urban and rural poor is a significant contribution to the life of Mexico.

Three successive waves of American Methodist activity reached into other parts of Central and South America in the nineteenth century. The first wave of missionaries which had arrived in Haiti in 1823 and in the Dominican Republic in 1834 pressed southward into Uruguay and Argentina, with MEC work beginning in both places in 1835–6. (The first church in Argentina was built in 1842.) The second wave is always associated with the missionary thinker William Taylor, whose work in Africa we have already touched upon. Under his inspiration Methodist churches were planted in Cuba in 1873, in Panama in 1877, in Peru and Paraguay in 1886, in Bolivia and Venezuela in 1890, and in Puerto Rico and Costa Rica in 1900. Back in the United States, Taylor founded the "Building and Transit Fund" in order to help Wesleyan and Holiness missionary personnel to become self-supporting. Contributing to this second wave were Wesleyan Methodists, Free Methodists, the Church of the Nazarene, and the Pilgrim Holiness Church. Taylor became their model whenever there was conflict, and many missionaries, local pastors, and lay people became Pentecostal rather than Methodist, especially after 1906.

The third wave of Methodist evangelistic work in Latin America was an internal missionary movement, only loosely connected with the main traditions of Methodism. José Míguez Bonino, the doyen of Methodist theologians in South America, has described at least three "faces" of Latin American Protestantism: the evangelical, the Pentecostal, and the ethnic. In Chile early Pentecostals were expelled from the MEC in 1907, and their

10. Methodist church, San Juan, Puerto Rico.

doctrines were condemned as anti-Methodist, "contrary to the scriptures and irrational"; today, some 75 percent of Chilean Protestants are members of the "Iglesia Metodista Pentecostal" in Chile. Although there are many middle-class Methodist churches composed of descendants of the early European and North American immigrants, Methodism more usually falls into Bonino's "ethnic" grouping, and for the most part the Methodist Church in South America manifests itself as the church of the poor. There are two aspects of this. In many countries, like Brazil, Methodism has forms of worship, preaching, and prayer that are in fact Pentecostalist. Such services attract the illiterate, who cannot read hymn-books or church bulletins, and the poor who have no Sunday-best clothes to wear. Such forms of worship awaken a sense in the oppressed and marginalized that they are children of God and part of the "familia di Dios," the family of

God. Powerful testimonies from across Latin America show Methodists with Pentecostalist tendencies working for the "abundant life" promised by Jesus, especially among women, immigrants, aborigines, and young people. At the same time, there is considerable awareness in Methodist circles of liberation theology, with its concern to transform harmful political and social structures. Latino/a Methodist liberation theologians like José Míguez Bonino of Argentina and Elsa Tamez, now teaching in Costa Rica, are well known outside South America for their contributions to social and ethical theory. Practical social action is undertaken by these newly empowered men and women, as for example in the case of Casimira Rodriguez who was awarded the World Methodist Council Peace Prize in 2003 for mobilizing domestic workers in Bolivia.

EUROPE

Europe became a significant mission field for Methodists when growing numbers of European immigrants in America came within the influence of the MEC and of the German churches that were associated with it (the Evangelical Association and United Brethren in Christ). Many of these new German-speaking American Methodists had a deep concern for their own people back home and deliberately returned to their places of birth in order to share their Christian faith. The influential figure in this process was the Tübingen-educated Wilhelm Nast (1807–1899), known as "God's bridge builder," who began his ministry working among German immigrants in the Ohio Annual Conference. By 1844 the General Conference was exploring ways of mounting a mission to Germany. In 1849, Ludwig S. Jacoby established a German-speaking Methodist mission station in Bremen, followed by Ludwig Nipert in Berlin in 1858. The United Brethren formally established a mission to Germany in 1869, and in the next year the first Methodist preachers arrived in Austria. Today there is a Methodist community of more than 100,000 in Germany and nearly 2,000 in Austria. British Methodists also maintained an interest in establishing missions on the continent, and initiated work in Italy in 1860 and in Portugal in 1871. In 1853 Ole Peter Person was assigned by the MEC to Norway; the first MEC society was gathered in Denmark in 1899. The Evangelical Association undertook a mission to Switzerland in 1865. The work of the MECS in Belgium, in the former Czechoslovakia, and in Poland grew out of its war relief ministries after the First World War. The United Methodist Northern Europe Conference embraces Methodist churches in Sweden, Denmark, Norway, and Finland.

Methodist work in Poland, Russia, and the Baltic states can be traced to the last years of the nineteenth century as a result of Swedish, Finnish, German, and American evangelistic activity. Methodism was surprisingly successful in the Baltic states, at least in the beginning, but suffered the full violence that marked the region in the twentieth century, struggling to endure the persecutions of Bolshevism and the conflict with Nazism. During this period, Methodist churches were destroyed and their communities were displaced by waves of invasion and occupation, Red Army and Nazi conscriptions, and battle casualties. In Latvia, Lithuania, and the western Ukraine Methodism was actually banned. The beginnings of Methodist missionary work in Russia were snuffed out in 1927, and were not renewed until after 1989, just before the breakdown of communism. With the watchword "to renew a mission suspended but never abandoned," the UMC has engaged in many initiatives to help restore the Methodist presence in the former Soviet Union. In addition to the efforts of the UMC, there has been notable support of the Russian Methodist communities by the Methodist Church in Korea, which has a significant missionary presence there. As the twenty-first century began, there were four Annual Conferences of Russian Methodists. Because this Methodist renewal is taking place in the historic territory of the Orthodox Church, great care is being taken to maintain good relationships with the Russian church authorities, and to foster Orthodox–Methodist dialogue. In Poland there are 4,000 Methodists linked with other Protestant churches in this predominantly Roman Catholic country. Methodist churches now operate with freedom in Estonia, Latvia, and Lithuania and are once again growing in numbers. Other significant Methodist initiatives are being worked out in Hungary, Bulgaria (where the number of Methodist congregations has grown from three when communist rule came to an end in 1991 to more than thirty today), the Federal Republic of Yugoslavia, and the Republic of Macedonia, and there is also a growing Methodist presence in Albania, Croatia, and Kosovo.

CONCLUSION

Methodist people around the globe cherish the stories of the men and women who came from other lands to share the Christian message with them. Many of these missionaries laid down their lives in order to preach the Gospel in foreign lands, and the places where these missionaries died have become Methodist shrines and pilgrimage sites. In 1995, the Chinese government itself rebuilt the grave of Samuel Pollard, which was destroyed by the Red Guards. Through these memories of the missionaries, world Methodism is linked directly with either the British Isles or with North America, and then back to the earliest Methodism of John and Charles Wesley.

But our missionary forebears were children of another time, and carried their own imperialistic or cultural baggage with them. Often they blundered because they had little anthropological training and were rarely self-critical about their own cultural norms and biases. But, for most Methodists around the world, deep affection for those who preached the Gospel in their midst overrides any resentment they might have about the way their culture was treated. One of the present writers remembers a Cree Indian minister of the United Church of Canada speaking affectionately about the early Wesleyan preachers in Canada: "They were great lummoxes," he said, "but they loved us."

In acknowledging his own indebtedness to his Methodist education Nelson Mandela reflects on the missionaries he knew in his youth. They are often criticized, he comments, for being colonialist and paternalistic in their attitudes and practices. "Yet even with such attitudes, I believe their benefits outweighed their disadvantages. The missionaries ran schools when the government was unwilling or unable to do so. The learning environment of the missionary schools, while often morally rigid was far more open than the racist principles underlying government schools."

The rigid and moralistic attitudes of the missionaries were sometimes internalized within the new converts, creating a bitter conflict that can persist to this day between Methodists in Africa, Asia, and the Pacific and their own cultures. Thus one Asian Methodist theologian speaks of the missionaries' form of faith "arriving with its attendant parochialism, dogmatism, cultural jingoism, secularism and materialism, demanding rejection of Korean indigenous values, customs, culture and faith." In contrast to this, he sets the vision of a "global and humane faith with its promises of appreciation and celebration of the best of Korean spirituality." The rejection of indigenous values and customs was repeated in many other countries, and theologians from these places are looking again at the resources that Methodist theology provides for a new missionary theology.

Throwing off the various forms of cultural domination is now happening rapidly in all kinds of situations. One African Methodist has written that, in the missionary era, "Africans were forced to live two lives at once. When they were in church, they had to sing like missionaries, and when they got home they were free to sing with liberty of movement in the accompaniment of the shaker, the drum and the rattle." The author of these words is himself working toward the renewal of native traditions of worship and music in the Zimbabwean church, and is finding ways for movement and ululation to become part of hymn singing, and for the use of drums to announce the high points of worship.

Everywhere in the non-Western world Christianity is taking on new forms of life very different from those of its origins in Europe or North America. Among them are the churches with their roots in the work of John and Charles Wesley who have new perceptions of how the Wesleyan heritage can be adapted and transformed to reflect and challenge their own cultural presuppositions and values. Doubtless these efforts would give the nineteenth- and early twentieth-century missionary people severe spiritual and mental indigestion. But it is clear that these are notable attempts at faithful interpretations of the Evangelical Arminian form of the Gospel that has been proclaimed in Methodism from the beginning.

CHAPTER 5

Methodist theology

As far as the central matters of theology are concerned, there is little that distinguishes Methodism from the broad spectrum of classical orthodox Christian doctrine, especially as it has been formulated by Protestants. Thus, the 1932 *Deed of Union* of the British Methodist Church affirms in its opening sentence: "The Methodist Church claims and cherishes its place in the Holy Catholic Church which is the Body of Christ. It rejoices in the inheritance of the Apostolic Faith and loyally accepts the fundamental principles of the historic creeds and the Protestant Reformation." Although they might not state it as explicitly as this, all major Methodist churches could make a similar assertion. The United Methodist Church, for example, affirms in its *Book of Discipline* that: "United Methodists profess the historic Christian faith in God, incarnate in Jesus Christ for our salvation and ever at work in human history in the Holy Spirit. Living in a covenant of grace under the Lordship of Jesus Christ, we participate in the firstfruits of God's coming reign and pray in hope for its full realization on earth as in heaven."

The UMC *Discipline* goes on to assert that American Methodism, like its British parent, claims "a common heritage with Christians of every age and nation," a heritage that is "grounded in the apostolic witness to Jesus Christ as Savior and Lord, which is the source and measure of all valid Christian teaching." A similar pattern of belief is found in Methodist churches around the world. Most often this is manifested by an affirmation of the authority of scripture, the historic creeds, and in many cases the Twenty-Five Articles of Religion (Wesley's own abridgement of the Church of England's Thirty-Nine Articles presented to the 1784 Christmas Conference). Along with all Protestant churches, Methodists affirm that salvation is by faith alone, that scripture is the sole principle upon which faith is based, that the priesthood of Christ has been entrusted to all believers, and that Christ alone is the head of the church.

Nevertheless, there remain some distinctive emphases in the Methodist understanding of the nature of the Christian faith, most of which have their roots in the teaching of John and Charles Wesley. The first set of emphases relates to the importance of "heart religion" with a corresponding prominence given to the relationship between faith and experience. A second group of "Methodist distinctives" is centered upon the "Arminian Evangelicalism" that sets Wesleyan Methodism apart from all forms of Calvinist Evangelicalism. A further set of emphases have as their focus doctrines variously known as "Christian perfection," "entire sanctification," "scriptural holiness," and "perfect love." All Methodist theology is imbued with a sense of the "optimism of grace" which refuses to set limits to God's power to transform individuals and societies. But in this case, as we shall see, there remains a division of opinion among John Wesley's heirs about the way in which God perfects holiness in the believer, and Methodist churches throughout the world are still divided over the significance of a "second blessing" and the degree to which instantaneous perfection should be understood as indispensable to true Christian faith and life.

The great themes of Wesleyan theology, especially as worked out by the Wesley brothers in their sermons, their hymns, their journals, and their other writings, are the subject of this chapter. Although it was never their intention to found a new denomination, both John and Charles Wesley lived to see the Methodist movement grow into something akin to a church, both in Britain and in the newborn United States of America, and the attitudes and beliefs of Methodists were as important to the Wesleys as were their pastoral care and spiritual formation. John Wesley in particular was concerned that the core understanding of Methodism should be firmly and fully enshrined in a set of doctrinal "standards."

Like every living religious tradition, Methodism is marked by change and development, and has responded to various forces, internal and external, exerted upon it. After its initial impetus, the trajectory of Methodist theology was subjected to both the gravitational pull of a desire to return to traditional Protestant thinking, and to the sharp crosscurrents of the theological culture in which it found itself. We shall see how at least some of these forces took Methodist theology off course in the nineteenth and twentieth centuries and, in later chapters, how more recently some Methodist theologians have been returning to the original sources of the tradition.

WESLEYAN THEOLOGY AGAINST ITS
EIGHTEENTH-CENTURY BACKGROUND

Many Methodist writers have tended to imply that the eighteenth century was a kind of spiritual wasteland, and that Methodism came to birth as an antidote to the utter spiritual desolation of the age. But, like most caricatures, this is neither very accurate nor very helpful in understanding the complexity of religious life in Enlightenment Britain. To be sure, there was much that was amiss in the life of the Church of England, not least serious problems of ecclesial administration. The last Convocation of the eighteenth century met in 1717, and ferocious internal disputes led to its dissolution by Prime Minister Robert Walpole (it was not to be reconvened until 1852). In the absence of overarching structures of governance, each Anglican bishop tended to do what was right in his own eyes. Since episcopal preferment was based on maintaining social and political connections, many bishops were creatures of the Whig establishment, and their decisions were more often motivated by political expediency than by pastoral or theological sensitivity. This is not to say that there were not many good bishops, among them Joseph Butler (1692–1752) of Bristol and Durham, author of *The Analogy of Religion*, the great scholar-bishop Edmund Gibson (1669–1748) of Lincoln and London, and Thomas Wilson (1663–1755) of Sodor and Man, whose acute concern with Christian education is embodied in his *The Knowledge of Christianity made Easy* published in 1755. Within this haphazard situation, clergy often made valiant efforts to care for their parishioners, ensuring that the sacraments were duly observed and that instruction for confirmation was given. Contemporary questionnaires and visitation reports of bishops and archdeacons show that, although worship in the parishes could at times be lifeless and stilted, very rarely had it died out altogether. The fact that John Wesley had such an easy supply of good-quality religious writing to recommend to his preachers in 1744 and again in 1746 is some indication of the religious vitality present in the church of his time.

Genuine seekers after God and godliness were numerous, and we may take Dr Samuel Johnson (1709–84) as representative of them; his unaffected piety produced prayers that are still regarded as classics of English devotional literature. Others turned their faithfulness into action for social improvement. Robert Raikes (1735–1811), a newspaper publisher in Gloucester, organized the first Sunday schools in 1780, and elsewhere men and women were setting up charity schools and hospitals. Notable philanthropists like Thomas Coram (*c.* 1668–1751) and Jonas Hanway (1712–86) established institutions like the Foundling Hospital for orphans (1741) and the Magdalene Hospital for prostitutes and other outcast women.

Many devout eighteenth-century Anglicans were affected by the currents of spiritual vitality that had been flowing into the British Isles from continental Europe. The revival of religion associated with Halle in Saxony and Würtenberg in southern Germany had emphasized "a religion of the heart" over the "religion of the mind" fostered by Enlightenment rationalism. In the *Pia Desideria*, Philipp Jakob Spener (1635–1705) had set out a program for renewal in the Lutheran Church, emphasizing Biblical authority and laying new stress on the priesthood of all believers and the religious responsibility of the laity. Spener's strategy for regeneration called for a program for training ministers to be preachers of *faith* rather than instructors in *doctrine*, and for groups known as *collegia pietatis* ("colleges of piety"): small gatherings of lay people meeting in their homes for study of the scriptures and for prayer. When his vision was rejected by the leaders of the Lutheran established church in Frankfurt, Spener moved to Saxony where he met August Herman Franke (1663–1727). Together they laid the foundations for the religious renewal movement known as Pietism.

Because Spener and Franke were demanding "real" instead of "nominal" Christianity, "inwardness" instead of ceremonial and formality, Pietism was always destined to present an implicit challenge to "Christendom" and to churches established by law as arms of the state. Pietism arose precisely within societies whose symbols (codes, creeds, cultural manifestations) had become moribund, where there was neither any sense of the need for crosscultural communication of the Gospel nor any wish to challenge established Christian structures. The old "corporativeness" (in which every person knew his or her place in society) was beginning to lose its power in continental Europe, and people had begun to sense that the "church" might not be coterminous with the "nation." Inexorably Europeans were moving into a time of cultural and religious pluralism and the spirit of the Enlightenment was increasingly lifting up the ideal of personal autonomy and independent decision-making. In such a situation, Spener had sensed the urgency of a positive reinforcement of Christian convictions, and his solution was to offer people spiritual nurture and mutual society within Pietist groups. The groups themselves became *ecclesiolae in ecclesia*, "little churches in the church," and they gave individuals a sense of being part of the "real" church within an apparently failing institution. This theological and organizational development had a significant impact on Methodism, which could hardly have arisen had it not been for the influence, on the one hand, of the "religious societies" in England and, on the other, the direct influence of the Moravian Pietists on the Wesleys themselves between 1735 and 1739.

Spener's Pietism was transmitted to England through the work of Anthony Horneck (1641–97), the widely popular preacher based at the fashionable Savoy Chapel in London from 1671 onwards. It was Horneck who first established religious societies within the Church of England, and had instructed that each of these be led by "a pious and learned divine of the Church." A first rule of these societies was: "All that enter the society shall resolve upon an holy and serious life." Much larger and more centralized organizations, such as the Society for the Reformation of Manners (1691), the Society for Promoting Christian Knowledge (SPCK, 1698), and the Society for the Propagation of the Gospel (SPG, 1701), arose out of the matrix of these small religious societies. So important were these gatherings, both large and small, that they were the subjects of a scholarly treatise, *The Rise and Progress of Religious Societies* (1712), by Josiah Woodward. The group that met in Fetter Lane described in chapter 1 was just one such Church of England society, even though it was deeply influenced by the Moravians in its theology.

To be sure, there had always been small religious gatherings for prayer, Bible study, and edification in the British Isles. These were especially important in the period of Puritan separatism, and would surely have been part of the living memory of John Wesley's parents. Such a group met for mutual spiritual improvement under the wing of the Puritan pastor-theologian Richard Baxter (1615–91), and his description is typical: "Every Thursday evening my Neighbours that were most desirous and had opportunity, met at my House, and there one of them repeated the Sermon; and afterwards they proposed what Doubts any of them had about the Sermon, or any other Case of Conscience, and I resolved their Doubts." The Wesley brothers would have come into direct contact with this kind of intimate religious gathering at the Epworth rectory, where a small religious society came into being in the year before John's birth. The key objective was clearly a search for "real holiness," and this idea of the need for an intentional form of Christian living had captivated John and Charles Wesley at an early age.

But the most decisive impact of the religious societies on Methodism came through the Moravian Brethren, a group that came into being under the direct influence of Count Nicholas von Zinzendorf (1700–69). Educated at Franke's seminary in Halle, Zinzendorf later established a settlement for emigrants from Austria (descendants of the Bohemian Brethren), on his estates at Herrnhut, eventually resigning from government service to engage in full-time pastoral care. Zinzendorf was deeply Lutheran and regarded his group as an *ecclesiola* within the established church rather than a church in its own right. At an early stage, Moravians became concerned with overseas missions, transforming themselves into *ecclesiolae* on the move; in 1732 two of the brethren went to the West Indies and in the next year others traveled to Greenland. According to the familiar story the fearlessness of a band of Moravian missionaries facing death in a storm at sea made the deepest impression on John Wesley. In Savannah, Georgia, he met the Moravian leader August Spangenberg (1704–92) who pressed the question, "Does the spirit of God bear witness with your spirit that you are a child of God?" Wesley replied in the affirmative, but also recorded his uncertainty: "I fear they were vain words." Nevertheless, the need for the kind of "heart religion" espoused by Moravian Pietism had now clearly laid hold on him.

By the end of 1737 John Wesley's mission to Georgia had failed and he returned, depressed and uncertain, to London. As soon as he arrived, he promptly began to meet with Moravian Peter Böhler ("February seventh, a day to be remembered," he would write in his *Journal*), who was preparing to make his own missionary journey to America. Böhler, a Lutheran minister who had been ordained as a Moravian by Zinzendorf, met with Wesley often during the next four months, and Böhler laid out for him the principles of Lutheran theology (in Latin, although Wesley had begun to learn German to speak with the Moravians and Böhler was learning English to speak with the people in America). During this time, Böhler incisively diagnosed the inherent rationalism of Wesley's piety: "*Mi frater, mi frater, excoquenda est ista tua philosophia*" ("My brother, my brother, that philosophy of yours must be purged away"), and then replaced by faith. We have already encountered Böhler's decisive counsel to John Wesley: "Preach faith until you have it," and it was under Böhler's influence that Wesley came to understand that true Christian faith was "a sure trust and confidence which a man hath in God, that through the merits of Christ *his* sins are forgiven and *he* is reconciled to the favour of God" (emphasis Wesley's). During this same time Charles Wesley also had a long conversation with Böhler about the nature of faith, so that he too "saw clearly what was the nature of that one true, living faith, whereby alone through grace are we saved." Through their preaching and their hymnody the Wesleys shared the rich heritage of Lutheran Pietism with their followers, and made it possible for the whole of British Christianity to come into contact with a vibrant European movement that anteceded Methodism. (This can perhaps also be identified as the moment when the work of Martin Luther was at last fully understood by English-speaking Christians.)

Wesley found the Lutheran teaching and Moravian practice, which he experienced both in the Fetter Lane society and in the society which was meeting in Aldersgate Street, so attractive that in July and August, 1738, he set off to visit the Moravian communities in Germany. But rather than confirming his views, this visit raised serious reservations in his mind, especially with regard to the Moravian understanding of faith as "assurance" and justification as "freedom from sin." He was to work his way through these questions, however, not by delving further into Lutheran Moravianism but rather by recapturing his own Anglican heritage. So, as tension with the Moravians in the Fetter Lane society was increasing at the end of 1738 and the beginning of 1739, John Wesley turned to *The Homilies of the Church of England* (1547), a set of doctrinal sermons written by Archbishop Thomas Cranmer (1489–1556) at the beginning of the English Reformation in order to make up for the educational or theological deficiencies of local parish clergy. Of the twenty-one sermons in the first book of the *Homilies*, Wesley was particularly affected by those "On the General Salvation of Mankind," "Of the True and Lively Faith," and "Of Good Works." He also looked again at another document central to the Anglican settlement of 1559, the *Treatise on the Laws of Ecclesiastical Polity* by Richard Hooker (*c.* 1554–1600), from which he rediscovered the necessity of a balance of scripture, tradition, and reason in developing one's faith. From both of these sources, Wesley found support for his increasing conviction that faith and works were inseparably linked, and in 1738 Wesley himself published an extract from *The Homilies* for the use of his followers.

To the rediscovery of his own Anglican tradition as an answer to what he considered the Moravian misperception of the relation of faith and works, Wesley added his own native confidence in the power of reason, also confirmed by Richard Hooker and the Cambridge Platonists (men like Benjamin Whichcote, Ralph Cudworth, and Henry More). Like them, Wesley could conceive of elements in revelation that were *above* human reason, but never anything which would be *contrary* to human reason. But Wesley still had the problem of faith to deal with, and it was the work of John Locke (1632–1704), the supreme figure in the intellectual project now known as the Enlightenment, who would help Wesley explicate his own sense of the relationship between faith and human reason. In his *Essay on Human Understanding* (1690) and *The Reasonableness of Christianity as delivered in the Scriptures* (1695), Locke had strongly affirmed that human beings can be said to "know" things through the use of reason. But at the same time he emphasized another key element in human understanding, namely *experience*. For Locke "experience" was a combination of *sensation* plus *reflection*, and no genuine knowledge (including scientific knowledge) was possible without it. Wesley was enormously taken with this idea, and Locke gave Wesley the confidence to proclaim that "religion and reason go hand in hand," and that to "renounce reason is to renounce religion."

But in order to apply this epistemological scheme to the specific case of *religious* knowledge, Wesley had to challenge Locke on one important point. Since it was obvious that the physical senses could not receive empirical information on the world of the Spirit, Wesley argued that human beings are equipped by their Creator with "spiritual senses" that are able to register spiritual reality in the same way that physical senses register material reality. Thus, human beings have "eyes to see" and "ears to hear" in the realm of the Spirit. But of course these spiritual senses are not what they were before the Fall of Adam, and this deformation results in a "spiritual blindness and deafness." In order to come to true religious knowledge, the spiritual senses needed to be brought back to life, reawakened from the habits of indifference and neglect. Through faith, Wesley believed, the "impenetrable veil" that stands between the spiritual and the material world is penetrated, and the result is a new sensitivity to the divine: "The eyes of understanding are opened," and the believer sees the "light of the glory of God in the face of Jesus Christ." Wesley became deeply convinced of the truth of the words of St. Paul: "for if any one is in Christ there is a new creation: the old has passed away, and behold the new has come" (2 Cor. 5:17).

Wesley did not create his augmentation of Locke's theory of knowledge out of nothing. His understanding of religious knowing echoes that contained in a treatise by a Greek patristic writer known to Wesley as Macarius the Egyptian (but now considered to be the work of a fifth-century Syrian monk), who describes this transformed spiritual perception as the birth of new senses: "For our Lord Jesus Christ came . . . to work a new mind, a new soul, and new eyes, new ears, a new spiritual tongue . . . that he may pour into them the new wine, which is his Spirit."

Macarius was not the only ancient writer upon whom Wesley would rely in the formation of his theological agenda. He was widely read in the Greek Church Fathers generally (he had, after all, been lecturer in Greek at Lincoln College, Oxford), and was especially interested in their expositions of the New Testament. Indeed, throughout his life we find insights drawn from the patristic corpus contributing to key moments in Wesley's religious development. In a 1738 *Journal* entry, for example, he recorded that during the day of May 24 (some hours before his Aldersgate experience that evening) the words of 2 Peter 1:4, "that you may become partakers of the Divine nature" (he transcribed them in Greek), were explicitly in his mind. This is a key text for the Greek Fathers; the idea of "partaking in the divine nature (*theosis*)" is central to their understanding of God's actions in the world, and it would become equally central to what Wesley was later to call "true genuine Christianity." Although there is little evidence that Wesley consulted the Greek theologians regularly, he did say that one of the chief privileges of a university education had been his introduction to the work of the Cappadocian Fathers, Basil (*c.* 330–79), Gregory of Nazianzus (329–89), and Gregory of Nyssa (*c.* 300–*c.* 95). All of these men were notable for their expositions of the work of the Holy Spirit as creator, life-giver, and perfector in the work of salvation. Macarius also stood within this school of thought, and some of the emphasis Wesley placed on the work of the Holy Spirit and the power of divine love to transfigure the material world can be seen in the selections he chose from Macarius's *Fifty Homilies* for inclusion in the first volume of the *Christian Library*. For both John and Charles Wesley the Greek slogan "God became what we are that we may become what he is" was supremely important, especially, as we shall see, in their exposition of the doctrine of sanctification.

THE MAIN THEMES OF WESLEYAN THEOLOGY

When John Wesley published the first issue of *The Arminian Magazine* in 1778, his choice of its title illuminates the chief theme of Wesleyan theology. Methodists were, it declared, "Arminians," and the implications of this self-description are crucial for understanding the theology that is embodied in the writings and hymnody of the Wesley brothers and the work of their chief assistants such as John Fletcher (1729–85). There is an anomaly here, however. While Wesley was certainly well aware of the theology of the man whose name he had borrowed for the title of the journal, the influential Dutch theologian Jacobus Arminius (1560–1609), Arminius's work was not a direct influence on Wesley's. Nor were the writings of the theological heirs of Arminius, the so-called "Remonstrants" who were condemned as heretics at the Synod of Dort in 1618–19 for their utter rejection of Calvinism. Wesley stood, rather, within that distinctly Anglican tradition represented, as we have seen, by the *Homilies* of the Church of England and the works of Richard Hooker. He did need, however, a term that would immediately distinguish the kind of evangelicalism that Methodists were to claim from that of their Calvinist opponents (both Methodists like George Whitefield and Howell Harris, and Anglicans like Thomas Toplady). The word "Arminianism" did just that, and many have considered the most accurate term for Wesleyan theology to be "Evangelical Arminianism," or the interchangeable term "Arminian Evangelicalism."

THE UNIVERSALITY OF SALVATION

The starting point of Arminian theology is the affirmation that God's grace is universally available to humankind, and that in no sense did God foreknow, elect, or predestine those who would be saved and those who would be lost. John and Charles Wesley abhorred what they referred to as the "horrible decrees" of Calvinism as an affront to the God of infinite love and mercy. In October 1778, an early issue of *The Arminian Magazine* carried a seventeen-verse poem by Charles Wesley, originally published in 1741–2 in his *Hymns of Everlasting Love*, as a polemic against the notion of divine election. It begins

> Father whose *everlasting love*,
> Thine only Son for sinners gave,
> Whose Grace to *All* did freely move,
> And sent Him down a *World to save*.
>
> Help us thy Mercy to extol,
> Immense, unfathom'd, unconfin'd;
> To praise the Lamb who *died for All*
> The *general Saviour of Mankind*.

The emphases are all Charles Wesley's (lest we mistake his point). To this constant insistence on universality, Charles adds the next quatrain:

> Thy *undistinguishing Regard*
> Was cast on *Adam's* fallen race
> For *All* Thou hast in Christ prepared
> *Sufficient, sovereign, saving* Grace.

Saving grace is stressed because Calvinist formularies like the Westminster Confession allowed that, while the non-elect might possess some grace or "common operations of the Spirit," only those predestined would be saved.

Others not elected, although they may be called by the ministry of the Word, and may have some common operations of the Spirit, yet they never truly come to Christ and therefore cannot be saved; much less can men not professing the Christian religion; be they never so diligent to frame their loves according to the light of nature and the law of that religion which they do profess, and to assert and maintain that they may is very pernicious and to be detested.

Such a view of the Godhead comes close to being blasphemous for the Wesleys. Accordingly Charles goes on in verse 14 to put the following words in the mouths of those who restrict the universal love of God, and who "think that Fury is in Thee / Horribly think, that God is hate!":

> Thou hast compell'd the lost to die,
> Hath *reprobated* from thy face
> Hath others sav'd, by them *past* by;
> Or mock'd with only *Damning Grace*.

Again the emphasis in the fourth line belongs to the original, and Charles Wesley adds a footnote at the end of this verse which explains that "damning grace" is "more usually call'd *Common Grace*." In the face of what appeared to him as blasphemous conceptions of God, Wesley affirms prevenient (or, in eighteenth-century language, "preventing") grace:

> Jesus hath said, we all shall hope,
> Preventing Grace for all is free:
> "And I, if I be lifted up,
> I will draw All Men unto Me."

The direct quotation here is from St. John's Gospel (12:32), and elsewhere in this poem Charles Wesley alludes to two other key verses from the same Gospel: "Behold the Lamb of God who takes away the sins of the world" (John 1:29), and "God sent his son into the world that the world might be saved" (John 3:16). For the Wesleys, God's concern clearly and unequivocally extends to the whole world, and not merely to a part of it; indeed, there is even hope, as the hymn suggests, "for those who will not come to him." Even for these, "the Ransom of his [Jesus'] life was paid."

This, then, is a central theological theme in "Evangelical Arminianism": God's love is universal. Because the whole world is the object of God's love, it necessarily follows that God intends salvation for the whole world. John Wesley gives the best expression to this idea of the universality of grace in his sermon *The General Spread of the Gospel*. Based on texts in the Book of Isaiah and in the Psalms, this sermon envisions a world in which both God's action and human action are caught up in God's reconciling purposes. This mutuality of encounter will produce not only a living "experiential" knowledge of God, but will also result in a state in which humankind will arise to an "unmixed state of holiness and happiness far superior to what Adam enjoyed in paradise." He says explicitly, "The loving knowledge of God, producing uniform, uninterrupted holiness and happiness, shall cover the earth, shall fill every soul of man." Wesley's is a truly optimistic eschatology that sees the restoration of all creation that could take place through the boundless love of God:

[H]e is already renewing the face of the earth. And we have strong reason to hope that the work he hath begun he will carry on unto the day of his Lord Jesus Christ; that he will never intermit this bless work of his Spirit until he has fulfilled all his promises; until he hath put a period to sin and misery, and infirmity and death; and re-established universal holiness and happiness and caused all the inhabitants of the world to sing together, Hallelujah! The Lord God omnipotent reigneth.

SIN AND ITS CONSEQUENCES

But there is an obstacle to such a vision ever becoming reality: the radical separation from God caused by sin and its particular immediate consequence, the loss of the image of God in which human beings were created. Indeed, it is only because of sin and separation from God that there is any a need for the Gospel at all. At this point Wesley repudiates the supreme confidence in human perfectibility that marked the eighteenth-century Enlightenment, asserting that "the grand fundamental difference between Christianity" and the "most refined heathenism" lay in the affirmation of original sin. All who denied this, he said, "are but heathens still." For Wesley, the consequences of sin are both personal and social, but they can be summed up by saying that sin results in a form of "practical atheism," in which men and women have no effective knowledge of God.

It is important to set Wesley's teaching about sin in its proper "Arminian" and "Evangelical" theological context. Despite the allegation that the Wesleys used the doctrine of hell-fire and everlasting punishment to frighten people into "getting saved" (as undoubtedly some of his contemporaries and great numbers of his successors have done), this is foreign to the thought of John Wesley. He takes no delight in speaking of the Fall and the consequent doom of humankind. Here is a minute from a very early Conference (in August 1745):

Q. Do not some of our assistants preach too much of the wrath, and too little of the love, of God?
A. We fear they have leaned to that extreme, and hence some of their hearers may have lost the joy of faith.

It appears that some still did not absorb Wesley's point here, and he was forced to return to it the next year:

Q. Why is it unsuitable to speak much of God's wrath, and little of love?
A. In general, this only hardens those who do not believe, and discourages those who do believe.

This sentiment was shared by Charles Wesley. There is only one hymn on hell in the *CHPM* and that is an extended meditation about the spiritual condition of those who are alienated from God: And even this hymn, in the end, moves toward encouragement: "I will improve what I receive, / The grace through Jesus given; / sure if with God on earth I live / To live with him in heaven."

At every point therefore the teaching of both John and Charles Wesley about sin has a therapeutic intention. The diagnosis (the condition of being in sin) has to be accurate and accepted, before the prescription (God's redeeming love) that leads to healing can be offered. With the teaching of St. Paul in his mind, "through the Law comes the knowledge of sin" (Romans 3:20), John Wesley affirmed that preaching of the Law was central to his own ministry and that of his preachers. And Charles Wesley similarly summed up the need of every Christian to have "the Law written in the heart / And a conscience with which to discern it." But both were equally aware that a true knowledge of sin emerges first from the encounter with God's gracious love in the Gospel. For John Wesley, the point of all Gospel preaching, not least preaching about original sin, was to extend God's offer of salvation, although he clearly has a particular model for understanding what salvation is and how salvation comes about.

SALVATION

Here we meet another distinctive feature of the Evangelical Arminian understanding of the Gospel. For most Protestant reformers and their successors, salvation has meant being forgiven by God, being pardoned by God, being justified by God. Indeed, these are often used as synonymous terms. When one is justified, one is first made an heir of eternal life or assigned a place in heaven, and therefore one is "saved" in the ordinary use of the term. But John Wesley used the word "salvation" in a much wider sense. In his sermon on Ephesians 2:8 ("Ye are saved through faith"), entitled *The Scripture Way of Salvation*, he poses the rhetorical question, "What is *salvation*?" His answer is clear and concise:

The salvation which is here spoken of is not what is frequently understood by that word, the going to heaven, eternal happiness. It is not the soul's going to paradise . . . It is not a blessing which lies on the other side of death, or (as we usually speak) in the other world. The very words of the text are "Ye *are* saved." It is not something at a distance. It is a present thing, a blessing which, through the free mercy of God, ye are now in possession of (emphasis in original).

Wesley's understanding of salvation was further clarified in a passage from his treatise *A Farther Appeal to Men of Religion and Reason*:

By salvation I mean, not barely, according to the vulgar notion, deliverance from hell, or going to heaven; but a present deliverance from sin, a restoration of the soul to its primitive health, its original purity; a recovery of the divine nature; the renewal of our souls after the image of God in righteousness and true holiness, in justice, mercy, and truth. This implies all holy and heavenly tempers, and, by consequence all holiness of conversation.

The analogy Wesley uses to make sense of the impact of God's saving acts on the human person is taken from the world of medicine. Just as the doctor uses medication for the healing for the body, salvation is understood as the *therapeia psuchēs* (therapy of the soul) that God effects in persons by the infusion of "true religion." Wesley speaks of faith as "God's method of healing a soul which is *thus diseased.* Hereby the great Physician of the Soul applies medicine to heal *this sickness*" (emphasis in original). For Wesley, this "restoration of the soul to its primitive health" will not only result in a person who is "saved" in the traditional sense of the word, but also a person who is possessed of "holy and heavenly tempers" in life.

John Wesley's view of salvation as essentially therapeutic resonates throughout his brother's poetry and hymnody, and in many verses throughout the *CHPM* we discover the theme of salvation as "soul healing." Here Charles addresses Christ the Healer:

> They that be whole, thyself hast said,
> No need of a physician have.
> But I am sick, and want thine aid,
> And want thine utmost power to save.

Charles asserts that "a word, a gracious word of thine / The most inveterate plague can cure" and calls upon the presence of Christ ("Come O my soul's Physician, thou!") to speak that word; this is paralleled by an invocation of the Holy Spirit in another of the hymns, where he addresses the "Spirit of health," who removes the "seed of sin's disease" as well as the "Spirit of finished holiness / Spirit of perfect love." These verses appear in the section in *CHPM* entitled "For Believers seeking Full Redemption," and point to the quest for "finished holiness" or entire sanctification as a major theme in Methodist spirituality.

REPENTANCE AS THE "PORCH OF RELIGION"

In his *Principles of a Methodist Farther Explained*, Wesley offers his own summary of the essential elements of his theology: "Our main doctrines, which include all the rest, are three: that of repentance, of faith, and of holiness. The first of these we account, as it were, the porch of religion; the next, the door; the third, religion itself." As we have seen, the point of the Law, for Wesley, is to lead to repentance when new Methodists discover the richness of God's grace in the love of Christ who died for them. Charles

Wesley described this (rather astonishing) experience in one of the most famous of all Methodist hymns

> And can it be that I should gain,
> An interest in the Saviour's blood?
> Died he for me who caused his pain
> For me who him to death pursued.
> Amazing love! How can it be,
> That thou, my God, should'st die for me?

For Charles Wesley, this experience of the radical, sacrificial love of God is a highly personal one, and intensely centered upon the Cross of Christ Jesus. The sense of contrition provoked by the experience of such "amazing love" leads to the birth of faith and trust, which his brother John described as the "door of religion." John Wesley's own "door" was the experience of the religious society meeting in Aldersgate Street, where the reading of Martin Luther's exposition of justification by faith fairly overwhelmed him. Luther had experienced his own struggle with the notion of the "justice," or "righteousness" of God, writing:

Then I grasped that the justice of God is that righteousness by which through grace and sheer mercy God justifies us through faith. Thereupon I felt myself to be reborn and to have gone through open doors into paradise. The whole of Scripture took on a new meaning, and, whereas before the "justice of God" had filled me with hate, now it became to me inexpressibly sweet in greater love.

The emphasis on repentance leading to justification by faith is, of course, in no way distinctive of Methodist theology. It belongs to the great tradition of the church. But John Wesley's approach to these doctrines had been filtered through the Protestant Reformation and the Moravian renewal, which became the lenses through which he read the Anglican formula: "We are accounted righteous before God only for the merit of our Lord and Saviour, faith, and not for our merits or deserving. Wherefore, that we are justified by faith is a most wholesome doctrine, and very full of comfort." Although it is through faith, and faith alone, that God justifies the sinner and although it is this justification alone that makes it possible for the sinner to live in the presence of God, it is only by the sheer mercy of God alone (and not by any effort whatsoever on our part) that faith is born in people. In the *Preface to the Romans*, Martin Luther declares: "Faith . . . is something that God effects in us. It changes us and we are reborn from God . . . Faith puts the old Adam to death and makes us quite different men in heart, in mind, and in all our powers; and it is accompanied by the Holy Spirit."

Wesley found himself in perfect agreement with this position, and never recanted it. In 1754 he wrote in his *Explanatory Notes on the New Testament* on Romans 3:24 that Christians

are justified – pardoned and accepted. *Freely* – Without any merit of their own, *By his grace* – not their own righteousness or work. *Through the redemption* – the price Christ has paid. *Freely by his grace* – One of these expressions might have served to convey the apostle's meaning; but he doubles his assertion, in order to give us the fullest conviction of the truth and to impress us with a sense of its peculiar importance. It is impossible to find words that should more absolutely exclude all consideration of our own works and obedience, or more emphatically ascribe the whole of our justification to free, unmerited goodness.

And in his preaching he set forth the very same doctrine: "Christian faith is . . . not only an assent to the whole gospel of Christ, but also a full reliance on the blood of Christ; a trust in the merits of His life, death, and resurrection; a recumbency upon Him as our atonement and our life, as given for us, and living in us."

But it was on this matter of "faith alone" that his nearly perfect agreement with the Moravians ultimately broke down. For many of Zinzendorf's followers, believers could accomplish nothing good whatsoever until the process of perfecting their faith was finished. The task of passively "waiting upon the Lord" superseded all works of piety and mercy. This dedication to "stillness," and the wanton abandonment of good works, was taking the doctrine of "faith alone" (*sola fide*) to a degree that Wesley could only regard as a form of antinomianism. It ran contrary to his Anglican upbringing and to all that he had learned from Catholic and patristic sources. It meant that the "door of religion" had become its terminus.

FAITH AS THE "DOOR OF RELIGION"

Very rapidly, however, Wesley's theological compass corrected itself, largely through his conviction that justification and sanctification were simply two sides of the same coin. That same act of faith that was the beginning of justification would also at the same time work a change in the human heart.

The same time that we are justified – yea, in that very moment – *sanctification* begins. In that instant we are "born again, born from above, born of the Spirit." There is a *real* as well as a *relative* change. We are inwardly renewed by the power of God. We feel "the love of God shed abroad in our heart by the Holy Ghost which is given to us."

This experience of the love of God produces "love to all mankind, and more especially to the children of God," and similarly expels "the love of the world, the love of pleasure, of ease, of honour, of money, together with pride, anger, self and every other evil temper." In other words, God not only "imputes" righteousness to newborn Christians, but also at the same time "imparts" righteousness to them. Not only are they *accounted* righteous, they are on the way to *becoming* righteous.

This is the exciting innovation in Christian theology and spirituality that some have hailed as the Methodist re-union of the Protestant and Catholic streams in Christianity. But Wesley's ideas here are intricate and subtle, and were frequently misunderstood by those who engaged in controversy with him. First he always insisted that the good works of men and women were accompanied by the grace of God even before justification. The whole work of God involves "preventing" (prevenient) grace:

> It will include all that is wrought in the soul by what is frequently termed "natural conscience," but more properly "preventing grace;" all the "drawings of the Father;" the desires after God which, if we yield to them, increase more and more; all that "light" wherewith the Son of God "enlighteneth every one that cometh into the world" (cf. John 1:9), showing every man "to do justly, to love mercy, and to walk humbly with his God."

Because of his clear sense that God's grace is present before human beings take a step toward it, Wesley is adamant (in direct contradiction of both Lutherans and Calvinists) that good works done *before* justification are never just "splendid sins." Wesley used the teaching of the Scholastics Thomas Aquinas and Duns Scotus, the Anglican *Homilies*, and Richard Hooker to assert that whenever human beings do what good they can, God will be present and bring those good intentions to good effect. (This is his translation of *Fac quod in te est, et Deus aderit bonae tuae voluntati* in his sermon *On Schism*.) Here we have Wesley the Catholic synergist, reaffirming the New Testament injunction to "work out your own salvation with fear and trembling, for God is at work in you" (Philippians 2:12). Wesley's pre-Aldersgate Street error was to imagine that this synergism was somehow transactional and that, if he worked hard enough at being virtuous, God would have to reward him. After 1738 he is still committed to synergism, but now faith is essentially *covenantal*, a matter of relationship with God, and has become what Wesley calls "*The great privilege of those who are born of God*" (the title of sermon 19), namely the fruition of perfect love, holiness, entire sanctification.

As a result of this reasoning Wesley can say that faith is "productive of all Christian *holiness*," rather than "of all Christian *practice*."

HOLINESS: RELIGION ITSELF

As we have seen, John Wesley was deeply attracted to the theological work of the fourth-century Greek Fathers. He found particularly compelling their conviction that one could be liberated from sinfulness by ceaseless concentrated prayer. When this takes place there comes about not merely a restoration of the divine image but a "new creature." From Gregory of Nyssa (333–95) Wesley gained a sense of the Christian life as dynamic, ever seeking fresh knowledge and insight.

This truly is the vision of God: never to be satisfied in the desire to see him. But one must always, by looking at what he can see, rekindle his desire to see more. Thus, no limit would interrupt growth in the ascent to God, since no limit to the Good can be found nor is the creasing of desire for the Good brought to an end because it is satisfied.

From Macarius, a follower of Gregory of Nyssa, Wesley took the image of the Holy Spirit always working within individuals to connect them with God, and the assurance that as persons respond to God, so God responds to them:

The life of God in the soul of the believer is the continual inspiration of God's Holy Spirit: God's breathing into the soul, and the soul's breathing back what it first receives from God . . . it plainly appears God does not continue to act upon the soul unless the soul re-acts upon God . . . he will not continue to breathe into our soul unless our soul breathes towards him again.

For Charles Wesley, too, the work of the Holy Spirit brings men and women into the reality of redemption and of a new creation. Over and over again the *CHPM* echo with invocations to the Holy Spirit, always in a fully Trinitarian context. Thus, Hymn 366 begins "Father of Everlasting grace, / Thy goodness and thy truth we praise," and then makes this great theological affirmation about the nature of the Spirit:

> Thou hast in honour of thy Son,
> The gift unspeakable sent down,
> The Spirit of life, and power, and love.

Then comes an invocation of this Spirit, whose presence results in the redemptive action described in the theology of the Greek Fathers, namely sharing in the divine nature.

> Send us the Spirit of thy Son
> To make the depths of Godhead known.
> To make us share the life divine.

Charles Wesley remains the best exponent of the Methodist teaching on holiness. For him, as for his brother John, holiness is a quality of the heart. It is freedom from all that diminishes human life; it is the fullness of love, and growth toward the "full stature of Christ":

> Give me a new, a perfect heart
> From doubt, and fear, and sorrow free
> The mind that was in Christ impart
> And let my spirit cleave to thee.

The hymn ends with the invocation:

> Thy nature, gracious Lord impart;
> Come quickly from above;
> Write thy new name upon my heart
> Thy new, best name of love.

This kind of plea for a whole new dimension of Christian experience is found in the best-loved and most widely sung of all Charles Wesley's thousands of hymns, "Love divine, all loves excelling." In the final verse, the singer asks God to:

> Finish then thy new creation,
> Pure and spotless let us be;
> Let us see thy great salvation
> Perfectly restored in thee;
> Changed from glory into glory,
> Till in heaven we take our place,
> Till we cast our crowns before thee,
> Lost in wonder, love, and praise.

More prosaically, Charles's brother John defined this holiness as "Christian perfection," as "loving God with all our heart, mind, soul, and strength." We find John Wesley's conviction about this kind of holiness as the spiritual goal for Methodists expressed as early as 1733 in his sermon *The Circumcision of the Heart*, preached five years before his Aldersgate experience. True holiness in these terms involved "training of all our affections on the will of God" and "having the mind in us which was also in Christ Jesus"; all this was possible because God had promised it was so. But there was always the question of whether this promise was intended to be fulfilled only in the end times, as a part of the "new heaven and new earth" described in the New Testament. Wesley was clear, however, that not only would God keep this divine promise of sanctification, but that that promise would be fulfilled for individuals in their lifetime. In his sermon *The Scriptural Way of Salvation*, Wesley says:

To this confidence, that God is both able and willing to sanctify us *now*, there needs to be added one thing more – a divine evidence and conviction that *he doth it*. In that hour it is done. God says to the inmost soul, "According to thy faith be it unto thee" [Mt. 9:29]. Then the soul is pure from every spot of sin; it is clean from all unrighteousness [cf. 1 John 1:9]. The believer then experiences the deep meaning of those solemn words, "If we walk in the light as he is in the light, we have fellowship one with another, and the blood of Jesus Christ his Son cleanseth us from all sin" [1 John 1:7].

The conviction that God intends human beings to be wholly renewed and as perfect "as your heavenly father is perfect" (Matthew 5:47) never left John Wesley. He was still preaching "by faith we are saved from sin, and made holy" in one of his last sermons, *On the Wedding Garment*, just a year before his death.

MISCONCEPTIONS ABOUT THE WESLEYAN TEACHING

But these Wesleyan convictions about the nature of sanctification have been misunderstood, even among Wesley's followers. These varied misinterpretations have turned on the ideas of "sinless perfection"; of perfection as instantaneous and once-and-for-all; on the idea that "attaining such perfection was a ground for boasting"; and that perfection was a personal possession. In much of his writing, John Wesley challenged the false conclusions drawn by some of his predecessors and distinguished himself from various schemes of the millenarian and perfectionist sects that have littered Christian history.

Neither of the Wesley brothers understood holiness in moralistic terms, as a force by which some real or imaginary fixed standards of right behavior were achieved, although many Methodists have since managed to use the doctrine of perfection to make themselves into joyless paragons of supposed virtue and wisdom. Neither did "Christian perfection" ever mean freedom from the unavoidable features of the human condition: "infirmities, ignorance, and mistakes." The important qualification lies in John Wesley's definition of individual sin as "voluntary transgression of a known law." Involuntary transgressions were bound to happen, and so too were mistakes. To the rhetorical question "Can mistakes flow from pure love?"

Wesley answers yes. The very temper that perfect love has of believing the best of all people "may occasion our thinking some men better than they really are."

Neither did the brothers think that entire sanctification was to be conceived as an action completed instantaneously and permanently, a condition that, once effected, remained an unchanging and utterly static mark of an individual believer. On the contrary, holiness was always a process, even if there were specific defining moments within that process. In the *Minutes* of the 1770 Conference, Wesley responded to his critics, who often asked, "Does not talking of a justified or a sanctified state, tend to mislead men? Almost naturally leading them to trust, in what was done in one moment?" The truer view is that "we are every hour and every moment, pleasing or displeasing to God, 'according to our works.' According to the whole of our inward tempers, and our behavior."

Wesley strongly advised people against glibly speaking of having experienced "entire sanctification." There may be times, John Wesley thought, when a person might say "I feel no sin, but all love. I pray, rejoice, and give thanks without ceasing. And I have a clear and inward witness that I am as fully renewed as I am justified." But even in these cases, he argued, it would usually be better to be silent, only sharing the experience as encouragement to others who were on a similar quest. But in any case persons believing themselves to have been sanctified should avoid all appearance of boasting, and speak always with the deepest humility and reverence. At the same time, the *Minutes* of the Bristol Conference in 1759 instructed anyone who had experienced sanctification: "let him speak more convincingly by his life than he can do by his tongue."

Last, but not least, for the Wesley brothers perfection does not end with the sanctification of individuals, but always moves toward the holiness of the whole of creation. John Wesley affirmed in his fourth sermon on *The Sermon on the Mount* that "Christianity is essentially a social religion, and that to turn it into a solitary religion is indeed to destroy it." He added:

By Christianity I mean that method of worshiping God which is here revealed to man by Christ. When I say this is essentially a social religion, I mean not only that it cannot subsist so well, but that it cannot subsist at all without society, without living and conversing with other men.

Although justification and new birth were to be seen as the beginning of a total change in the habits and characters of individuals pursued in fellowship with other believers, it followed that individual transformation would widen out until all life is transformed and the whole earth is full of "lovely tempers." To make this crystal clear John Wesley amended some verses by Henry More (1614–87) and included them in the *CHPM*:

> On all the earth thy Spirit shower,
> The earth in righteousness renew;
> Thy kingdom come, and hell o'erpower,
> And to thy sceptre all subdue.

John Wesley then refers to the power of the Holy Spirit to reverse "every law of sin" and unite all things in faith and love:

> Yea, let thy Spirit in every place,
> Its richer energy declare,
> While lovely tempers, fruits of grace,
> The kingdom of thy Christ prepare.

As we shall see in chapter 9 on social ethics, this commitment to an earth renewed in righteousness has never been absent from Methodist teaching, making the Wesleyan tradition different from all others that have taught and preached an other-worldly salvation.

THE DIMINISHING EMPHASIS ON EVANGELICAL ARMINIANISM IN THE NINETEENTH CENTURY

In 1871, in the preface to the third edition of his widely influential *Theological Essays*, Frederick Denison Maurice wrote about Methodist theology:

Immensely valuable as I hold the Methodist preaching of the last age to have been, with the Evangelical movement in the Church and among the Dissenters which was the result of it, – utterly dead as I conceive the faith of the English nation would have become without its rekindling of it, – I cannot but perceive that it made the sinful man and not the God of all Grace the Foundation of Christian theology.

By "the last age" Maurice is not referring to the times of John and Charles Wesley, but rather to the first fifty or sixty years of the nineteenth century, and he is quite accurate in lumping the Methodists with other Evangelicals, both those within the Anglican communion and those in the various nonconformist groups in this period. By the middle of the nineteenth century, the theology of Methodist preachers had become almost indistinguishable from that of these other Evangelicals in their focus upon "the chain of iniquity" that bound humankind as a result of the Fall of Adam and Eve. The distance between this sense of human depravity and the Wesley brothers' emphatic insistence on the doctrine of prevenient grace represents a serious diminishment of the ideas of Evangelical Arminianism which had marked the Wesleyan Methodist movement from its beginnings. It was as if the separation of the Wesleyan Methodists from Whitefield and the Calvinists had never taken place.

Reasons for this decline are not hard to find. Even in Wesley's time, there were many new recruits to the Wesleyan movement who had been nurtured in the Dissenting traditions and whose views tended toward Calvinism. In the period immediately following Wesley's death some of these people were coming to hold leadership positions in the Conference. In *Are Methodists Dissenters?* published in 1793, Samuel Bradburn (1751–1816) claimed that Methodism was essentially Presbyterian in character, a claim that had Wesley been alive he would surely have challenged vigorously. Although a friend and confidant of John Wesley, Bradburn urged his fellow Methodists to accept that the leading principle of Christianity was original sin, and that because of this strong hierarchical forms of leadership were needed for the Methodist societies.

Another factor in this move away from Evangelical Arminianism was the need for a systematic and orderly statement of Methodist doctrine, one that would be more directed to the community within the chapels than to the unevangelized world outside. In 1831 Richard Watson (1781–1833) offered his three-volume *Theological Institutes* to a receptive Wesleyan community (they had elected him president of Conference in 1826). What is most remarkable about the *Theological Institutes* is the paucity of references to John Wesley. Watson's theology was defensive and apologetic, intended to preserve the faith and keep it pure. He moved away from the Wesleys' experiential mode of doing theology to an orderly, thoroughly formulated theological system. For this defense of Christianity Watson used the extensive resources of the older Puritan and Dissenting divines, rather than Anglicans and the early church writers, and we increasingly hear their voices in the various sermons and treatises of the Methodist groups as the century progressed. Maurice correctly saw that the emphasis on the penal substitutionary view of the atonement that marked the wider Evangelical movement had been adopted by most Methodist theologians and preachers. The editor of a connexional magazine of the period exemplified this trend when he said that "Christ died in our stead, not only for our benefit."

The other leading theologian of the Wesleyan Methodists in the nineteenth century was William Burt Pope (1822–1903), whose *Compendium of Christian Theology* (1880) aimed at representing Methodist theology as "scriptural," "catholic," and "orthodox." Pope was deeply involved in the struggle by Victorian Wesleyan Methodists to insist that they were not a sect but truly part of the One Holy Catholic Church. This led Pope to write theology that drew on the universal resources of the Christian faith rather than upon John and Charles Wesley, who are seldom mentioned in his pages. But Pope never abandoned the central emphases of Methodist theology and his work did move away from understanding the atonement as the propitiating of an offended God to the doctrine of the Fatherhood of God and the universality of the Christian message. There is a well-known story of his persuading the Catechism Committee of the Wesleyan Methodist Church to define God as "Our Father," instead of as "An infinite and eternal spirit." Had Maurice not died before Pope's *Compendium* appeared, he might have altered his judgment of nineteenth-century Methodism.

William Burt Pope prepared the way for the work of John Scott Lidgett (1854–1953) who returned to the central Wesleyan doctrines. Much influenced by Maurice, Lidgett's two influential works – *The Spiritual Principle of the Atonement: As a Satisfaction made to God for the Sins of the World* (1898) and *The Fatherhood of God* (1902) – offer an authentic Methodist expression of what he himself called, in the title of a smaller book, "The Victorian Transformation of Theology." Both *The Spiritual Principle of the Atonement* and *The Fatherhood of God* celebrate an understanding of God more in terms of divine parenthood than of the majestic sovereign ruler of the Augustinian and Calvinist traditions. Lidgett set out his thesis thus:

The work of justifying "the ungodly" . . . is fatherly rather than forensic or even Kingly. Justification is forgiveness, but it is much more. It includes re-instatement . . . "Justification" and "adoption" may be taken as practically equivalent . . . The former is judicial, but by reason of its result in the reception of sonship, cannot be separated from its source in Fatherhood.

But Pope and Lidgett's attempts to hold on to Wesley as a source of Methodist theology ultimately failed, at least for their immediate successors, as Methodism moved into the twentieth century. Acutely aware of the implications of modern science and modern psychology, as well as of the rise of biblical criticism, they saw little help from Wesley for their immediate concerns. In fact the Primitive Methodist biblical scholar Arthur S. Peake (1865–1929) proposed that *The Explanatory Notes on the New Testament* be dropped from the list of doctrinal standards of the proposed reunited Methodist Church. In the British Isles there was a wholesale abandonment of Wesleyan theology. Methodist theologians, from James Hope Moulton (1863–1917) onwards, were Methodists engaged in the great mainstream areas of theology. Often their chosen fields were biblical studies, for example Vincent Taylor (1887–1968) and Charles Kingsley Barrett (b. 1917), and church history, for example E. Gordon Rupp (1911–86) and Philip Watson (1909–83). Many others have been leading scholars in various other disciplines. But their work belongs to ecumenical scholarship rather than to Methodist traditions, and assessment of their work belongs elsewhere.

A similar abandonment of John Wesley's theological ideas manifested itself in the American Methodist churches. One interpreter has seen a shift in the nineteenth century from "revelation to reason," from "sinful predicament to moral character," and from "free grace to free will." The leading Methodist systematic theologians of that period became increasingly concerned with apologetic questions (the so-called conflicts between science and religion and sociological and psychological interpretations of religion), and their writings offered broadly based defenses of Christianity. Part of this apologetic was the adoption of the idea of divine immanence, leading to a quite different emphasis on religious experience from that of the Wesley brothers.

Perhaps the outstanding American Methodist theologian of the later part of the century was Borden Parker Bowne (1847–1910). For him "personality" became a central conceptual key and the key to the solution of all epistemological problems, one which would enable faith to rest on a steady yet flexible foundation. Commentators see this position, known as "Boston personalism," as profoundly Methodist because its cornerstone was grace: "for grace characterizes God, the mode of creation and the relationship with human beings." Because there was no reference in his writings to the acts of a transcendent God, Bowne was tried for heresy at the MEC General Conference in 1904. In particular he was charged with denying the Trinity, miracles, and substitutionary atonement. At his trial he was acquitted, a verdict that established the MEC as open to theological inquiry and reconstruction.

This freedom has been the Methodist style in the USA throughout the twentieth century, and American Methodism has produced constructive theologians who have been active within most of the distinctive schools of systematic thinking in the past century. They have for the most part been entirely happy to do this, and have clothed themselves in widely diverse theological fashions: among them liberalism, biblical theology, Barthianism, radical theology, existentialism, process theology, neo-Pietism, and even fundamentalism. American Methodist preachers may be found expounding almost any of these systems.

But a kind of mismatch has been observable whenever Methodists have attempted to put on the clothes of movements that have their roots elsewhere. In this chapter we have pointed briefly to some of these roots: the holding together of prevenient and saving grace: the middle path between "faith alone" and "moralism"; the balancing of the "Catholic" and the "Evangelical"; the holding in tension of revivalism and sacramentalism. The leading American Methodist theologian of the second half of the twentieth century, Albert C. Outler (1908–89), once wrote that "Methodism's share in the history of theology has yet to match its true potential." Great ecumenist that he was, he knew that the Methodist doctrinal perspective "was not meant to stand alone." It works best, he declared, in a wider and more catholic context." Talking to fellow Methodists in 1969 he described his own vision for the renewal of Methodist theology in an ecumenical context:

This cannot mean an antiquarian return to Wesley or to anyone else as an arbitrary authority. Wesley was the first to repudiate *that* sort of thing. Even so, there is something about his way of doing theology that is still open to us as a paradigm: (1) to ground it all in Scripture; (2) to match it all against the centuries and the Christian consensus; (3) to keep chording the keys of grace and agency together; (4) to remember always, the aim of it all: effective mission in the world, effective service to the world for which Christ died. For us and for our future is there a conceivable alternative more promising?

In the chapters that follow we shall look at particular aspects of the Methodist tradition: common life, spirituality, worship, social ethics, and ecumenical and interfaith relations. We shall see how Methodists all around the world have done and are still "doing theology."

CHAPTER 6

The common life of Methodism

Protestant churches differ from one another not only in their histories, their doctrines and their forms of worship, but also in the way in which they choose to organize and structure their ecclesial life (usually referred to as their "polity"). Some denominations are radically democratic, with each local church an autonomous and self-governing structure. By contrast, the polity most characteristic of Methodism is a more centralized one, with somewhat hierarchical, "top-down" structures of supervision. For most Methodist bodies, the overarching governing structure is the Methodist Conference, which meets periodically to do the business of the church. As we have seen, such Conferences go back to John Wesley himself, who was concerned for the exercise of proper authority over and discipline among Methodist preachers as his movement began to grow.

The first Methodist Conference met for six days in June 1744 and its initial task was to establish who would be considered to belong to it. In the event, six Anglican clergymen and four laymen, all of these traveling preachers, were declared to be members of the 1744 Conference. But the question of membership never went away, and after Wesley's death the question of lay representation in the Conference became a hotly debated issue. The *Minutes* of this first Methodist Conference, like all the early Conferences, are recorded in a characteristic "question-and-answer" format, and these *Minutes* became part of the foundational documents of Methodism. In 1773 Wesley collected all the early Conference *Minutes* into one volume, known as the *Larger Minutes*, to which reference was constantly made in establishing precedents for the establishment of Methodist doctrine and practice. The *Larger Minutes* have continued to be employed by Methodists engaged in discussions of Methodist theology, ethics, and ecumenical relations.

All sorts of matters were addressed in the question-and-answer pattern of the early Methodist *Minutes*. A discussion at the very first Conference, which took place on Friday June 29, 1744, concerns the question of incorporating non-ordained but full-time agents into the ministry of the Methodists:

Q.1. Are Lay Assistants allowable?
A. Only in cases of necessity.
Q.2. What is the Office of our Assistants?
A. In the absence of the minister, to feed and to guide, to teach and to govern the flock.

In the same way, the Conference laid out the assistant's tasks: (1) to expound every morning and evening; (2) to meet the united societies, the bands, the select societies and the penitents every week; (3) to visit the classes (London excepted) once a month; (4) to hear and decide all differences; (5) to put the disorderly back on trial, and to receive on trial for the bands or society; (6) to see that the stewards and the leaders, schoolmasters and housekeepers, faithfully discharge their several offices; (7) to meet the stewards, the leaders of the bands and classes weekly, and overlook their accounts. For the next hundred years this would be the pattern for Methodist itinerant preachers.

The first Conference had as its principal focus "What to teach? How to teach? What to do?" and every Methodist Conference since has been concerned with similar fundamental questions. In August 1745, the second Conference debated theological issues, providing guidance to the theological neophytes so recently enlisted into the full-time lay ministry. One instruction to these preachers has been quoted by every generation of those concerned with the training of Methodist preachers: "You have nothing to do but save souls. Therefore spend and be spent in this work. And go always, not only to those who want [in modern English 'need'] you, but to those who want [need] you most."

On the matters of "How to teach?" and "What to do?" the Conferences in 1746 and 1747 addressed issues related to the advancement of Methodism. As we have seen, on a visit to Bristol in 1739 John Wesley had become convinced of the benefits of open-air preaching, and now the *Minutes* record Conference's commitment to this method of spreading the Gospel:

Q.1. Have we not limited field preaching too much?
A. It seems we have: Because our calling is to save that which is lost. Now we cannot expect the wanderers from God to seek us. It is our part to go and seek them.

As a result, a systematic organization was established for field preaching. There were to be seven "circuits," or "preaching rounds." The assistants appointed to these rounds became known as "circuit riders" (a little later the title "assistant" was to be reserved to the preacher-in-charge of each

THE LORD'S DAY PLAN

OF THE

WESLEYAN METHODIST PREACHERS,

IN THE WITNEY CIRCUIT.

"For we preach not ourselves, but Christ Jesus the Lord; and ourselves your servants for Jesus' sake." II Corinthians, Chap IV. V. 5.

1832. PLACES.	TIME.	JULY 22	29	AUG 5	12	19	26	SEPT 2	9	16	23	30	OCT 7	14	Preachers.
WITNEY ..	10½, 6, 2½	2/8	1/1	1/1s	2/15	2/2	1/1	1/3	2/2	2/2q	1/9	1/1s	2/2	2/22	
BURFORD	2½ 6	3	2s	20	1	12	2t	9	1	15q	2	22	1	10	**1** Brocklehurst,
‖ FINSTOCK	10	1	16	2SS	3	1	7	2	15	1q	12	2	10	1	**2** Loutit,
CHARLBURY	3 & 6	1	20	2s	9	1	11	2	7	1q	3	2	15	1	3 Joseph Early,
FREELAND	2½	2	15	11	2s	20	12	1	5	16q	1	3	9	2	4 T. Buswell,
HANDBOROUGH..	6	14	15	11	6	20	12	17	5	16q	18	3	9	19	5 G. Thomas,
NORTHLEIGH....	6	5	9	22	11	6	14	15	16	18q	10	20	12	13	6 W. Gardner,
STONESFIELD ..	2 / 6	13	12	16	3	9L / 9A	22	19	15	20q	11	10	14	5	7 W. Willis,
SOUTHLEIGH	6	15	17	5	8	21	6	P	20	17q	13	14	3	11	8 W. Pritchett,
COGGS	2½ / 6	15 / 14		5 / 15		21	5	P / 9		17q	6	14 / 20		11	9 James Marriott,
‖ ALVESCOTT.....	2½	9	23	4	7	15	23	5	7	4q	20	23	7	P	10 G. Crockett,
‖ BAMPTON	6	9	11	4	13	15	17	5	18	4q	20	19	21	P	11 P. Archer,
RAMSDEN	3	18	10	13	12	9	7	11q	16	19	22	21	P	17	12 W. S. Allen,
HAILEY ...	10½ / 6	18	10	13	20 / 12	9	P	11q	3 / 16	19	22	21	6 / P	17	13 J. Luckett,
‖ ASTHALLY	2½	7	19	21	23	13	18	6	P	7q	5	9	11	20	14 W. S. Pett,
MINSTER..........	6	7	19	21	23	13	18	6	P	7q	5	9	11	20	15 John Marriott,
LEAFIELD	2½ / 5	11	P	14	16	17	19	18	6	13q		21	12	5 / 3	16 T. Brooks,
CRAWLEY	2½ / 6	11	P	14	16	17	19	6		13q	21	P		5 / 3	17 D. Webb,
NEWLAND........	6	19	5	6	20	19	15	3q	13	11	9	8	17	21	18 R. Wright,
BARRINGTON...	9 / 5	20	2	7	1s	23	2	P	1	9q	2	7	1	4	S. Perkins,
TAYNTON	10½ / 2	20	2	7		23	2	P	1	9q	2	7	1	4	20 J. W. Hankins,
WESTWELL........	5	4	23	9	7	4c	23	20	7	23	4	18	7c	23	21 E. Mumford,
CURBRIDGE	2½	P	11	3	13	5	17	21	18	14q	15	19	17	21	22 R. T. Heel,
CHILSON	6	22	16	10	P	22	16	12	10	22q	16	P	10	12	23 W. H.
DUCKLINGTON ...															
Lessons for the Lord's Day Morning.		Jeremiah xi, John xi.	Jer. xxv. John xviii.	Jer. xxxiv. Acts iv.	Lam. ii. Acts xi.	Daniel ii. Acts xviii.	Daniel xii. Acts xxv.	Amos iii. Matthew iv.	Micah ii. Matthew xi.	Zeph. iii. Mal. xviii.	Zech. xiv. Matt. xxv.	Zech. xii. Mark xiv.	Malachi I. Mark xi.	Malachi iii. Luke iv.	

REFERENCES:— ‖ At the places marked thus ‖ the Preachers are requested to meet the Class, immediately after the public Service.
A. Anniversary Sermon in behalf of the Chapel.
Q. Quarterly Collection in behalf of the Circuits' Itinerant Ministry.
S. Sacrament of the Lord's Supper.
L. Love Feast.
S. S. Sunday School Sermon.

1. The Quarterly *Fast* is September 28th ; to be regarded as a day of *special intercession* for the outpouring of the Holy Spirit.
2. Our next Quarterly Meeting will be at *Witney*, on Monday, September 24th.—The Local Preachers to meet at *One*, and the Society Stewards at *Four* o'Clock, P. M.
3. Every Preacher is requested to look at his Plan *before* preaching, and to publish when there is a Collection, the Sacrament, or Love Feast, the following Sabbath.
4. N. B. It is fully expected that every Brother will attend to his own appointments or *himself* get an approved Substitute.

[J. SHAYLER, PRINTER, WITNEY.]

11. An English circuit plan for 1832, showing the pattern of rotation of preachers around the various congregations in the circuit.

circuit). Soon the need for cohesion among these circuits began to be felt, so in 1748 a pattern of "quarterly meetings" was put in place. Within five years the system of quarterly meetings was firmly established and involved considerable numbers: all the itinerant preachers, the local (or non-itinerant) preachers, the society stewards and class leaders, and (as property increasingly came to be owned by Methodist societies) the trustees of chapels and preachers' houses. The new office of "circuit steward" was created, and each circuit reported to the annual Conference, describing growth in membership and evangelistic initiatives.

In British Methodism, this four-times-a-year pattern of gathering all local Methodists was to last until 1976, when a major overhaul of Methodist Church structures took place. In American Methodism the vast distances between the settled communities often meant that the quarterly meetings were folded into camp meetings, and became significant occasions for worship and preaching. On both sides of the Atlantic these meetings of the people to do the business of the church revealed and nurtured gifts of leadership. Ordinary men and women became accustomed to administration, often carrying considerable financial responsibility within the Methodist connexions. Quarterly meetings gave Methodist men and women the opportunity to formulate persuasive arguments and engage in public discourse, and these skills were brought to their participation in the wider life of the community. Lay participation in the quarterly meeting certainly helps to account for both the widespread influence of Methodists in the trades union movement in the UK, and the disproportionate number of Methodist civic leaders in the young American republic.

The building blocks of these circuits were the societies, like the ones John Wesley had known in Epworth and Fetter Lane and which he himself had established at the Foundery. Here the contrast with George Whitefield is sharp. Whitefield preached everywhere he could, but put no structures in place through which those converted by his preaching might be united and nurtured. Other revivals similarly failed to provide after-care for those who responded to the preaching. When Wesley visited Pembrokeshire in South Wales, he was disturbed to find no visible evidence of the revival that had allegedly taken place there just a few years before. "Preaching like an Apostle," he commented, "without joining together those that are awakened, and training them up in the way of God, is only begetting children for the Murderer."

So John Wesley adopted (and adapted) the shape of the religious societies that were already in existence, and which had so deeply influenced and molded his own life of faith. New adherents to Methodism were not allowed to lose themselves in a private sense of the special favoritism that God had shown toward them, and as Wesley gathered converts in Bristol, Newcastle and London he set up local societies for them. The emotional force involved in being saved at an afternoon or evening meeting was tested by the requirement of attendance at a meeting very early the next morning for instruction in new patterns of life that conversion required. Only then were the new converts admitted as members of the society.

Almost immediately, these new Methodists were given a set of instructions about the shape of their new life and the discipline that would regulate it. These were embodied in the *General Rules of the Methodist Societies*. There were extensive negative rules:

(1) against the taking of the name of the Lord in vain (2) against profaning the day of the Lord (3) against drunkenness, buying or selling of spirituous liquors (4) against slave holding, the buying or selling of slaves (5) against fighting, quarreling, brawling, brother going to law with brother, returning evil for evil (6) against the buying and selling of goods that have not paid the duty (7) against the giving or taking things on usury – that is unlawful interest (8) against uncharitable or unprofitable conversations (9) not to do to others what we would not want them to do to us (10) no putting on gold and costly apparel (11) against taking of diversions which cannot be used in the name of the Lord (12) against singing those songs or reading those books which do not tend to knowledge of God (13) no softness and needless self-indulgence (14) no laying up treasure on earth (15) no borrowing without the probability of paying.

Many of these rules are couched in eighteenth-century language, and reflect a keen sense of the temptations and vices of the street culture of the rapidly growing cities. But even today none of them seems too quaint or arcane: the injunction prohibiting buying and selling goods on which the duty has not been paid is still instructive to those tempted by tax avoidance schemes.

Of equal contemporary value are the eleven positive rules. In them, Wesley insists that Methodists are to show their faith:

(16) by doing good as far as possible to all men (17) doing good to their bodies, by giving food to the hungry, by clothing the naked, by visiting or helping them that are sick or in prison (18) by instructing, reproving, or exhorting all we have any intercourse with (19) by doing good, especially to them that are of the household of faith (20) to live by all possible diligence and frugality.

To achieve any success in abiding by the *General Rules*, Methodists were to "(21) run with patience, taking up their cross daily." This means that they would have to avail themselves of "the means of grace," namely:

(22) attending all the ordinances of God (23) attending the ministry of the word (24) and the Lord's Supper (25) family and private prayer (26) searching the scripture (27) fasting: according to the practice of the early church from waking to mid afternoon.

The sanctions for any breach of these rules were clear and unambiguous: exclusion from the society. In Wesley's plain language:

If there be any among us who observes them not, who habitually breaks them, let it be known unto them who watch over that soul as they who must give an account. We will admonish him of the error of his ways. We will bear with him for a season. But, if then he repents not, he hath no more place among us. We have delivered our own souls.

Such requirements prevented eighteenth-century Methodism from ever becoming a mass movement. In Newcastle in 1743 Wesley read the *General Rules* and then promptly excluded sixty-four members from the society: all those guilty of cursing, swearing, Sabbath-breaking, drunkenness, wife-beating, lying, railing, idleness and laziness, lightness and carelessness. Eight years later Wesley was able to triumph in the success of this seemingly harsh course of action. Describing his societies in Yorkshire in 1751 he says, "I found them all alive, strong, vigorous of soul, blessing, loving and praising God their Saviour."

From the beginning they had been taught both the law and the gospel. "God loves *you*; therefore love and obey *Him*; Christ died for *you*: therefore die to sin. Christ is risen: therefore live to God. Christ liveth evermore: therefore live to God, till you live with him in glory." So we preached; and so you believed. This is the scriptural way, the Methodist way, the true way. God grant that we may never turn from it, to the right hand or to the left.

This tight discipline accounts for the discrepancy in statistics in this early period, which reflects the difference between the relatively small numbers of members reported to the Conferences compared with the huge numbers of people who heard Methodist preaching.

At the beginning of the movement, Wesley seems to have laid more emphasis on the subgroupings within the societies known as the "bands." These met daily in order to obey the scriptural instruction "confess your faults to one another, and pray for one another that ye may be healed." Here, as we have seen before, Wesley is using the word "healing" as synonymous with "salvation," and he constantly emphasized that Methodists would need each other to diagnose their spiritual infirmities: "For till we are sensible of our disease it admits of no cure," he argued in the sermon *The Repentance of Believers*. Within a framework of trust, one man might speak lovingly to another man, or one woman to another woman, of deeply rooted sins. In many cases, the hymns Charles Wesley was writing were intended explicitly for these Methodist band meetings:

> Help us to help each other, Lord,
> Each other's cross to bear,
> Let each his friendly aid afford,
> And feel his brother's care.
>
> Help us to build each other up,
> Our little stock improve;
> Increase our faith, confirm our hope
> And perfect us in love.

Wesley's set of questions to be used in band meetings presents a formidable challenge to members: "What known sins have you committed since our last meeting? What temptations have you met with? How were you delivered? What have you thought said or done, of which you doubt whether it be sin or not? Have you nothing you desire to be kept secret?" Confronted with such interrogations, members of the bands might well have been dismayed, and some of the more unusual manifestations of Methodist religious emotion occurred in the context of the bands rather than in the context of public preaching. Members were reported to have been "seized with strong pain" or "wounded by the sword of the Spirit." Because of this genuine possibility of emotional excess, as well as the intimate nature of the discussions, the bands were always divided along gender lines, and single people met separately from married people. Although the bands themselves are no longer a part of Methodist experience, it is still common for many Methodists to use the expression "in band" to indicate the need for the utmost confidentiality.

Many of Charles Wesley's hymns give words to the emotional release of those who found new freedom in Christ in the band meeting. The much used hymn, "And can it be that I should gain / An interest in the Saviour's blood" (CHPM 193) voices the sense of pardon, liberation, and courage experienced in the band.

> Long my imprison'd spirit lay
> Fast bound in sin and nature's night,
> Thine eye diffused a quick'ning ray.
> I woke; the dungeon flamed with light,
> My chains fell off, my heart was free,
> I rose went forth, and follow'd thee

No condemnation now I dread.
Jesus and all in him, is mine.
Alive in him, my living Head,
And clothed in righteousness divine,
Bold I approach the eternal throne,
And claim the crown, through Christ my Own.

As the movement developed, most of these hymns were used within another manifestation of Methodist common life, namely the class meeting. In many ways the popularity of the classes rendered the bands superfluous, and by the end of Wesley's life the decline of the band system was already underway, much to his dismay. Three years before his death, he lamented in a letter to William Simpson in Yarm that "no circuit did, or ever will flourish, unless there are Bands in the large Societies."

We have seen how Captain Foy in Bristol had suggested collecting a penny a week from United Society members in order to deal with the debt upon the Bristol New Room. John Wesley saw the weekly visit of the class leaders as "the very thing we wanted." "The Leaders," he wrote, "are the persons who may not only receive the contributions, but also watch over the souls of their brethren." It became obvious that collecting the pennies each week could be done more easily if the class members were to gather weekly in one place. The class leader became now not a mere collector of class pennies but more significantly a shepherd of the little flock committed to him or her. Unlike the bands, membership of classes was based on where people lived and was not divided according to gender. While there was a strict requirement that a Methodist had to be a member of a class in order to be a member of the society, membership in a band was an optional extra.

Early Methodism was thus built upon ideals of mutual openness and vulnerability. Spiritual growth was a group activity, not the "flight of the alone to the alone." As Wesley himself stressed: " 'Holy solitaries' is a phrase no more consistent with the Gospel than holy adulterers. The Gospel of Christ knows of no religion but social; no holiness but social holiness." Within the class and band meetings, and in early Methodism generally, "sin" was not so much about the failings of individuals but was focused rather on those things that distort and disrupt community life. Among these, the chief failing was pride, but equally dangerous were envy, covetousness, hypocrisy, gossip and double-dealing, all of which made fellowship impossible. In the Christian believer these had to be replaced with the virtues of "social grace" (Charles Wesley's expression) through which God might

> Our friendship sanctify and guide,
> Unmix'd with selfishness and pride,
> Thy glory be our single aim!

The *CHPM* offered these early Methodist communities ways of praying for "the social grace" through such verses as this:

> Move and actuate, and guide;
> Divers gifts to each divide:
> Placed according to thy will,
> Let us all our work fulfil.

A later verse in the same hymn portrays the ideal Methodist community:

> Sweetly may we all agree,
> Touch'd with softest sympathy,
> Kindly for each other care,
> Every member feel its share.

And it seems that frequently members of classes and bands did indeed become little communities of grace which embodied these ideals. One participant in early Methodism said about them: "these little parties, and Classes and Bands, are the beginning of the heavenly society in this lower world."

The responsibility for ensuring that these lofty goals were kept before class members belonged to the class leaders. These men and women were just as important in the early growth of Methodism as the itinerant preachers. Some were upper-middle-class like Elizabeth Ritchie (1754–1835), later Mrs. Mortimer, who was the daughter of a Yorkshire surgeon. She exemplifies the degree to which the responsibilities of the office were taken to heart. Appointed a class leader in London in 1777, she was, a friend wrote, "impressed with its importance and deeply sensible of her incompetency to fulfil its duties without much Divine assistance." In Dublin, Henry Brooke, an artist and scholar and friend of John Wesley, led his class with charm and vivacity, sharing in his class, according to a contemporary observer, his "large acquirements of knowledge without the parade of learning." Like Elizabeth Ritchie, many class leaders were well-educated women who found class-leading a natural outlet for their talents: Lady Darcy Maxwell (1742–1810) in Edinburgh, Hester Ann Roe, later Mrs. Rogers (1756–94), and Mary Bosanquet (1739–1815), the wife of John Fletcher, and many others, were equally impressive, and studies of how they offered Christ in their classes are part of the treasury of Methodist devotional literature. Some class leaders had multiple classes in their care, like a veteran soldier

James Field in Ireland, and William Carvasso (1750–1834), a Cornish farmer, whose own account of his life in the *Memoir of Mr. William Carvasso: Sixty Years as a Class Leader in the Wesleyan Methodist Connexion* is a major source of information about class meetings at the turn of the nineteenth century.

This tradition of class leading continued into the nineteenth century. In 1854 Edward Corderoy of the Lambeth Chapel in South London wrote *A Memoir of Father Reeves the Methodist Class Leader: a Brief Account of Mr William Reeves: Thirty-Four Years a Class Leader in the Wesleyan Society in Lambeth*. Corderoy describes an illiterate young countryman "without God and without hope, softened through affliction," who found his way to the newly opened Lambeth Chapel in 1808.

It was the first Monday evening in December: he was entirely unknown to preacher and congregation, but the service was for him, as though no one else was present; he listened – he trembled. The message to the Laodicean church [sc. in Revelation, 3] was read: the tone struck sharply and deeply on his conscience; it appeared as though the Saviour once more uttered the words – "Behold I stand at the door and knock; if any man hear my voice and open the door, I will come in to him and will sup with him and he with me." Here was Christ's appeal – here the sinner's opportunity. The young man opened his heart to the heavenly visitant, tears of repentance were shed, holy resolutions formed, and the way of life deliberately and decisively chosen.

This characteristic conversion story is authentically told, although in the third person; as a fellow class leader in Lambeth, Corderoy would have heard it many times from Reeves' own mouth. What is more important, however, is the wide range of social consequences resulting from this kind of critical turning point in people's lives. When he arrived at the door of the Lambeth Chapel, William Reeves was, in nineteenth-century language, a "mechanic" – a wheelwright and coachmaker – and by working from six in the morning to eight at night he could earn forty shillings a week. But upon his conversion he realized that this regime left him little if any time to visit the members of his class, and he soon reduced his working week, with a reduction in his wage of six or seven shillings a week, a substantial sum then. Beginning as a prayer leader, and learning to read at the same time, in 1818 he was appointed a class leader. Reeves continued in this chosen path until his death in 1852, acquiring on his way the honorific nickname "Father."

Three excerpts from the *Memoir* of Reeves' life as a class leader will convey a sense of the common life of the Wesleyan Methodists of this period. First they were devoutly loyal to the tradition they had received. Corderoy records that "on no account would [Reeves] sanction the use of hymns that were not found in our own collection" (i.e. the *CHPM*), and comments:

This conduct of brother Reeves did not arise from bigotry; though he knew nothing better than the Methodism which he loved, and nothing richer than the experience of the Wesley hymns, his endeavours were mainly to repress certain extravagances, both in tune and words, in which many zealous people are too apt to indulge.

This careful attention to order within the class meetings is not abnormal: enthusiasm in its more vigorous manifestations was always carefully monitored. Whatever the practices being developed in other sections of Methodism, the English Wesleyan tradition restrained inordinate emotion.

Second, this was a period of rapid expansion in British Methodism, and the *Memoir* of Father Reeves describes this growth within one London Methodist community. Reeves conducted two classes, one on Sunday afternoon, the other on a weekday. Writing of the Sunday afternoon class, Corderoy remarks that as early as 1822 it had grown so large that it had to be divided: "This Class remained ever after a very large one; though repeatedly divided, yet it constantly grew. It was admirably trained; and in late years, out of eighty members on the books at one time, more than seventy have been known to present themselves for their quarterly tickets." Dividing the classes was a necessity: Reeves himself recorded that for the members "it was a tearing asunder": "I cannot forget my feelings, when I saw their love to one another, and their grief at the thought of parting. They could not have overcome the trial if they had not seen the necessity for separation, for they were now fifty in number."

Third, the class meetings were never merely an evangelistic tool. Reeves and his contemporaries pressed the claims of "entire sanctification." Thus in 1844 Reeves records in his journal that for some weeks he had been longing for "a clearer testimony from the Spirit of my entire sanctification": "I pleaded hard with the Lord for it, through the precious blood of Jesus and glory be to my heavenly Father, he very soon granted me the desire of my heart, though so unworthy, and filled my soul with perfect love. Blessed be the name of the Triune God for his unspeakable love to me."

This experience was confided simply to his journal; he made no boast of it in public, much in accordance with Wesley's own teaching. But it infused his teaching style, so much so that he could record a Sunday class meeting in 1848 when his people, "who had long enjoyed peace through believing," were now led

in an extraordinary and earnest manner to cry for perfect love; and although there were so many, yet there was but one heart, one soul, one voice. "Love, perfect love," was the cry of all; and, Glory be to God, we did not cry in vain; the spirit of love was so poured out upon us that we scarce could part. This Sabbath has been a foretaste of the Sabbath above.

To be sure Corderoy is describing this old class leader in the hagiographical style much loved in mid-nineteenth-century Methodism, but he does record an outsider's point of view. All the talk in Lambeth on the evening that William Reeves was killed, knocked down by a bullock-cart, was of his death. "Dead!" said a Lambeth Walk shopkeeper – "who is dead?" "Mr. Reeves." "What! The little old man with the umbrella, that was always going about visiting the sick?" "And thus faithfully," says Corderoy, "was his character sketched by one who was little interested in the religious motives which actuated our friend, but who noticed and admired his life of devotion."

The esteem in which people held their leaders can be seen in this poem printed in the *Wesleyan Methodist Magazine* in 1841:

> When I first joined Zion's band,
> Who kindly took me by the hand,
> And prayed that I might faithful stand?
> My Class Leader!
>
> Who bade me flee from Satan's wile,
> And shun the world's alluring smile,
> Nor let its charms my soul beguile?
> My Class Leader!
>
> When'er my wand'ring footsteps stray
> From Wisdom's sweet and pleasant way,
> Who over me doth weep and pray?
> My Class Leader!
>
> And when with me life's dream is o'er,
> And I shall weep and sigh no more,
> O may we meet on Canaan's shore,
> My Class Leader!

But there is evidence in these verses of something else. One commentator notes the sentimental individualist piety expressed here; that there is no reference to the place of the class meeting in promoting mutual accountability and the preparation for worthy participation in the means of grace. At this point in mid-nineteenth-century Wesleyan Methodism the class meeting as an institution is beginning to collapse. Increasingly in this period, in both the British Isles and in North America, there are accounts of dull and lifeless class meetings, replete with sanctimonious moralizing, which members found increasingly burdensome to attend.

As the Methodist movement grew, John Wesley would add yet another layer to this system of societies, bands and classes, namely, the "select

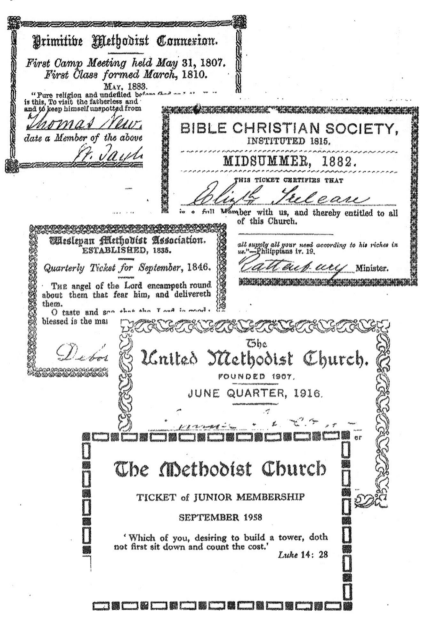

12. Class tickets were originally introduced by Wesley in 1741, to be issued to members of Methodist societies in good standing by preachers following a quarterly examination.

bands" or the "select societies." Their purpose was two-fold. First, they provided spiritual advice to those who had experienced "sanctifying grace." As such, the select bands were highly elitist, designed to encourage special Methodists "to press after perfection; to exercise their every grace, and improve every talent they have received." Wesley saw the select societies and bands as a kind of inner cabinet where he could share his own spiritual life, a "select company to whom I might unbosom myself on all occasions, without reserve." Some sense of what it was to be a member of a select band is reported by Mary Bosanquet. Her band met every other Wednesday evening to pray for "an outpouring of sanctifying grace and purity of heart." In her reminiscences of these band meetings, we get a sense of the near-mystical bliss she experienced: "O! the sinking into nothing before God my spirit used to feel! Of all the meetings I ever was employed in while in Yorkshire, I know not I ever felt my soul so conscious of the Lord's approval as in these." Although this strand of perfectionism in Methodism has been lost at different periods, it has never been wholly abandoned, and we will see it return to the surface again in the Holiness movement of the nineteenth century and in modern phenomena such as the popular Emmaus Walks within the American Methodist churches.

The Wesleys recognized that not all those who embark on the Christian journey could consistently lead lives worthy of the Gospel, that they could at any time become "backsliders" (this was an aspect of their Arminianism). But these wayward individuals could also at any time repent and "come home." For persons in this kind of spiritual condition the Wesleys devised the "penitent bands." Penitents were said to be those for whom "the exhortations and prayers used among the believers did no longer profit," and who "wanted advice and instructions suited to their case." The bands set up especially for them helped them to affirm their desire for God, offer them hope and guide their steps toward recovering the experience of salvation. No less than twenty-one hymns in the *CHPM* are concerned precisely with such penitents; Hymn 180, for example, offers appropriate vocabulary for a person seeking restoration:

> Son of God, if thy free grace
> Again hath raised me up,
> Call'd me still to seek thy face,
> And given me back my hope;
> Still thy timely help afford,
> And all thy loving-kindness show.
> Keep me, keep me, gracious Lord,
> And never let me go!

Music, hymn singing, and prayer each played a role in these meetings, and Charles Wesley recorded in his *Journal*, "At eight in the evening I met the people crowding to our lecture at the Foundery (the meeting of the penitents, it was called). Now all sorts come, whether in the Society or out of it." Clearly by this time the penitent bands had become a means of spiritual seeking for a much wider audience.

These structures were all in place as Wesley neared the end of his life and were transmitted to North America with Philip Embury, Barbara Heck, Robert Strawbridge, Francis Asbury, and others. Class and society meetings nourished the first Methodists in the Caribbean, in South Africa, in India, in Sri Lanka, and in Australia. But, as we have seen, these meetings did not survive through the nineteenth century. When Methodism on both sides of the Atlantic began to take the shape of regular denominations, it was proposed by leading ministers that Methodist membership no longer be tied to membership in and attendance at class meetings. In British Methodism the ideal of meeting in classes was reasserted in 1889, but by 1890 the "class-book" system of recording membership was replaced by a roll-book of members of the congregation. Against this tide, the 1932 Deed of Union affirmed the importance of the class meeting, and said that all Methodist members should have their names entered in a class-book. But the class meeting was no longer central to Methodist life. The desire for fellowship remained strong, however, and various movements sprang up to meet this need. One of these, the Wesley Guild, dates back to 1896 and has had a lasting influence on British Methodism. The phenomenon of the adult Sunday school class in American Methodism has also been a means of nurturing faith and in some ways carried on the work of the class meeting.

The ideal of Methodist people meeting in small groups to support and encourage members on the spiritual journey has often allowed the Methodist Church to survive when other larger ecclesial institutions have failed. For example, in the remarkable story of the survival of the Methodist witness in the Baltic states of Estonia and Latvia, and in Bulgaria, class meetings sustained men and women when the church itself was being suppressed and could not meet for public worship. In recent years David Lowes Watson has reexamined Methodist class and band meeting structures, arguing that an indispensable feature of the Wesleyan ideal is "mutual accountability." Watson and others have worked in recent years to renew Methodist life in North America and elsewhere through the renewal of the kind of "covenantal discipleship" that was embodied in the classes and bands.

Beyond Britain and the United States the class meeting ideal survived in different cultural forms. We have noted that very considerable growth of the Methodist Church in Korea has largely been dependent upon class meetings, so much so that other Korean Protestant churches have adopted them. In Latin America they have been influenced by liberation theology and have taken the form of "base communities" in which members meet for Bible study and strive to discover ways to put their discipleship into practice. The same theory that lies behind the class system can also be seen in the para-church movement which influenced wide segments of British Christianity in the 1970s and 1980s, and more recently the widespread proliferation of "house-churches," both those attached to larger ecclesial structures and those which exist as separate entities.

SUNDAY SCHOOLS

While Robert Raikes (1735–1811) of Gloucester is usually credited with the first Sunday school in 1780, Methodists often claim this honor for Hannah Ball (1733–92), a Methodist class leader in High Wycombe who established classes for the religious education of children in 1769. In her *Journal* for 1775 she recalls that she was used to "praying with some children which I meet every Sabbath day to instruct in the principles of Christianity." She also wrote to John Wesley about meeting with these children twice a week, Sundays and Mondays, in which she endeavored to teach them the rudiments of the faith as a part of her own "desire to promote the interest of the Church of Christ."

In a time before public education, the work of the Sunday school was at first directed to the education of poor children (in Raikes' words "ragged, rough, dirty urchins") whose parents could not afford the cost of schooling. It met on Sundays because these children often worked every other day, and attendance at worship was often also required of the pupils. Gradually, increasing numbers of Methodist preachers and class leaders took this work on as part of their responsibilities, and the names of many notable Methodists are remembered in the history of Sunday school education. John Wesley had insisted that the members of the Holy Club engage in teaching the "children of the poor," and it is not surprising that he approved of and encouraged this movement, believing that it was important to "instill the principles of religion" into the minds of young people. Sunday schools, he wrote, were the "noblest specimens of charity" toward those who were in need. His own experiments in fee-paying schools, two institutions for day students and boarders, Kingswood (established in Bristol in 1748) and the Foundery, were designed to teach the sons of Methodist families "in every branch of useful learning." Wesley's persistent interest in these educational institutions is obvious from his journals, and the successor of the Kingswood School (now located near Bath) continues to this day. Those taught to read and write in Methodist Sunday schools, and to articulate the faith that was in them often became Methodist leaders in their own right, and contributed to the "upward mobility" that marked nineteenth-century Methodism.

In North America a similar pattern was established, although public schooling had a firmer and earlier foothold than in the British Isles. By 1900, the Sunday school movement had become a well-established Protestant phenomenon, led by laypeople and often housed in purpose-built school buildings. Graded Sunday school curriculum material began to dominate the output of religious publishing houses. Methodist Church buildings also accommodated themselves to the importance of the Sunday school in the life of the church, giving rise, for example, to the so-called "Akron Plan" design for churches, with folding wooden panels that could be used to separate or combine the Sunday school space and the main sanctuary. As we shall see, the growth of the Sunday school movement also put pressure on Methodist worship, with the increasing demand for family services, "rally days," passing out parades (Sunday school graduations), children's sermons, "junior church," and more recently various forms of "all-age worship."

Sunday schools for all age groups have also become the primary means of fellowship in North American Methodism, where it is common to have two morning services, the first fairly early and the second mid-morning. Between the two services are sandwiched the adult Sunday school classes as well as the graded Sunday school for children. In smaller churches there will be only one service preceded or followed by Sunday school.

THE CONFERENCE

One major innovation of the Wesleys has survived almost intact to the present time and is integral to the common life of most forms of Methodism in the world. The Annual Conferences, we have already noted, began in 1744 with just ten members. Today there are thousands of Annual Conferences around the world which exercise oversight over the affairs of the Methodist people. The technical term for this oversight is *episcopē*, or supervision of the discipline and doctrines of the Christian community. *Episcopē* has been part of church life from the New Testament period, and for many Christian traditions (Roman Catholics, Anglicans, and the Orthodox, for example) it has been located in a single person, the *episcopos* or "bishop." At the Reformation, the followers of John Calvin came to believe that *episcopē* did not reside in a single person but rather in the whole body of the *presbyteroi*, or elders, resulting in a system of church government known as Presbyterianism. Others at the time of the Reformation believed that the place where *episcopē* was most properly worked out was in the life of the local congregation, and congregational forms of government are also commonly found within the spectrum of Protestant polity. As we have seen, Wesley's deepest conviction about his own ordination turned on seeing the words *episcopos* and *presbyteros* in the New Testament as equivalent terms. Methodist church government can therefore be described as a modified Presbyterianism, in which all ministers are of equal rank. When Methodists enter into discussions about church union this understanding of church government becomes a key issue.

Since 1744 the Annual Conferences throughout world Methodism have taken it as their responsibility to ensure that right doctrine was taught, that the worshiping life of the church was as well ordered as possible and that ethical and moral standards were faithful to this understanding of church order ("What to teach? How to teach? What to do?"). Under the first heading, the Conferences have often both defined and interpreted the doctrines of the church, and from time to time this has entailed removing those thought to be in error from the preaching ministry. Second, the Conferences have determined what forms of worship and common prayer might be used in their areas of jurisdiction. Third, they have also paid continuous attention to questions of mission and outreach as well as to opportunities of mutual care and aid between the churches in their areas, enabling the more prosperous to come to the aid of those in need. In the case of the autonomous Conferences in all parts of the world the decisions of the Conference are final, and the slogan "Conference is master in its own house" is a very familiar cry in these independent bodies. The supreme authority of Conference means that it is the focus of Methodist common life. Ministers and societies are linked through the Conferences in one connection.

There are some variations in the polity of the American tradition of Methodism. From its inception in 1784 the Methodist Episcopal Church, true to its name, tended to emphasize the role of the bishop in its governing structures. Men like Asbury and Whatcoat reinforced the sense of personal authority when they took full responsibility for selecting, training, ordaining and stationing the circuit riders. But at the same time the 1784 Conference, consisting of "the body of traveling elders," had itself elected Asbury and Coke as their superintendents, and thereafter met annually to vote on changes in the *Discipline*, or rule-book of the church. In 1792 they created, in addition to these Annual Conferences, a quadrennial General Conference consisting of all the ordained traveling preachers in the denomination. But as Methodism grew and spread across the continent, and as the number of preachers increased, the size of this quadrennial Conference became unwieldy, and the early American Methodists created a delegated General Conference to meet every four years. The General Conference had and still has some restrictions on its powers. It cannot, for example, alter doctrine or change the basic polity of the church.

Annual Conferences have remained important to the core identity of the Methodist Church, its people, and its ministers. The Conference remains, as it was from the beginning, the place of membership of Methodist ministers, both elders and deacons; Methodist clergy are accountable to their Annual Conferences from whom they annually receive their appointments to their pastoral charges. A normal question put to Methodist ministers around the world is "To what Annual Conference do you belong?"

As American Methodism spread across the world it was obvious that the General Conference would not be able to cope with the distinctive needs of the new Christian communities. Accordingly the idea of the Central Conferences was born. Today there are some seven Central Conferences organizing United Methodist work in more than twenty-two nations. As the twenty-first century begins, these Central Conferences have a combined membership of more than 1.3 million. This represents 13 percent of the total membership of the UMC. These Central Conferences are fully represented in the General Conference, and their bishops are full members of the Council of Bishops.

Alongside the Conference structure, in American Methodism there has always been a second "constitutive principle," that of the general superintendency of all the bishops meeting in Council. They are charged with planning, in the words of the UMC Constitution, "for the general oversight and promotion of the temporal and spiritual interests of the whole Church." Unlike Anglican or Catholic bishops their *episcopē* does not entail sacramental authority and does not therefore make them a distinct third order of ministry along with deacons and elders. Consequently it has no connection with the older understanding of the apostolic succession as guaranteeing the fundamental continuity of the ministries of the church. Methodist bishops remain part of the body of elders and are elected and consecrated to their work. As in secular forms of democracy, they depend far more on the "consent of the governed" than on authority given "from above."

It may be said that American Methodism (in most of its forms, including the EUB and the African-American churches) has created quite a distinctive form for the office of bishop. These men and women have enormous influence through their constant travel and ubiquity. General Conference meets only every four years and in the intervening time the bishops give a sense of unity to the UMC. They speak, intervene, encourage, preach, administer, and chair boards and commissions. In 1992 they were further charged with the responsibility "to guard, transmit, teach, and proclaim, corporately and individually, the apostolic faith." Such activities make for the coherence of the "connection" in American Methodism.

CONNECTIONALISM/CONNEXIONALISM

The distinctive form of ecclesiology within the Methodist traditions resides in its "connectionalism" (we now choose to use the American spelling for the sake of convenience). It has always been clear to followers of the Wesleys that to be a Christian community involves a total sense of interconnectedness and interdependence with other Christian communities. For Methodists, the Christian Church is not considered to be some loose network of independent congregations, owing allegiance perhaps to some distant church dignitary. On the contrary, Methodists, in all times and places, have been certain that the Bible gives as little evidence of solitary communities as it does of solitary religion. Charles Wesley's hymn "All praise to our redeeming, Lord" captures this organic sense of the mutuality of the Christian life:

> The gift that he on one bestows,
> We all delight to prove;
> The grace through every vessel flows,
> In purest streams of love.

Everything in the Methodist ethos contributes to this interdependency. The authority of the Conference, the traditions of itinerant superintendency exemplified by John Wesley himself in Britain, and by Francis Asbury in the USA (and, as we have just seen, developed so very strongly in the American tradition) are hallmarks of connectionalism. The nature of the itinerancy of the Methodist preachers who were received into "Full Connection" formed another strand of the interconnectedness. The common bonds of discipline and the transferability of membership from society to society all reinforced the sense of mutual belonging.

Methodist theologians found eloquent ways to express their commitment to this sense of mutuality. Here is a voice from mid-nineteenth-century

Wesleyan Methodism, that of Alfred Barrett (1808–76) of Richmond College, London:

A single Christian, yea, or a single Christian church, is a puny thing standing all alone, and does nor see and feel and know *all* the Gospel, because the eye of the understanding and the heart of others is needed for this purpose. Christ intended the soul of his people to cohere, in order that while they were mutually loving, they might mutually teach.

Another Wesleyan Methodist, Benjamin Gregory (1820–1900), the British connexional editor, grounded his view in Trinitarian theology, writing that "Christ Himself declared that the unity of the Godhead in the three persons of the Trinity is at once the archetype, basis and consummation of the unity of the Church." He continued:

As the life of the believer is to be manifested to the world, so it is designed that the unity of the Church shall be manifested to the world. It is no part of his plan that His body should be disjointed, that His church should be split up into rival, mutually repellent or even isolated and altogether mutually independent fragments.

This sense of connectionality was never completely lost, even in nineteenth-century and twentieth-century British Methodism, which had turned its back on Wesley in other matters. It was taken for granted that connectionalism would prevail within the new Methodist Church of 1932. For a number of reasons, it was strongly reinforced in the British Methodist Church's 1999 ecclesiology report, *Called to Love and Praise*. Interdenominational relationships had strengthened with the emergence of the Local Ecumenical Projects (LEPs), and ecumenical partners were keenly interested in the ways Methodists did things. Roman Catholics too were rediscovering Methodism as an dialogue partner, and many called for conversations on connectionalism. In addition there were certain stresses and strains caused by the restructuring of the British Methodist Church in the 1970s that (together with a sharp downturn in membership) were leading to serious questioning of the relevance of connectionalism and to anxieties about the tendency of some large local churches to adopt a more congregational form of polity. *Called to Love and Praise* embraced connectionalism wholeheartedly. It was said to "enshrine a vital truth about the nature of the church" because it witnesses to "a mutuality and interdependence which derive from the participation of all Christians in the very life of God himself." Echoing (though not consciously) both the nineteenth-century theologians we have just mentioned, the report stated that individual churches do not function effectively in isolation, failing either to see or to set priorities in mission and service. The report also felt able to commend the connectional principle to other churches and suggested a new openness to possibilities of reconciling connectionalism with other forms of church order and discipline. Although connectionalism "naturally excludes both independency and autocracy as models of church government" it was certainly in the minds of the authors of the report that this statement might not necessarily exclude reasonable local self-determination on the part of congregations or some forms of personally focused ministries of oversight. The way to further discussion with Methodism's ecumenical partners was left wide open. The section in *Called to Love and Praise* on connectionalism concluded with a statement about global concerns: "at this international level, the connexional [sic] principle propels Methodist churches towards a sharing of resources which crosses both denominational and national boundaries."

Called to Love and Praise did not refer in any detail to American Methodism's more fully worked-out logic of global connectionalism, expressed through its General Conference and its Central Conferences. This significant failure indicates something of the depth of mutual incomprehension of the two great traditions.

For American Methodists, as much as for their British counterparts, connectionalism arises directly from a concern for mission and evangelism. The historic roots of American connectionalism reach far back into the beginnings of Methodism, when there was no established church, no central planning from any ecclesiastical body, and no way of ordaining ministers for the new territories. In this wide-open new world, the Methodist way of forming religious societies, sending preachers as and where they were needed, and of adapting ministry to particular situations made a great deal of sense. It was equally important that these new societies and their preachers were bound to each other by shared disciplines of holy living and right thinking, not least because it helped to combat the sense of isolation experienced by frontier preachers. The sense of solidarity with other Methodists was the particular gift that Francis Asbury offered both the societies and the preachers as he traveled the entire connection. The benefits of not being alone soon appealed to other groups, and German immigrants adopted connectionalism as the organizational pattern for the Evangelical Association and the United Brethren Societies. Connectionalism also appealed strongly to the newly free African Americans.

Even though the language of "societies" and "class meetings" dwindled in importance in Methodist self-consciousness many decades ago, the Methodist churches of the USA are still organized and interrelated as local units of a much greater connection, guided and nurtured as we have seen by both the General Conference and the constant "general superintendency" of the House of Bishops. The whole point of such interconnectedness is that all local churches are seen to be fundamental units of the church's mission; in the words of a report of the General Council of Ministries in 1994: "The local church congregation is the primary base for ministry and mission and the foundation for everything that happens in the church."

The implications of such a conception are farreaching. Connectionalism links every local Methodist church in the USA, with congregations represented in each of the seven Central Conferences overseas. So, for example, what happens in faraway places is felt in the Methodist life-stream to be of equal importance to what is happening in the next town or neighborhood. The House of Bishops gave expression to this feeling in a 1990 document *Vital Congregations – Faithful Disciples:* "Through our mutual support as congregations in covenant, we share resources and hold one another up in the joys and sorrows of ministry. Together we undergird the whole outreach of the church."

To be sure there are many imperfections in the ways resources are shared, both within the USA and between the USA and its Central Conferences. Under discussion in 2004 is a proposal to gather a hundred or more leaders from all parts of the world to form a "connectional table" which would be charged with coordinating the sharing of resources. There is much work to be done, but the logic of American connectionalism is clear and Methodists of the British traditions need to take counsel with their American colleagues if they are to move "towards a sharing of resources which crosses both denominational and national boundaries."

Of course, the common life of Methodism is represented in more than a particular set of organizational or institutional structures. Connectionalism has embodied certain distinctively Methodist values in matters of justice and peacemaking "on the ground," and classes and bands have nourished particular forms of Christian piety. In local congregations, forms of preaching, hymn singing and common prayer have shaped the lives of generations of men and women. It is to these questions of spirituality, worship, and social ethics that we turn in the following chapters. In all of these, however, the Methodist emphasis on mutual accountability and interdependence that we have seen in the structures of Methodist polity are in evidence.

CHAPTER 7

Methodist spirituality

We have been looking at Methodism as a worldwide religious tradition with a particular history, organizational structures, and doctrinal standards. But in many ways the Methodist movement was in its beginnings primarily a *spiritual renewal* movement. Indeed, one collection of eighteenth-century English devotional writing calls this whole period the "Age of Wesley," with John Wesley standing as the prototype for the quest for God and for godliness in the midst of Enlightenment rationalism. But the spirituality of Wesleyan Methodism has never been, even in its inception in the Oxford Holy Club, a monolithic entity, and it has begotten over the years a host of adjectives to describe it: mystical, perfectionist, experiential, penitential, social, pragmatic. In some ways, all of these adjectives can be accurately applied to Wesley's original vision for Christian spiritual revival, and some Methodist groups have been able to maintain the creative tension between and among them. At other times, however, one or another of these aspects of Methodist piety has been lifted up and emphasized to the exclusion of others, producing a spiritual tributary off the Methodist mainstream. The Holiness movement, with its emphasis on perfectionism, is one example.

The evidence for Methodist piety is abundant. Having early on identified his principal task as the spread of "Scriptural holiness," John Wesley often focuses on the importance of the inner life as he reflects in his *Journal*, offers advice in his letters, and admonishes Methodist societies and congregations in sermons and treatises. In every generation, Methodists have echoed this deep concern for the inner life in their own writing, and Methodist spiritual autobiographies are plentiful. As we shall see, during many periods of Methodist history journal-keeping has been considered to be an essential spiritual discipline, allowing people not only to ruminate on their own walk of faith, but also to share it with others. Journals and diaries were often passed down in families, and the reflections of notable men and women were published for the edification of a wider readership. In the eighteenth and nineteenth centuries, the obituaries of pious Methodists were staple offerings in the pages of popular religious magazines, and these eulogies regularly detailed the spiritual exercises, good works, prayer lives, and deathbed insights of thousands of otherwise ordinary men, women, and children. While much of this material is clearly stereotyped and hagiographical, it does tell us a great deal about the spiritual aspirations (if not the spiritual reality) of the Methodist people in any given period.

At the same time, the structures and theological formulations of Methodism can also be "read" for their devotional implications: the importance of the classes and bands in the quest for holiness, the link made in John Wesley's theological treatises between the means of grace and care for the poor, the material artifacts that Methodists passed on from generation to generation, and similar resources arising from the various parts of worldwide Methodism. So, for example, the 1780 *CHPM* can be seen as an encapsulation of Methodist spirituality at a particular time and place, with its contents so organized as to describe the journey of the Christian soul. After exhorting and beseeching a sinner to return to God, the hymns move on to describe the pleasantness of religion, the goodness of God, death, judgment, heaven, hell. "Formal" and "inward" religion are then contrasted, followed by prayers for repentance. There are hymns for mourners convinced of sin and brought to the new birth, for those convinced of backsliding – and their recovery – and then for believers, rejoicing, groaning for full redemption, saved and interceding for the world. The fifth part allows the singer to intercede for the world. Then the society meeting and its tasks are described: giving thanks, praying, parting. Taken together, these various kinds of resources can help us to gain a sense of the shape and content of Methodist piety.

THE CONTEXT OF WESLEYAN SPIRITUALITY

While many Methodist authors have wished to view the world into which the Wesleys were born as something of a spiritual desert and Methodism as a vital oasis, as we have seen this is hardly the case. The Puritan religious experiment of the previous century had not only been aimed at a reformation of doctrine and worship, but at a reformation of piety as well, with a deep concern for individual spiritual responsiveness to the unmerited grace of God. With the rise of lay literacy, devotional books were now not only in the hands of clergy and academics, but of ordinary people as well; John Bunyan's *Pilgrim's Progress*, for example, was a huge popular success, and the compelling story of Pilgrim's journey to the Promised Land gave readers a model for the soul's journey toward God. Anglican spiritual literature was also plentiful, and the devotional poetry of George Herbert, the meditations on ecclesiastical order of Richard Hooker, and Jeremy Taylor's treatises on *Holy Living* and *Holy Dying* were all available to those who wished to live a more intentional form of Christian life.

But just as political instability had called forth new patterns of spirituality in the seventeenth century, the social and intellectual instability of the eighteenth century also resulted in new spiritual needs. With the shift in population from countryside to city, the closely knit family and community structures of traditional Britain began to break down. Worse still, the urban deprivation occasioned by low wages and an overburdened infrastructure, and the rural deprivation created by the lack of sufficient work to go round and the safety-net of the extended family, all combined with a rigid class system, had cast many people into a state of unrelenting poverty. In the midst of this was a rising merchant-industrial class, who were seeking somehow to interweave their own spiritual and financial aspirations, and a ruling class who feared that their inherited privilege might not be as secure as they had imagined.

This was, of course, also the period during which the impact of empirical science and rationalism was creating that great intellectual project known as the Enlightenment that would come to define the philosophical character of the eighteenth century. While the theologians of the continental and English Reformations had insisted that no human faculty could be relied upon for the knowledge of God, since all had been infected by sin (or, in the language of Calvin, were "depraved"), Enlightenment rationalism saw the human senses, and preeminently human reason, as created by God and therefore a path to religious insight. Reason was a reflection of the *imago dei*, the image of God, in which humanity was created, and thus was elevated to a place of honor.

But could the existing structures of the Christian Church respond to the new spiritual needs occasioned by this rapid realignment of traditional social and intellectual categories? On the simple level of access the answer is clearly "no." Should even half the people in any given parish have wished to attend the parish church on a Sunday morning, there were simply not enough seats to accommodate them. In addition, very little of the seating in churches came without a cost (the pew rental system was in full swing) and that cost was usually well beyond the means of the poor. While many clergy were diligent men who had the best interests of all their parishioners at heart, the general perception was that the parish church was simply an extension of and most responsive to the religious needs and demands of the aristocratic upper classes (who were in most cases directly responsible for clerical appointments and advancement). Into this vacuum stepped the Wesley brothers and their followers with a new understanding of "heart religion."

Often this "heart religion" of the Wesleys is set in direct conflict with what was portrayed as the prevailing "head religion" of his time. But there had certainly been forms of affective piety which had marked the century prior to Wesley and which carried on throughout his lifetime. The Society of Friends waited patiently in silence for the promptings of the Spirit, the religious revival in Scotland in the 1630s had produced converts struck down unconscious with emotion, Lutheran Pietists urgently sought holiness through a disciplined, communal life, and continental Quietists emphasized the spiritual benefits of meditative prayer and contemplation. Adherents to all of these movements, and many others, were not content with superficial piety, but sought a relationship with God that engaged the whole human personality. As one scholar of spirituality says, "by the early decades of the eighteenth century, there was scarcely a religious community in Western Europe that had not been affected by the religion of the heart movements." But the extraordinary intersection of the kind of evangelical piety embodied by the Wesleys and a world on the verge of modernity would give Methodism a potency that has allowed it to cross temporal, social, and geographical boundaries for over two an a half centuries.

A significant part of the power of John and Charles Wesley's spiritual vision was that it was both integrated and integrative, seeking to involve all the various facets of human existence in a balanced way. In addition, it gave people a clear set of spiritual disciplines in a chaotic world, a warm and cohesive social network in a time of intensified social dislocation, and, perhaps most essentially, a sense of their value as persons and of the importance of their spiritual and economic needs. All around, in the words of one historian, "the image of God was being restored in the downtrodden and oppressed, the fatherless and widows were being comforted, and prisoners and the sick visited with kindness on an unprecedented scale." The Methodist spiritual renewal enabled people who had no stake in the wider society to feel a new sense of belonging and of status, and in fact the growth of Methodism almost exactly paralleled the growth of industrialization in the British Isles.

SOURCES FOR THE PIETY OF JOHN AND CHARLES WESLEY

The roots of John and Charles Wesley's spiritual vision are notoriously difficult to untangle. Much of it can be traced to their upbringing in the

Epworth rectory, and especially to the influence of the redoubtable Susanna. Here was surely born the notion of the importance of small group meetings for mutual counsel and spiritual nurture, of the disciplined devotional life, and of searching the scriptures diligently in order to discern the will of God. And Samuel Wesley, although less often cited, must also have been an influence, particularly in his scholarly attention to ancient sources of the Christian tradition. Both parents brought a self-conscious and intentional attachment to the Church of England, an attachment that ran contrary to the inclinations of their own Puritan parents. This notion that the call of God takes priority over any personal inclination, societal expectation, or even ecclesiastical authority was surely confirmed when Susanna took responsibility for the pastoral care of the Epworth congregation in her husband's absence.

Some sources of Christian piety that would ordinarily have been of genuine interest to someone of Wesley's spiritual inclinations were not fully embraced because of his essential distrust of all forms of Dissent. For example, the importance of the indwelling Spirit to George Fox and the Society of Friends should have provided a treasury of insight on the matter of the Wesleyan doctrines of holiness and perfection, and indeed many Quakers were attracted to Methodism in its early days. But even though John Wesley's encouragement of pious admonition within classes and bands mirrors the Quaker practice of mutual reproof among members, the Quaker emphasis on radical freedom and equality was contrary to Wesley's more authoritarian temperament. Much more congenial was the spirituality of ·Roman Catholics and of the Eastern Fathers. We know that at Oxford he had read Thomas à Kempis's *Imitation of Christ* and other early and medieval spiritual classics.

The state of Anglican spirituality was certainly never quite as moribund as some Methodists have made it out to be, and small grassroots meetings for prayer and mutual society were clearly active before Wesley established his own classes and bands. We have seen that the society meeting in Fetter Lane was one such, as was the one which gathered at Aldersgate Street, where John Wesley had found his own heart to have been "strangely warmed" in May, 1738. Devotional writings from the Elizabethan period of Anglican piety, and later William Law's *Serious Call to the Devout and Holy Life* (1728) and Jeremy Taylor's *Rules and Exercises of Holy Living* (1650) and *Rules and Exercises of Holy Dying* (1651), provided a treasury of spiritual insight from which Wesley freely drew. Just before Wesley's time, Thomas Comber (1645–99) and others had given much thought to the ways in which the church's worship could be used as a "school of prayer" for Christian believers. But despite these significant resources, much of the spirituality of the eighteenth century, whether Anglican or Reformed, retained an aura of "elitism," and this can be seen in the ongoing debate over the matter of religious enthusiasm.

THE PERILS OF "ENTHUSIASM"

Throughout the early decades of the eighteenth century, in both England and America, many pastors, spiritual guides, and church leaders warned against the dangers of "enthusiasm." In the wake of the revivalist preaching of George Whitefield and the First Great Awakening in America, New England Congregationalists like Charles Chauncy (1705–87), who led the staunch anti-revivalists, and Jonathan Edwards (1703–58) who, while defending the revival, was distrustful of enthusiasm as a religious manifestation, wrote extensively on this matter. At the same time in the British Isles, "enthusiasm" fell under similar suspicion, both within the Church of England and among Scots Presbyterians. Not only, the opposition argued, might enthusiasm result in social and political chaos, but it also had the potential to lead people to be deceived, since the claims made as a result of religious enthusiasm (the assurance of salvation, for example) could not be substantiated intellectually. As Chauncy explained, "The enthusiast mistakes the workings of his own passions for divine communications, and fancies himself immediately inspired by God, when all the while he is under no other influence than that of an over-heated imagination."

Such objections did not end with Wesley's death. As late as 1820 an Anglican biographer of John Wesley, Robert Southey, voiced his own objections to Methodist spirituality:

His [Wesley's] system . . . enjoined a perpetual course of stimulants, and lest the watch-nights and the Love-Feasts, with the ordinary means of Class meetings, should be insufficient, he borrowed from the Puritans one of the most perilous practices that ever was devised by enthusiasm, the entering into a covenant, in which the devotee promises and vows to "the most dreadful God."

These kinds of concerns over the perils of enthusiasm are too numerous to be ignored, and they have dogged the footsteps of Methodists for over two centuries. Methodists were all too often, in the words of one American camp meeting song, "despis'd . . . because they shout."

The Wesleys themselves were clearly concerned about this matter of enthusiasm, that the religious enthusiasm of their followers might replace "true religion" and their work be undone. While John Wesley believed that both the witness and the fruits of the Spirit were at the heart of religious experience, he looked to scripture to distinguish "true" from "false" signs of the Spirit. He was clear that even though people might find themselves "shedding tears, falling into fits, or crying out these are not the fruits [of the Spirit]"; in such circumstances people were required to evaluate "the whole tenor of their life; *till then* many times wicked; *from that time* holy just and good" (Wesley's emphasis). But he was also certain that the fruits of the Spirit and the witness of the Spirit went together, and that the cultivation of "rightly disposed spiritual senses" was the task of every Christian.

But the charge of promoting enthusiasm against Wesley and his followers was inevitable. As sensitive as he was to the dangers of enthusiasm, Wesley had also to argue against those who, although they believed in the objective *reality* of the Spirit, denied the *witness* of the Spirit in the present day. Wesley knew that the "Spirit of God, sharply convicting the soul of sin, may occasion the bodily strength to fail." He was equally clear that it is precisely "the witness of the Spirit" in individuals that confirms Christian doctrine. Certainly, those activities which Chauncy, Edwards, and other critics of the more overt manifestations of revival portrayed as the causes of enthusiasm were the very things that the Wesleys saw as indispensable to the task of spreading "scriptural holiness." These especially included small, quasi-public, lay-led groups, hymn singing, and extended periods of contemplative prayer, although Wesley sought to curb undisciplined enthusiasm in these settings by giving his preachers, class leaders, and the societies and bands strict rules for behavior and doctrine.

If Wesley shared in the concern over unregulated enthusiasm, he identified another, perhaps even more dangerous, religious possibility that he wished his followers to avoid: that of indifference. He firmly believed that the substitution of the outward trappings of religion for the heart of Christian piety was the enemy of all true Christian experience. In his writings and sermons John Wesley sought a middle course between these two extremes: between "mere formality" on the one hand and "the wildness of enthusiasm" on the other. While Methodist piety was always to be heartfelt and witnessed to by manifestations of the Spirit, it was to be neither unstable nor unpredictable, but rather as a "tree firmly rooted, not to be shaken by any tempest." Enthusiasm and indifference were, for Wesley, "danger on the right and on the left," and it is because of the continuous attempt to walk the line between them in the spiritual life that Wesley has been famously characterized as a "reasonable enthusiast."

Throughout the years that followed Wesley's death, even fellow Methodists began to criticize the tendency of their co-religionists to extravagance in their responses to the Spirit, especially in the context of public worship. In his *Methodist Error; or, Friendly Christian advice to those Methodists who indulge in extravagant emotions and bodily exercises* (1814), the early nineteenth-century theologian Richard Watson admitted that while such activities as shouting may be acceptable in small meetings, during contemplative prayer, and in the process of Christian conversion, they have no place in services of worship in church. He pointed to a continuing controversy within Methodism between those who viewed themselves as more "respectable" and "sober and steady," and the "common folk" who were prone to zealousness in expressing "the most heedless emotion" in worship. (Watson identified the latter as those of the lower classes, the "illiterate Blacks," and those with "uninformed minds.") This ongoing debate between, as one commentator describes them, Methodist "shouters" and Methodist "formalists" would run as a thread through the whole of the nineteenth century, as the influence of the camp meetings on the one hand, and the increasing desire for respectability, on the other, would shape the piety of large portions of the Methodist movement.

WESLEY AND THE RELIGIOUS AFFECTIONS

While John Wesley and his early followers were suspicious of enthusiasm, at the same time they were clear that religion must penetrate the whole person and must direct every thought and action. Even before Aldersgate, Wesley's exposure to rationalist empiricism convinced him of the responsive nature of the human affections (to the things we love and desire most deeply), and this contributed to his growing sense of needing to "feel" the love of God. Most scholars of Methodism would agree that the Aldersgate experience was the moment during which Wesley's intellectual conviction about the need for God's grace to penetrate every human faculty became a reality in his own life. As he reflected on both his belief in and his experience of the fully engaged response of mind, will, and heart to the love of God, Wesley began to frame a mature model of Methodist "heart religion," and in this the religious affections played a key role.

The kind of affective religion that Wesley seeks, then, cannot be known through logical reasoning, but only through what Wesley refers to as "a kind of intuition." He most often describes this as the experience of a "heavenly, healing light" that breaks in upon the soul, and a "feeling that the love of God has been showered on the human heart." As people become convinced through these experiences of God's pardoning love for them, they are prodded to exercise their affections, gradually shaping them into "holy tempers," or enduring dispositions to love. While all this happens as an act of the Spirit that can never be coerced, in Wesley's vision of heart religion the means of grace were central. As believers participated in spiritual disciplines, the Lord's Supper, the love-feast, and Bible reading, they exposed themselves to the empowering presence of the Spirit and as a result their affections were shaped and strengthened into Christ-likeness. As this took place they were gradually freed to love both God and neighbor fully.

The religious affections, then, are an alternative way of knowing for John Wesley. If it was true, as his philosophical mentors following John Locke were fond of saying, that there was "no idea in the mind that is not first in the senses," then the question of how the believer "knows" the love of God was something of a problem. Our ordinary senses could lead us to knowledge in the material world, but in order to have knowledge of God there must be "spiritual senses." It is the religious affections, those things in the human heart that respond to the love of God, that he believes to be these "spiritual senses." What warms the heart so "strangely" (or spiritually) is an encounter with God that convinces a person at the core of his or her being that, in the words of one of Charles's hymns, "Thy nature and Thy name is Love."

Certainly the best description of Wesleyan spirituality is that it is a spirituality of love. Wesley remained constant in his conviction that love should rule over every aspect of the Christian life:

Let love not visit you as a transient guest, but be the constant temper of our soul. See that your heart be filled at all times, and on all occasions, with real, undissembled benevolence; not to those only that love you, but every soul of man . . . Be not straightened or limited in your affection . . . but let it embrace every child of man. Everyone that is born of a woman has a claim on your good will.

This is clearly a description of a Christ-like character, and it is growth toward the "full stature of Christ" that he sees as the key to responding to God and human beings with unfailing love. Like Thomas à Kempis before him, Wesley never believed that to be an imitator of Christ meant that Christians must duplicate the actions of Jesus Christ, but rather that they be filled with Christ-like love for all and allow that love to shape the whole of life.

The last verse of CHPM 508 for use during the celebration of the love-feast makes the point that love is the beginning and end of Methodist spirituality:

> Hence may all our actions flow;
> Love the proof that Christ we know;
> Mutual love the token be,
> Lord, that we belong to thee:
> Love, thine image love impart
> Stamp it on our face and heart!
> Only love to us be given –
> Lord, we ask no other heaven.

If love is at the center of Methodist piety, other characteristics of mind, heart, and action radiate out from that center in concentric circles. As he wrote in the sermon *On Zeal*:

In a Christian believer *love* sits upon the throne which is erected in the inmost soul; namely, love of God and man, which fills the whole heart, and reigns without a rival. In a circle near the throne are all *holy tempers*; longsuffering, gentleness, meekness, fidelity, temperance; and any other were comprised in "the mind which was in Christ Jesus." In an exterior circle are all *the works of mercy*, whether to the souls or bodies of men. By these we exercise all holy tempers; by these we continually improve them, so that all these are real *means of grace*, although this is not commonly adverted to. Next to these are those that are usually termed *works of piety*; reading and hearing the Word, public, family, private prayer, receiving the Lord's Supper, fasting, or abstinence. Lastly, that his followers may the more effectually provoke one another to love, holy tempers, and good works, our blessed Lord has united them together in one – the *Church* (emphases in original).

This focus on love in Methodist spirituality has had important practical consequences for mission and for ecumenical and interfaith relations. John Wesley argued for the crossing of boundaries on the basis of love in the text he used for his sermon *Catholic Spirit*, "if your heart be right with my heart," and Methodists in all generations have tended to recognize and value the spiritual paths chosen by others whose lives are centered on God's love. Thus, for example, Methodist missions in India were greatly aided in the beginning of their work by the correspondence between the bhakti ("love-devotion") thread in Indian thought and the emphasis on the mutual love between God and human beings that is so prevalent in Charles Wesley's hymns. As one commentator says, "It is not accidental that probably still the finest translation of those Hindu poems of passion for God is the pioneering work in *Hymns of the Avatars* published in 1929 by the Methodist J. S. M. Hooper." The numbers of Methodists who have been involved in interfaith and ecumenical work is explained not only by Methodist doctrinal emphases, but by immersion in a particular kind of devotion that is rooted in love.

THE HALLMARKS OF WESLEYAN PIETY

The strength of Methodist spirituality lies both in the stability of this central core of love and in its essential adaptability to changing times and circumstances. This adaptability is always set, however, within a particular set of Methodist devotional parameters, and Wesleyan piety can be said to have a number of persistent features that tie Methodists around the globe to their origins in John Wesley's devotional insight. Seven characteristics, all of which have their roots in the writings of John and Charles Wesley, may be seen to be at the core of Methodist piety. In any given period, or in any given local situation, one or more of these may be downplayed and others emphasized. But none is ever completely absent from a piety that identifies itself as Methodist.

Biblical spirituality

It may seem self-evident to say that one of the hallmarks of Methodist spirituality is that it is biblical; to one extent or another, all Christian piety can be described in this way. In this sense Rule 26 of Wesley's *Rules* for the Methodist societies is in accordance with the Christian tradition: Methodists are to engage in "searching the scripture." But the way in which Methodists ground their spiritual life in the Bible has a particular character, and certain texts have had special prominence in Wesleyan piety. Many of Charles Wesley's hymns (and those of other Methodist hymn writers) are paraphrases of or expansions on biblical verses, and the combination of singing, reading, and meditating on the scriptures, and hearing them proclaimed in public meetings, gives the Bible a peculiarly penetrative power in the Methodist imagination.

Certainly those biblical texts that speak of the love of God in Christ have a special place in the spiritual life of Methodists everywhere. But Methodists have also seemed to be able to take quite different texts and to find in them the same message: that at the center of all things is the redemptive love of God for every person. Take, for example, Charles Wesley's hymn on the text from Genesis that describes Jacob wrestling with the angel (Genesis 32:24–32). In this hymn, in the original version fourteen verses long, Charles casts the singer in the role of Jacob, who speaks to the one wrestled with as a "Traveller unknown":

> Come O thou Traveller unknown,
> Whom still I hold, but cannot see!
> My company before is gone,
> And I am left alone with thee;
> With thee all night I mean to stay,
> And wrestle till the break of day.
>
> I need not tell thee who I am
> My misery or sin declare;
> Thyself hast called me by my name,
> Look on thy hands, and read it there.
> But who, I ask thee, who art Thou?
> Tell me thy name, and tell me now.
>
> In vain thou strugglest to get free,
> I never will unloose my hold!
> Art thou the Man that died for me?
> The secret of thy love unfold:
> Wrestling, I will not let thee go
> Till I thy Name, thy Nature know.

Here the singer, like Jacob, demands a blessing, but also demands to know the name and the nature of the contender. It is here that the hymn diverges from the Genesis text; the singer asks the contender to speak, and to "tell me if thy Name is Love."

> Yield to me now – for I am weak;
> But confident in self-despair!
>   Speak to my heart, in blessings speak,
> Be conquer'd by my instant prayer:
> Speak, or thou never hence shalt move,
> And tell me if thy Name is LOVE.

It is only then that we learn the identity of the one with whom the singer wrestles.

> 'Tis Love! 'tis Love! Thou diedst for me:
> I hear thy whisper in my heart!
>   The morning breaks, the shadows flee,
> Pure, Universal love thou art:
> To me, to all, thy bowels move –
> Thy Nature and thy Name, is Love.

This kind of imaginative, Christological reading of the Old Testament text, which can be alarming to those of more literalist tendencies, is common in Wesleyan spirituality. The Bible is not read so much for information about "what really happened," but as a treasury of spiritual insight to be plundered by those to whom it has been given. So it is not at all seen as inappropriate that the journey taken by Jacob in wrestling with the angel in Genesis is here reinterpreted as the journey of the Christian soul toward the recognition of Christ's redeeming love for all people.

In order to look to the Bible for spiritual insight in this way, Wesleyans have had to know the Bible, and we have many, many accounts of men, women, and children whose familiarity with the Bible is remarkable. In the nineteenth century, laywoman Jane Treffrey was reported to have always knelt while reading her Bible, and by the end of her life had read it through twenty times over in this manner. She may have had Charles Wesley's hymn in mind:

> When quiet in my house I sit,
> Thy Book be my companion still,
> My Joy Thy sayings to repeat,
> Talk o'er the records of Thy will,
> And search the oracles divine,
> Till every heartfelt word be mine.

For Methodists, the idea that the Bible is not primarily the church's book, nor the clergy's book, but is *their* book, is extraordinarily strong. The superabundance of Methodist "Bible study" materials, for both individual and group use, is testimony to the place of the Christian scriptures in the shaping of Wesleyan piety. No major Methodist gathering would be seen to be complete without the incorporation of a period of Bible study of some sort into the proceedings.

Prayerful spirituality

At the center of Wesley's vision for the disciplined spiritual life was prayer. "Prayer," he wrote, was "the grand means of drawing near to God"; the other means of grace are only useful insofar as they "are mixed with or prepare us for this." There is no single entry in Wesley's diary where he does not mention having prayed, usually several times in the day; the entry for Wednesday, May 24, 1786 is typical:

4 [am]. Prayed; Matthew 13:3 etc., Select Society; journal. 8. Tea, religious talk; prayer. 9. Journal; necessary talk (religious); at Mrs. B—'s; prayer. 10. sins! Letters. 12. Walked. 1:15. Dinner; Magazine. 3. Read notes; R. W.; letter; prayed; 2 Corinthians 5:1, etc.! supper, religious talk; prayer. 9.30.

Often this prayer was indeed meditation on texts from scripture, in this case morning prayer centered on Matthew 13:3 and prayer in the evening on 2 Corinthians 5:1. Wesley's early study of Greek patristic writers gave him a sense of the ascetic ideal, and he often speaks of praying in solitude. But equally often we find references to his practice of praying in company with others, and one can imagine the company gathered with Wesley at eight o'clock on the morning described above taking tea together, engaging in "religious talk," and saying their prayers.

As far as can be gleaned from their journals, the early Methodists, while not as "Methodical" as the Wesleys, spent the first hour each day engaged in private prayer. One such is Henry Longden writing in 1778:

I determined to divide each day into portions that one positive duty might not interfere with another and than nothing of importance might be neglected. Accordingly, I rose at five and spent an hour with God. From six to seven I devoted to business allowing myself frequently a few minutes for secret prayer.

Similarly, the *Memoir* of the life of Jane Treffry, whom we have already met reading her Bible while kneeling, describes her own practice of daily prayer:

It was her practice, first to renew her covenant with God, with great solemnity, and then after having referred to the ordinary topics of thanksgiving and intercession in a very extensive and minute manner, for the members of her own family, ministers, especially those in whom she had recently noticed anything which she judged inconsistent with the sacred office, particular places and Christian Societies, etc., etc. Into all these and many other subjects, she went with all possible minuteness, mentioned the name, described the state and confessed the sins of each, and upon each implored suitable blessings.

The Obituaries in the *Arminian Magazine* (and later in the *Methodist Magazine*) stressed the centrality of a prayerful relationship with God as the mainstay of the Christian life. In these memorials, the deceased is eulogized not only for diligence in works of mercy, but for diligence in prayer, and often the prayers said in the last days of life are transcribed and reported.

The importance of assenting fully to whatever one prays was clearly part of John and Charles Wesley's spiritual heritage. The story is told of his mother Susanna refusing to say with her husband the prayers appointed in the Prayer Book for the Protestant King William of Orange (she had remained loyal to the exiled Catholic King James), and on one occasion even separating from her husband on this account. The goal of all Methodist prayer is that it be "sincere" and "heartfelt," with the expectation that the words and intentions will move from the lips into the heart and there become established, shaping holy dispositions.

Prayer is seen in Wesleyan spirituality to be a truly egalitarian activity; neither learning nor status is considered necessary for one to be powerful in prayer. Indeed, it is often those poorest in the material things of this world that have the riches of prayer entrusted to them. As the nineteenth-century Irish Methodist writer William Arthur says in his widely influential *The Tongue of Fire* (1856):

The gifts of prayer are part of the work and prerogative of the Holy Ghost . . . in no form is the tongue of fire more impressive, more calculated to convince men that a power above nature is working than when poor men, who could no more preach than they could fly, and could not suitably frame a paragraph on any secular topic, lift up a reverent voice among a few fellow Christians, and in strains of earnest trust, perhaps of glorious emotion, and even of sublime conception of things divine, plead in prayer with their Redeemer.

Within the democratic social milieu of the class and band meetings, the gifts of prayer were shared equally among members. Pious conversation and godly admonition, the needs of members and the needs of the world, the pricking of the conscience, and the thanksgiving for God's blessings received all fed into prayer in these gatherings.

Joyful and optimistic spirituality

If Methodist piety is a heart-felt piety, then the character of much of the experience is one of joy and optimism. A Methodist, John Wesley said, is "happy in God, yea, always happy." In his description of a meeting of the Fetter Lane society at which a number of former members of the Holy Club were present, Wesley recalls an experience of this kind of religious ecstasy:

About three in the morning, as we were continuing instant in prayer, the power of God came mightily upon us, insomuch as *many cried out for exceeding joy*, and *many fell to the ground*. As soon as we were recovered from shock and amazement at the presence of his majesty, we broke out with one voice, "We praise thee, O God, and we acknowledge thee to be the Lord" (our emphases).

The wellspring of this persistent joy is the intense awareness of divine providence, the experience of saving grace, and the freedom of new life in Christ. Charles Wesley's hymns return over and over again to the happiness of the Christian believer:

> Since the Son hath made me free,
> Let me taste my liberty;
> Thee behold with open face,
> Triumph in thy saving grace,
> Thy great will delight to prove,
> Glory in thy perfect love.

Persons reconciled in Jesus must, he affirms in the next verse, expect to experience all the gifts of grace, "All the joy, and peace, and power, / All my Saviour asks above / All the life and heaven of love."

When John Wesley himself speaks of character of Methodist "heart religion," he too often refers to this joyful response to the Gospel. In a mature reflection on the kind of piety he envisions for his followers, he says:

This is the religion we long to see established in the world, a religion of love and joy and peace, having *its seat in the heart*, in the inmost soul, but ever showing itself by its fruits, continually springing forth, not only in all innocence . . . but likewise in every kind of beneficence, spreading virtue and happiness all around it.

Ironically this joyful and optimistic form of piety was rooted in close attention to the reality of sin and the necessity of penitence. This is not the "dark night of the soul" of the medieval mystics but rather part of a continual cycle of contrition and joy that Wesley may well have absorbed from reading both Richard Hooker and William Law. It is a powerful demonstration of God's love: "It is a consequence of our knowing God loves us, that we love him, and love our neighbors as ourselves . . . this is religion, and this is happiness, the happiness for which we were created." This joyful love is likened to the love between parents and children, and John Wesley preached on the text of Luke 12:7 ("we are his children") no less than forty-five times.

There is strong evidence that ordinary Methodists often experienced this kind of joy in their spiritual lives. For example, in 1854 a Mrs. John Bangs had responded to Methodist preaching and joined a Methodist class meeting in New York City. It is reported in her obituary in the *Christian Advocate and Journal* that she "continued to seek, and one Sabbath she requested to join the Class as a seeker and was admitted. After returning home her distress of mind increased until the next morning, when while engaged in prayer and reading the Scriptures, her soul was brought into unspeakable enjoyment in believing." Over and over in biographies, autobiographies, journals, and diaries we find Methodists striving to describe that "cheerful piety, habitual pleasure in devotion and consequent settled self-enjoyment,"

which John Wesley maintained to be "the inheritance of the true Christian."
While Wesleyans might lament their sins and their lack of progress toward
true holiness, there appears to be no persistent "dark night of the soul" in
Methodist piety. Because God's unfailing grace and love are always felt to
be out ahead of believers, pulling them forward into God's future, there is
a kind of native optimism in Methodist spirituality. Methodist Christians
like Grace Murray, later Grace Bennet (1716–1803), built their lives on this
kind of piety. She left this dying testimony:

> I would have no encomiums passed on me; I AM A SINNER, SAVED FREELY BY
> GRACE: Grace, divine grace, is worthy to have all the glory . . . Some people I have
> heard speak much of our being faithful to the grace of God; as if they rested much
> on their own faithfulness: I never could bear this; it is GOD'S FAITHFULNESS to
> his own word of promise, that is my only security for salvation.

In the American context, with its persistent emphasis on productivity and
expansion, this deep Wesleyan optimism fueled a conviction that any situation could be transformed into an opportunity for growth and transformation. As Methodism moved through the nineteenth and into the twentieth
century, this optimistic spirituality undergirded all the various social movements in which Methodists became involved: abolition, women's suffrage,
temperance, and labor reform. Methodists in every time and place have
been empowered by this optimistic spirituality, and have been fully convinced that, in seeking to transform the world, they are contributing to the
mission of God to renew and reconcile all things.

Pragmatic spirituality

There was nothing considered so "crass" or "worldly" that it fell outside the
scope of Methodist spirituality. Wesley wrote about everything, from the
use of money to the advisability of drinking tea to the employment of what
would later be called electro-shock therapy. The question "How should we
pray?" was always intertwined with the question "What are we to *do?*" In
Hymn 515 in the *CHPM*, Charles Wesley asks this central question directly:

> Holy Lamb, who thee confess.
> Followers of thy holiness,
> Thee they ever keep in view,
> Ever ask, "What shall we do?"

Wesley's was a spirituality of overall stewardship, and Methodists have
often been convinced that deeds of mercy rank above deeds of piety. The
Methodist lives in the understanding that to do good (and conversely to

do no harm) is as pleasing to God as prayer and worship. This kind of embodied discipleship can be attempted irrespective of one's strength of belief or depth of experience: the beginner gains knowledge of God and the ways of God by attending to the small things in life, in decisions made about the spending of time, effort, money, and attention.

The *General Rules for the United Society* (fully set out on pp. 122–3) enshrine this pragmatic tendency in early Methodism: Rules 6 and 7 warn members against the "buying and selling of goods that have not paid the duty" and against "the giving or taking things on usury – that is unlawful interest"; Rule 15 makes it clear that no member of a Methodist society should engage in "borrowing without the probability of paying." In these early days at least, failure to meet these standards was not simply viewed as "conduct unbecoming of a Methodist," but more clearly as an impediment to spiritual progress. In commending the *Rules* to Methodists, Wesley was clear that "The walking herein is essentially necessary, as to the continuance of that faith towards everlasting salvation." For the very same reasons, Methodists were enjoined to avoid extravagance; John Wesley's Rules 10 and 20 for the Methodist societies state that members were not to put on any "gold and costly apparel" and were "to live by all possible diligence and frugality."

The spiritual significance of the stewardship of resources can be seen in Wesley's advice on the use of money. He says that money in the hands of God's children is

food for the hungry, drink for the thirsty, raiment for the naked. It gives to the traveller and the stranger where to lay his head. By it we may supply the place of a husband to the widow, and of a father to the fatherless; we may be a defence for the oppressed, a means of health to the sick. It gives ease to them that are in pain. It may be as eyes to the blind, a set to the lame; yea, a lifter up from the gates of death.

This is a deeply sacramental view of the use of one's possessions, carrying with it the sense that anything in the material creation has the potential to be a vehicle for the loving presence of God.

This is perhaps why Methodists have so often used physical objects to call to mind higher things and to shape dispositions toward holiness. For example, John Wesley's deathbed words were reported to have been: "The best of all is – God is with us!" and quite soon the Staffordshire potters (among whom Methodism had taken root strongly in the early days of the movement) were making teapots, plaques, and bowls with this phrase emblazoned on them, and Methodist homes on both sides of the Atlantic used these as decorative reminders of the spirit of their founder. This tendency toward "pious materialism" has continued throughout Methodist history, with the proliferation of decorative religious items in Victorian homes, and later the ubiquitous presence of Warner Salman's "Head of Christ" and Dürer's "Praying Hands" in Methodist domestic design.

At its worst, this pragmatic streak in Wesleyan spirituality has the capacity to turn into heavy-handed moralism or asceticism, with abstinence practiced for its own sake rather than as a vehicle for "spreading the love of God abroad." Whenever attention to the use (or non-use) of things has become viewed as simply a mark of holiness rather than as an exercise in "practical divinity," Methodists have loosened their attachment to their Wesleyan spiritual roots.

Social spirituality

Much of the potency of the Methodist spiritual path in its early days came from the fact that it rested within a protective subculture that quickly became an alternative both to the old system of patriarchial dependency and to the isolation of urban life in the new cities and industrialized villages. Classes and bands, society meetings, and family prayer all contributed to a network of relationships of mutual care and interdependency. While small religious meetings were not invented by Methodism, they were a central and persistent feature of Methodist culture for several generations, and helped to shape a deeply rooted understanding of the communal context of Christian spirituality.

John Wesley's conviction that there was, as he put it, "no holiness but social holiness" was established early in his life. While a Fellow at Oxford, he had read newly published books by William Law (1686–1761): *On Christian Perfection* (1726) and *A Serious Call to the Devout and Holy Life* (1729). Both these works helped to shape his spirituality and his sense of the higher Christian calling. In 1732, Wesley even traveled to visit Law, who introduced him to the work of the medieval mystics that would inform much of his devotional theology. But eventually they would part company over one central point: the emphasis Law placed on the "solitary" life as the model for all true Christian piety. As Charles Wesley put it, Methodists were

> Not in the dark monastic cell,
> By vows and grates confined.
> Freely ourselves to all we give,
> Constrained by Jesu's love to live
> The servants of mankind.

In the system of classes and bands, the Wesleys' commitment to "social holiness" was given visible form. Here people gained not only a Christian education, but a devotional family in which they could develop a strong sense of their value as persons. In the Methodist Society the spiritual and economic needs of members were looked upon as equally important as their spiritual needs, and people worked together toward the creation of a new social fabric of mutual care.

Certainly each believer had a personal responsibility for his or her own spiritual life. But always there would be mutual encouragement on the journey toward holiness, and mutual admonition when impediments to holiness were perceived. Each Methodist is considered in some way accountable for the spiritual lives of others, whether these are friends, family, or fellow members of the congregation. Rule 18 of the *Rules for the Methodist Societies* admonishes members to be diligent in "instructing, reproving, or exhorting all we have any intercourse with."

The spiritual power of a common voice expressing love and devotion is often expressed in Charles Wesley's hymns. In one hymn for the love-feast, Methodists are described as "partners of a glorious hope," and are enjoined to "lift your hearts and voices up, / Jointly let us rise, and sing / Christ our Prophet, Priest, and King." Somehow, devotional deficits in any one individual are compensated for by the faith and piety of the whole company of believers.

Disciplined spirituality

John Wesley himself has been described as a man of "almost ferociously disciplined personality and character," and in his own life modeled this discipline throughout the course of his ministry. He is estimated to have preached 45,000 sermons and traveled more than 250,000 miles, often in extraordinarily difficult conditions. Until the end of his long life he rose early, fasted regularly, and prayed ceaselessly. In Oxford, he and his brother gathered around them people equally convinced that the Christian path was a narrow one, and the Oxford Holy Club can be characterized, first and foremost, as a society for mutual encouragement in living out the disciplined Christian life. That sense of the necessity of discipline in the quest for spiritual growth has pervaded the Methodist movement to the present day.

Several of the classical spiritual disciplines were seen to be of particular usefulness in Wesleyan piety. Fasting and other exercises in abstaining from food and drink were heartily commended by Wesley and other early

Methodists. In Rule 27 of the *Rules for the Methodist Societies*, John Wesley enjoined members to fast "according to the practice of the early church from waking to mid afternoon"; at the same time he instituted a "public fast in the first Friday after Michaelmas and every other regular quarter-day" among his followers, and these dates were announced on most circuit plans, even though the practice was gradually abandoned. In the *Sunday Service for the Methodists in North America*, John Wesley commends fasting "all Fridays in the Year, except Christmas Day," and describes those who are overly fond of alcohol in the harshest possible terms: "an enemy of your country," "an enemy of God," a "beast" fit for "every work of the Devil." Most early Methodists saw fasting as a joy, however. Hannah Ball, the founder of the first Methodist Sunday school, recording a fast day in November 1769, says "This is a fast-day to my body, but a feast-day for my soul," and she reports feeling an "unusual freedom of spirit and communion with God."

Among the most persistent spiritual disciplines among Methodists has been the keeping of journals and diaries. In every period of Methodist history, men, women, and children have tracked their progress toward holiness by writing regularly and then meditating on their entries. These journals were not simply reports of how each day was passed, but were extensive works of devotional prose: the journal of Mary Lyth of York, although incomplete, still comprises twenty large volumes. John Gladwell, a mid-nineteenth-century English Methodist, treats his journal as a conversation partner, much as he would a member of his class or band meeting:

August 21st, 1821: When I look upon the day that is past, I see that I have not glorified God in all that I said and did, so much as I might have done; and when I look forward, I think the same more consistently; but how strange is this still desiring, and never attaining! O Lord, help me to resolve in thy strength; for vain is the help of man!

23rd: To-day I am found still complaining. The world takes up too much of my attention; and I am often unnecessarily engaged in trifling conversation, which is injurious to my advancement in the divine life. Lord, "to whom shall I go but unto thee? thou hast the words of eternal life." O do thou take me unto thy fold! Did not my redeemer suffer for me? Did he not rise again? And is he not pleading my cause above? O yes! Then, Lord, I come to thee: help me to do it in an acceptable manner.

This type of entry, which has the quality of a prayerful dialogue with God, is reduplicated in the first-person writing of Methodists around the globe. Because of the concern of Wesleyan leaders for extending the benefits of education to all classes of people, the keeping of journals and diaries became a means of combining religious instruction with exercises in reading and writing, thus spreading the discipline widely among Methodists. After a period of decline in the middle of the twentieth century, journal- and diary-keeping has recently experienced something of a revival, especially among American Methodists.

More recently, other kinds of disciplines have been important to Methodists. The Upper Room, based in Nashville, Tennessee, publishes an extensive range of materials for the use of those wishing to reclaim the classical spiritual disciplines. On the local level, such things as labyrinth walks, extended periods of meditation on Biblical texts, and Lenten fasts are finding their place in the devotional lives of Methodist people around the world.

Perfectionist spirituality

The same writers (Thomas à Kempis, William Law, and Jeremy Taylor) who convinced the young John Wesley that he should not be satisfied with being "half a Christian" also convinced him that to give the whole heart to God and to be perfected in love was not only a possibility, but should be the quest of every true Christian believer. This is clear as early as 1733 in a sermon entitled *The Circumcision of the Heart*. Circumcision of the heart, Wesley says, is "that habitual disposition of soul which in the Sacred Writings is termed 'holiness,' and which directly implies the being cleansed from sin, 'from all filthiness both of flesh and spirit' . . . the being 'so renewed in the image of our mind' as to be 'perfect, even as our Father in heaven is perfect.'" Six years later he elaborates this idea of being "perfected in love" in his treatise *The Character of a Methodist*:

A Methodist is one who loves the Lord his God with all his heart . . . soul . . . mind . . . and strength . . . Perfect love having now cast out all fear, he rejoices evermore. And loving God, he "loves his neighbor as himself," he loves every man as his own soul . . . All the talents he has, he constantly employs according to his Master's will . . . he thinks, speaks, and acts adorning the doctrine of God our Savior in all things.

We have seen that Wesley taught that the Christian cannot be perfect in knowledge or be free from infirmities and weakness. But the Christian can be perfect in love and charity and, as such, can reach a state in which no intentional sin is committed. "If we walk in the light," Wesley says, "we are children of the light . . . It remains then that Christians are saved in this world from all sin, from all unrighteousness; that they are now in such a sense perfect, as not to commit sin, and to be freed from evil thoughts and evil tempers." When one is in a state of Christian perfection, one loves God with the whole heart, mind and strength, and there is no temper in the soul which is contrary to love. For Wesley, to deny this possibility would be to deny the sufficiency of God's empowering grace, to make the power of sin greater than that of grace. But, for Wesley, even this kind of perfection was not to be understood as the ultimate goal of the Christian spiritual life. He admonished his followers: "Yea, and when ye have attained a measure of perfect love . . . think not of resting there! That is impossible. You cannot stand still; you must either rise or fall."

Much of this perfectionist strain in Methodism has a distinctly eschatological character. While Methodists may strive for perfection in this life, for most, true holiness will be achieved only after death. Charles Wesley puts this prayer in the mouths of Methodist hymn singers:

> Rising to sing my Saviour's praise,
> Thee may I publish all day long,
> And let Thy precious word of grace
> Flow from my heart, and fill my tongue,
> Fill all my life with purest love,
> And join me to Thy church above.

In John Wesley's model of the relationship between the striving for holiness in this life and its perfection in the life to come, all human love is likened to a river, which will in time flow homeward into the endless ocean of God's eternal love. "The sea," Wesley wrote, "is an excellent figure of the fullness of God, and that of the blessed Spirit. For as the rivers all return into the sea, so the bodies, the souls, and the good works of the righteous return into God to live there in [God's] eternal repose."

This assurance never exempts Methodists from striving for true holiness; but it does offer some confidence that, even if the goal is not reached in any given lifetime, God will absorb and perfect the striving.

The various structures of Wesleyan Methodism were intended as aids to those who were pressing toward perfection and Charles Wesley taught them to sing:

> Christ from whom all blessings flow,
> Perfecting the saints below,
> Hear us, who thy nature share,
> Who thy mystic body are.
>
> Join us in one spirit join,
> Let us still receive of thine;
> Still for more on thee we call,
> Thou who fillest all in all.

In the classes and bands, members encouraged one another so that all might partake of sanctification, and evidence of holiness was examined and evaluated. Had one become truly a "cheerful and uncoerced servant of heavenly tempers, and still more the adoring and free servant of the Sovereign Will"? Does one "shrink from the touch of sin which sometimes approaches to pain"? Revival meetings also tended to hope for this result, and Wesley himself credited a revival at Otley in 1763 for increasing throughout the Methodist societies "the number of those people who believed they were saved from sin." This event precipitated the publication in 1766 of his *Farther Thoughts on Christian Perfection.*

If it was possible to live a life so filled with the love of God that intentional sin has no place in it, then the reality of sin needed to be addressed, not only theologically, but experientially. In some spiritual traditions, an overconcern with sinfulness turns rather dour and dark; but this is not the case in Wesleyan spirituality. The possibility of sanctification kept this tendency at bay. Certainly Methodists were encouraged to engage in persistent examination of conscience:

> If to the right or left I stray
> That moment, Lord, reprove.
> And let me weep my life away,
> For having grieved Thy love.
>
> Give me to feel an idle thought
> As actual wickedness,
> And mourn for the minutest fault
> In exquisite distress.

But as important as this process is, it is never regarded as an end in itself, either as a method for breaking the human will or for impressing on people that they are, in John Calvin's words, "worms five feet tall." It was rather a necessary step in the soul's progress toward holiness, with the love of God always drawing the believer toward Christ-likeness.

As one would expect, the more Calvinist Methodists such as George Whitefield tended to believe that human perfection of any sort was an abominable notion, and even within Methodism this spiritual quest for "entire sanctification" has been the subject of endless debate. The continual controversy clearly weighed on John Wesley's mind. In 1768 he wrote to his brother Charles, saying:

I think it is high time that you and I, at least, should come to a point. Shall we go on asserting perfection against all the world? Or shall we let the matter drop? We really must do one or the other, and, I apprehend, the sooner the better. What shall we jointly and explicitly maintain concerning the nature [of holiness], the time (now or by and by?), and the manner of it? instantaneous or not?

But they did not "let the matter drop," and as we have seen the assertion by Wesley at Whitefield's funeral that he and Whitefield had always "preached the same doctrine" led to a further divergence of the Wesleyans and Calvinist branches of Methodism. Equally troubling, however, were those Wesleyans who wished to give the extraordinary marks of instantaneous sanctification (dreams, visions, and ecstasies) a special status, over and above the marks of conversion, within the Methodist societies. The Wesleys were adamant that all were progressing toward holiness and that to create a "two-tier" Methodism was misguided and divisive.

These debates over sanctification were fully engaged when Methodism began to spread throughout America, and this ensured its importance in the New World. Memoirs of those who claimed to have been sanctified entirely, such as that of Thomas Rankin (1738–1810), were enormously popular in the colonies, and the graphic descriptions of experiences of instantaneous sanctification fueled the revivals that spread up and down the east coast of America in the 1770s and 1780s. As we shall see below, there would come a point at which the holiness strain in Methodism, rooted in Wesley and carried forward in the camp meeting revivals, would travel in its own direction in America, resulting in a division first between "Holiness" and "non-Holiness" Methodists, and eventually between Methodist and Holiness churches.

Was John Wesley really convinced that Christian believers could be wholly directed by "the humble, gentle, patient love of God, and our neighbour, ruling our tempers, words, and actions," and thus achieve entire sanctification or "Christian perfection"? Certainly he believed the journey toward sanctification is one to which all Christians are called, and was not to be considered an exceptional reality for Wesley. But clearly only very few individuals ever attained this kind of "Christ-likeness"; John Wesley never claimed to have reached the state of perfection himself, and certainly never attached it to his 1738 experience at Aldersgate Street. He did, however, report knowing of those who had reached the kind of Christian maturity in which love governed each thought and deed, and it was that possibility which fired the spiritual imaginations of many of the Wesleyan movement in the next century.

A DIVERGENT FORM OF METHODIST SPIRITUALITY

Nearly one hundred years after John Wesley's Aldersgate experience, a twenty-nine-year-old American woman underwent what she described as "entire consecration." Phoebe Worrall Palmer (1807–74), the daughter of a devout Methodist family in New York, had a public ministry which spanned the next thirty-seven years of her life, during which she wrote, lectured, preached, and organized a movement centered on the Methodist doctrine of sanctification. It would be difficult to find a nineteenth-century woman with wider and more persistent religious and social influence: she stands at the fountainhead of the numerous Holiness denominations, she shaped American higher education through her many contacts with college and university presidents, and she paved the way for the widening of opportunities for professional ministry for women. For our purposes, she has been described as the "missing link between Methodist and Pentecostal spirituality."

Phoebe Worrall seems to have been a precocious and pious child, and in 1827 married Walter Clark Palmer (1804–83), a physician who shared her attachment to the Methodist Church. They had six children, three of whom died in infancy. In 1837, Palmer began the Tuesday Meetings for the Promotion of Holiness in her home; these meetings were characterized by fervent prayer, scripture study, and witnessing to the work of the Spirit. Gradually an international network of Tuesday Meetings was established which would continue for sixty years; by 1886 at least 238 such meetings were being held around the globe. These meetings attracted a committed core of Methodist intellectuals, as well as leaders from a wide spectrum of American Protestantism. Palmer's own powerful intellect and charismatic presence made her not only a guiding light of the Tuesday Meetings, but a respected and much sought-after revival preacher.

Much of Palmer's influence came through her writing, and the *Way of Holiness*, first published in installments in 1842–3, sold nearly 25,000 copies in the first six years after its publication. Her spirituality centered on the universal availability of the promises of the Gospel and the desire of the Spirit to reclaim the whole person. Certainly in this emphasis Palmer retained the Wesleyan spiritual optimism and its pragmatism, and combined it with a very American sense of progressive possibility. She thought of the sacrificial life of the Christian as continually being "laid on the altar," and was never in doubt that God had made a covenant to accept that sacrifice. She herself had been convinced that her own sanctification had come only when she had detached herself from affection for husband and children in order to obey the Christian injunction to reserve her highest love for God. She writes of the singular love she felt on the day on which she experienced entire sanctification: "I am wholly thine! – Thou dost reign unrivaled in my heart! There is not a tie that binds me to earth; every tie has been severed, and now I am wholly, wholly thine." Because of this link between holiness and sacrifice, Palmer argued that the experience of sanctifying grace would never lead believers away from the world, but would rather lead them more deeply into it in ministries of social action. Palmer herself founded important organizations for mission to the poor and the sick.

The wider Holiness movement that rose up out of Palmer's work resulted in a number of Holiness churches, and eventually influenced the modern Pentecostal movement beginning in the early twentieth century. But, as one observer has said, "it would be difficult to identify any Protestant denomination of mid-nineteenth century America or Britain that did not feel her influence." This occurred through seminary education and Holiness camp meetings and conferences such as those in Vineland, New Jersey, and Keswick, England. Palmer's spirituality almost exactly matched the spirit of her age, with its essential optimism and progressivism, and her belief in the perfectability of human beings was ideally suited to rapidly industrializing nations. Most of these churches which trace their origins to Palmer's preaching would not call themselves Methodist, although all recognize their indebtedness to Wesleyan spirituality. The Pentecostal and Pilgrim Holiness churches, the Churches of the Nazarene, the Apostolic Faith Movement, the Four-Square Gospel Church, the Church of God (Anderson, Indiana) and the Church of God (Cleveland, Tennessee) are all churches within this wider Holiness tradition.

Belief in the possibility of sanctification, and of the demands of sanctification, also led Palmer's followers to an egalitarian stance with regard to ministries within the church. The denominations that arose from the work of Palmer and the mid-nineteenth-century "Holiness revival" consistently raised the status of the ministry of women to a central place in church life. Phoebe Palmer argued that God had from the church's very beginning blessed women with gifts of the Spirit and that the hastening of the Kingdom of God would depend on their efforts.

When the founder of our holy Christianity was about leaving his disciples to ascend to his Father, he commanded them to tarry at Jerusalem until endued with power from on high, And of whom was those company of disciples composed? . . . here were both male and female disciples . . . they are waiting from the promise of the Father.

The waiting disciples, men and women alike, received the promised gift of the Holy Spirit, and her confidence in this fact undergirded Palmer's belief in the worthiness of women both to preach and be ordained. But many "conscientious and sensitive Christian women," she knew, "have actually suffered more under the slowly crucifying process to which they have been subjected by men who bear the Christian name than many a martyr endured in passing through the flames." Palmer herself was not especially known for her advocacy of women's ordination, and was convinced from her own experience that combining marriage, motherhood, and Christian work was possible.

In Palmer's work and preaching we see how a single emphasis within Wesleyan spirituality, in this case the deep inclination toward Christian perfection, can be taken up and made the center of a new spiritual track. As we have seen, this was the time of an increasing desire for respectability among British and American Methodists, and many were appalled by the emotional excesses of Holiness revivals. While they acknowledged that sanctification was a part of their own doctrinal inheritance, they were inclined to leave it in a subordinate place in their own piety. One might ask what the current shape of Methodism might have been if it had been able to contain Palmer's Holiness emphasis within its own boundaries.

CONCLUSION

The various strands in Methodist spirituality that we have highlighted, when held in a creative tension with one another, have given it an extraordinary strength and resiliency, and over the course of its history Methodism has adapted to a wide variety of circumstances. But at its core it has been a remarkably stable spiritual tradition. Just as Methodists are a people who have tended to *think* about God in particular ways, they are also a people who have tended to *approach the active relationship* with that God in particular ways. This results in particular habits of prayer, particular devotional disciplines, and particular links between prayer and action. But the line between Methodist piety and other aspects of the tradition is never clear-cut. As one Methodist historian has said:

Some Methodists . . . have found in their tradition a source of precedents which have guided their participation in one or another specific project; others have reflected in their characteristic activities some enduring feature of Methodist institutional history; still others have found in the Wesleyan past a source of theological insight; and many others have borne, often unwittingly, the dispositional residues for their formation within local Methodist congregations.

The pragmatic strain in Methodist spirituality has meant that almost everything can be seen to have devotional implications: doctrine, money, church life, and history. In addition, Methodists carry with them a set of expectations about what kinds of spiritual experiences they might have: the expectation that one can have an experience of a kind of penetrating, saving grace, a loving presence of God that draws people toward holiness, the expectation that others are put into believers' lives to aid them in the journey, the expectation that the will of God can be known. All of these combine to form a particular kind of outlook and attitude toward the interior life.

If there is a single, brief description of Methodist spirituality, then, it is a disciplined commitment to a lifelong pursuit of holiness in the framework of mutual accountability. As one of Charles Wesley's hymns has it, Methodists are to be "Vessels, instruments of grace" and are to live out their lives, as Charles says, "Twixt the mount and multitude, / Doing or receiving good: / Glad to pray and labour on, / Till our earthly course is run."

We have seen that the mission statements of Methodist churches around the world reflect this spirituality.

CHAPTER 8

Methodist worship

The fervent, extempore praying at a revival meeting in the American Midwest, the formal dignity of a celebration of holy communion in North Yorkshire, the pregnant silence of a watch-night service in a township near Johannesburg, the spirit-filled singing of Afro-Caribbean Sunday worship in Port-au-Prince: to the casual observer, the only thing that links these diverse and distinctive forms of Christian common prayer is that in each case the congregation gathered identifies itself as "Methodist." Coming together for prayer in common has always been central to Methodist life, but like its polity, praxis, and theology, Methodist worship has been shaped by its history of controversy and by the various contexts in which it has established itself. While the identity and unity of some worldwide communions of churches are largely determined by the maintenance of standardized forms of liturgy (albeit often with local variations), Methodist unity tends to be expressed in other ways, and tolerates a wide variety of patterns of worship. This variety does, however, retain certain distinctive features that can be described as identifiably "Methodist."

This common liturgical thread is especially evident whenever a particular Methodist denomination sets out to develop official or semi-official service materials. Decisions made about which rites to include, about the shape and content of these rites, about such things as calendars, lectionaries, and hymns, and about the overarching questions of appropriate leadership for worship, are rooted in a number of different kinds of commitments. Certainly there is serious attention paid to the principles on which John Wesley and the other early Methodists shaped common prayer for the Methodist societies; but at the same time there is deep concern for the more local, indigenous patterns that have marked the Methodist worship of the particular people who will be using the services. In addition, Methodist involvement in ecumenical matters turns the eyes of those writing and revising services of worship toward the wider liturgical consensus, toward bilateral agreements, and toward the trajectories of national and international conversations. And there is always a desire to employ the artistic and literary gifts of those who respond creatively to the demands of the contemporary cultural context, and who seek new forms of expression for key biblical and theological motifs.

Some services used by contemporary Methodists, such as the Covenant Service used at the beginning of each new calendar year, are distinctively Methodist and can be traced back to the liturgical work of the Wesleys themselves. Many of these have been brought by Methodist churches as their distinctive contribution to the new service-books of united denom-inations such as the Church of South India. Other services (baptism and the Lord's Supper, for example) are common to all Christians, but are given a Methodist "slant" in their form and content. Others have been shaped by Methodist participation in ecumenical conversations, and by a willing-ness to find a compromise with dialogue partners in matters of worship by giving up some of their own liturgical distinctives for the sake of a wider Christian unity.

In many cases, however, Methodist worship has become "inculturated" to the social and ethnic context in which it finds itself. So, for example, worship in a given African-American Methodist Church may look more like worship in an African-American Baptist or Presbyterian Church than worship in an Anglo-Methodist Church. Sometimes Methodist worship absorbs features of the dominant *religious* culture of which it is a part: the worship of Methodists in Britain has stayed closer to its Church of England roots than has the worship of their American cousins; Methodist worship in the southern United States has taken on elements of Southern Baptist worship; Methodist worship in South America has been influenced by the prevailing Pentecostalist religious sensitivities. Some of this adaptation is simply a natural result of living in a particular culture; some is the result of a more deliberate missionary strategy. In either case, while we do find certain aspects of worship that can be identified as being within a "Methodist tradition," the story of Methodist worship is as complex and multifaceted as the story of Methodism itself.

WORSHIP IN EIGHTEENTH-CENTURY ENGLAND

It can certainly be argued that, had Church of England worship been meeting the spiritual needs of large numbers of people, the Methodist revival would never have taken hold as strongly as it did. At the most basic level, it was very difficult for many people to attend worship services in their parish churches because of insufficient seating. Much of this was the result of the rapid urbanization of English society which began in the middle of the century. By 1817, for example, the population of Manchester, in the north of England, had grown to 100,459 and yet there was accommodation in churches for only 14,850. Equally difficult was the situation in Marylebone, a London suburb, where there were 60,000 inhabitants in 1811 and seats in the parish church for only 900. In addition, most of the seating that did exist came at a cost: "pew rents" were almost invariably imposed and free seating in Anglican parish churches was scarce.

But, at a deeper level, to many people on the fringes of political, economic, or social power, Anglican worship was a part of the overall structure of the Establishment, and an extension and expression of privilege. Most ministers were appointed by noble families and chartered institutions (the universities, for example) that "held the living" within a given parish, and in order for clergy to rise within the ecclesiastical system, deference to their patrons was a necessity. The "liturgical spirituality" of eighteenth-century Anglicans (as well as eighteenth-century Presbyterians) was generally quite low, with many viewing attendance at services of Christian worship more as a pious duty or a means of maintaining necessary social structures than as food for the hungry soul. Sacramental piety also tended to be rather tepid. Many students of the period have noted the general neglect of the celebration of communion, and recent studies have determined that the Lord's Supper was held on average only three or four times per year in most Anglican parish churches. In Presbyterian churches the devotional focus tended to be on an individual's worthiness for receiving communion, and a great deal of attention was paid to the penitential preparation for the Supper during the "sacramental seasons" which immediately preceded the celebration of the sacrament. Baptism was normally a private event, with only the immediate family and godparents of the child present. The overall "temperature" of Christian worship in this period was also rather cool, with rational, erudite sermons and rites that made little appeal to the human emotions.

One can see, given the dominant liturgical culture, the ways in which Methodist worship in the early years met the desire of many people for a more heartfelt form of Christian worship, with fervent hymn singing, prayer, and preaching, and rites of baptism and the Lord's Supper that were treated seriously. Indeed, this has been the appeal of Methodist worship in every generation, especially among those who have felt the need to integrate heart, mind, and affect in the worship of God. The other integration found in Methodist worship that was only rarely made in the Christian worship of the eighteenth century was that between worship and the needs of the world. (One of the exceptions would have been the silent worship of the Society of Friends.) Indeed, collection for the poor as a part of Sunday services was one of the early Christian practices that Wesley revived in an age when it was largely neglected by the Church of England.

CHRISTIAN WORSHIP AS CONCEIVED BY THE WESLEYS

John and Charles Wesley were reared in a family that centered its life on the worship of the church. Their father Samuel would have had oversight over Sunday and daily worship, the festivals, and the pastoral rites of baptism, marriage, and burial in the parish of Epworth. The Wesley children would have learned to read from the Bible and probably would have known the words of the Book of Common Prayer by heart at an early age. Although the various theological parties within the church represented some diversity in ritual, a certain equilibrium had been reached and the virulent debates over worship that had marked the seventeenth century had largely disappeared.

While the Wesleys were not raised in a period of wholesale liturgical revision, they were part of a culture that was fascinated by "tinkering" with the church's official rites. Attempts to bring the services of public worship more nearly into conformity with scripture, with the practices of the ante-Nicene church, and with the subtle shifts in Anglican theology, were the pastime of many Church of England clergy and intellectuals. As a young man John Wesley himself had been concerned with restoring primitive Christian liturgical customs (he reports in his diary in 1736 that he had "revised the Common Prayer Book"), and his sojourn in Georgia allowed him to experiment with some of these revisions, although they were hardly well received by the local population. Although he was devoted to the shape and language of the Prayer Book rites, as the Methodist movement grew Wesley became increasingly convinced that as long as worship conformed to the principles of the faith, to Scripture, reason, and ecclesial tradition, variety in styles and patterns of worship was acceptable. It is probably safe to say that he would apply the same principle to worship that he applied to doctrine and religious opinion: "Everyone must follow the dictates of his own conscience in simplicity and godly sincerity. He must be fully persuaded in his own mind, and then act accordingly to the best light he has." Wesley's essential pragmatism also allowed him to judge worship by the degree to which it produced spiritual benefits in the worshiper: an increase in faith, in Christian insight, and in works of mercy.

Methodist worship in the early days of the movement took place in a variety of different settings. Wesley encouraged members of Methodist societies to worship on Sundays and feast days in their own parish churches, and to receive communion there regularly. In classes and bands and in select societies prayer in common occupied ordinary weekday meetings, and at quarterly meetings of circuits services of worship were particularly meaningful occasions. Special services, such as the love-feast, watch-nights, and the Covenant Service were distinctively Methodist forms of common prayer, and had enormous significance in the formation of Methodist identity.

As more and more adherents to Methodism saw the Methodist Society as their primary religious affiliation, however, Methodist worship on Sundays began to be both widely desired and widely practiced, not least at Wesley's own chapels, the Foundery and later the City Road Chapel. Because the "spread of Scriptural holiness throughout the land" was never to be hindered because of a lack of suitable buildings, preaching and other services of worship were regularly held in the open air, in private houses, and in public buildings of various kinds. But although the Wesleys strongly resisted the notion of local Methodist gatherings as "parishes," and preachers as "pastors," as the eighteenth century went on the principal worship experience for many Wesleyans was regular Sunday worship in designated Methodist buildings set apart for that purpose.

Even so, in Mr. Wesley's day, especially in the early period, the normal Methodist would have been a member of the Church of England, where she attended Sunday services, and where she was married, had her children baptized, and was buried. In addition, she attended meetings of the Methodist society one or more times a week where she would hear sermons and exhortations. She sang the hymns written by the Wesleys, using them both as private devotional aids and as a part of common worship in society meetings, class and band meetings and quarterly meetings of the circuit, and gathered with the community for special services, such as the Covenant Service, the love-feast, and the watch-night service.

REVISION OF THE BOOK OF COMMON PRAYER

The time would come when John Wesley himself would undertake the task of a more thorough revision of the Book of Common Prayer than he had attempted as a young man, and it is here finally that we see his liturgical instincts embodied in actual proposals for Christian public worship. As we have seen, the situation in America after the Revolution required singular measures in order to hold the Methodist societies there within the Wesleyan doctrinal framework. In 1784, John Wesley produced an abridgement of the 1662 Book of Common Prayer (hereafter BCP) which he entitled the

Sunday Service of the Methodists in North America (hereafter SS), and which was accepted by those gathered in Baltimore for the Christmas Conference between December 27, 1784 and January 3, 1785. The roots of this work lie deep in Wesley's Oxford days, when the members of the Holy Club were trying to pattern their worship after the early church, while maintaining their ties of love and loyalty to the BCP.

In a letter written at Bristol dated September 10, 1784, and addressed to "Dr. Coke, Mr. Asbury and our Brethren in America," Wesley describes the "very uncommon train of providences" which led the Methodists in America to be "disjoined from their mother-country" and in a place where bishops had no legal jurisdiction. His pastoral concern in ordaining clergy and devising the service-book for American Methodists is clear: "for some hundred miles together there is none either to baptize or to administer the Lord's Supper." With Methodists in the new United States now "totally disentangled both from the State and the English Hierarchy," Wesley thought they were "at full liberty, simply to follow the scriptures and the primitive church." But at the same time that "liberty" may not have been as "full" as we might imagine, for he certainly intended that his followers in America should adopt the ritual he proposed. Wesley declares in the preface to the SS that he knows of

no LITURGY in the world, either in ancient or modern language, which breathes more of a solid, scriptural, rational Piety, than the COMMON PRAYER of the CHURCH OF ENGLAND. And though the main of it was compiled considerably more than two hundred years ago, yet is the language of it, not only pure, but strong and elegant in the highest degree.

He goes on in the preface to outline the changes he has made to the 1662 rites (to which he says he has made but "little alteration").

1) most of the holy days (so called) are omitted, as at present answering no valuable end, 2) the service of the Lord's Day, the length of which has been often complained of, is considerably shortened, 3) some sentences in the offices of Baptism, and for the Burial of the Dead, are omitted, And 4) Many Psalms left out, and many parts of the others, as being highly improper for the mouths of a Christian Congregation.

These included thirty-four psalms entirely excised and many other verses left out, such as the last verse of Psalm 137 that declares that "happy shall they be who take your little ones and dash them against the rock!" (Psalms 137:9).

But a closer look at the SS itself reveals further, if perhaps more subtle, differences from the BCP on which it was based. Clearly this is a book primarily intended for congregational worship on Sundays, with provision made for such pastoral needs as marriage, the burial of the dead, and ordinations, and including brief orders for morning and evening prayer. Some elements in the BCP are removed entirely, such as the rite for the Visitation of the Sick. Although the ritual in the SS is intended to be followed closely, there is an indication that the preacher should "throw up an Extempore Prayer" at the Lord's Supper and during weekday gatherings. One can even see places where his rather disastrous pastoral experience in Georgia influenced changes in the BCP original. For example, in Savannah he had had a very difficult time convincing his congregation that the only "proper" mode of baptism was by submersion in water, and in the service for the baptism of infants in the new SS, sprinkling is allowed as an alternative rite.

The SS went through four further editions (with very minor emendations) passed by the American Conference in 1786, 1788, 1790, and 1792. But after John Wesley's death it almost immediately fell into disuse, except for Wesley's twenty-four Articles of Religion (an abridgement of the Church of England's Thirty-Nine Articles of Religion) and a brief compilation of "sacramental services," both of which remained appended to successive editions of the *Discipline*. (They were not, however, reproduced in any "people's book" such as a hymnal or service-book.) There were several reasons for this abandonment of the SS. Increasing numbers of Methodists in America had had no previous familiarity with the Book of Common Prayer, and so the foundational rites and liturgical principles, as well as the language, of the SS services were strange to them. Although Wesley had urged his ministers to "administer the Supper of the Lord every Lord's day," the pastoral circumstances in the new United States made that extremely difficult and the more informal style of public worship in America played a part as well. So, while Methodists in America continued to use Wesley's rites for the Lord's Supper, baptism for both adults and infants, marriage, burial, and ordinations, most ministers believed that "they could pray better, and with more devotion, while their eyes were shut, than they could with their eyes open."

In 1789, the MEC bishops and presiding elders, meeting again in Baltimore, and recognizing the particular demands that the American situation presented, declared that: "The exercise of public worship on the Lord's Day shall be singing, prayer, and reading of the Holy Scriptures, with exhortation or reading a sermon, in the absence of a preacher." We can see that if Methodist worship as Wesley conceived it has been characterized as a creative combination of the formal (Eucharist-centered) and the joyfully informal (preaching-centered), it was the latter that was transplanted more successfully into the American situation. And as the Second Great Awakening began to sweep westward, the informal exuberance of Methodist worship would be further emphasized.

To accommodate the growing Methodist diaspora, in 1786 Wesley published an edition of the *Sunday Service of the Methodists* for use by Methodists "in His Majesty's Dominions." Differences in settlement patterns resulted in various degrees of warmth in its reception: in the Caribbean Methodist churches, for example, the reading of prayers was more often the norm than extempore prayer. It is difficult to say to what extent *The Sunday Service* was used in Wesleyan Methodism more generally. The numerous editions through which the SS went indicate some popularity for the book, but it seems likely that in England, at least before Wesley's death, the Book of Common Prayer was more generally used than the *Sunday Service*, if only for the administration of the sacraments and pastoral rites. In 1885, a minister in England writes of Wesley's service book: "We confess that, for ourselves, we never found any difficulty in using it" (indicating that others had had difficulty), and that although it may "curtail some ministers' evangelical exuberance," it allows them to "proclaim with positiveness and universality the glorious gospel amnesty."

THE LORD'S SUPPER IN EARLY METHODISM

The Methodist revival has been described as not only an evangelical revival but a sacramental revival as well, and the two aspects of Wesleyan piety were intimately linked with one another. The general neglect of the sacrament in most parish churches was compounded by a highly penitential piety, which kept people away when it was held, for fear of unworthiness. Although the Wesleys' sacramental piety was strong, and although they have been described as "High Churchmen," theirs was not the kind of neo-medieval restorationism of the nineteenth-century Oxford Movement. It was more nearly a repositioning of the sacraments as the chief means of grace in the Christian life. The Supper was, as John Wesley described it, "the grand channel whereby the grace of His Spirit was conveyed to the souls of all the children of God." Among the most important disciplines for the members of the Oxford Holy Club was the regular attendance at communion, and the stated disciplines of the Methodist societies include the admonition that Methodists should "be constant and well-prepared in attending the Most Holy Sacrament at every Publick occasion."

Certainly, the more open, joyful, and welcoming attitude toward the sacrament on the part of Methodist preachers had singular effects, and in response to Methodist preaching, huge crowds came to receive communion. John Wesley reports in his *Journal* for 1790 such an occasion when he was preaching in Dublin: "I went to the Cathedral. I desired those of our Society, who did not go to their parish churches, would go with me to S. Patrick's. Many of them did so. It was said the number of communicants was about 500, more than went there in the whole year before Methodists were known in Ireland." Other claims in his *Journal*, for example, that "eighteen clergymen helped me distribute communion to 1,100 people" and "it was supposed that we had 1,000 communicants and I believe none went empty away," are common. The large numbers of people could sometimes create a problem of discipline as their interest began to wane, and it seems that the practice of hymn singing was seen, to some extent at least, to be a creative solution to this problem. In 1756, John Fletcher advised Wesley that "as the number of communicants is generally very great . . . [you might] interrupt, from time to time, the service of the Table, to put up a short prayer, or to sing a verse or two of a hymn." (It is hard to say whether Wesley actually took this advice.)

ADMISSION TO COMMUNION

John Wesley himself had been admitted to communion by his father at the parish church at Epworth when he was nine years old, having clearly demonstrated his worthiness on this matter of admission to communion. Through his theological and devotional reading he had become aware of the practice of the early church and among the Orthodox churches, which allowed children to receive communion as soon as they had been baptized. But, at the same time, as a priest of the Church of England he would have been compelled to bar children from the Table until they had been confirmed. He is, however, known to have admitted children as young as eight or nine years of age upon evidence of genuine responsiveness to the Christian message, but he clearly expected that these children would immediately come under the discipline of the Society which would guide them toward mature faithfulness. Neither the BCP catechism nor the confirmation rite was included in Wesley's *Sunday Service* for American Methodists, although his reasons for omitting them are nowhere stated. Perhaps he believed that Christian instruction would normally be dealt with in the society (and especially in classes and in families), and that the catechetical structure of the whole of Methodist practice made a separate rite for confirmation unnecessary.

John Wesley was probably more concerned with ensuring the adequate preparation of members of Methodist societies for receiving communion. As we have seen, he had already been in some difficulty over the issue of admission to communion while in Georgia, when he refused communion to Sophie Hopkey. He recognized his error, writing many years later "Can anyone carry High-Church zeal further than this? And how well I have been beaten with my own staff!" But the devotional preparation for communion was another matter, and one that claimed his persistent attention.

Clearly, meetings of the Methodist classes and bands were, at least in part, occasions for the preparation for communion, with mutual admonition and examination of conscience necessary components of this preparation. But more likely than not, in the early days of Methodism, this was preparation for receiving communion in members' own parish churches. But gradually, as Methodists began to be less and less welcome at the parish altar, and later as they were developing an unmistakable church life of their own, they sought to celebrate the sacrament of the Lord's Supper in their own societies. Again, it was within classes and bands that preparation was made for communion, and this was assured by the possession of a "communion token" or "class ticket." But the large crowds that came to communion services in response to Methodist preaching were another matter, and accusations that the Methodists were promoting "indiscriminate communion" were rife. Of course the Wesleys' own deep desire to remain within the Church of England made all of these issues about the integrity of the sacrament somewhat difficult. If Methodists began receiving communion outside the structures of the Church of England there was a serious question about their ability to sustain the intention so clearly stated in Charles Wesley's hymn quoted on p. 245.

But the question of who should receive communion never went away, and during the second half of the nineteenth century the admission of non-members to the Lord's Supper gave Wesleyan Methodism much concern. By that time, there were large numbers of people who worshiped with the Methodists and attended services of the Lord's Supper, but who did not attend the class meetings and whose names were not inscribed on the rolls. Such people were allowed to apply for a note of admission to the sacrament, although these tickets, while renewable quarterly, were not supposed to be issued indefinitely. More recently, with the increasing pluralism and mobility that have marked modern societies, the problem of "open" and "closed" communion has been a matter of controversy in Methodist churches around the world, with a number of important issues being discussed. Should baptized children be admitted to communion, or is an explicit "profession of faith" a necessary prerequisite? Should non-baptized adults be received at the Table? Should those of other faith traditions be invited? How do the divisions between and among Christians play themselves out at the Eucharist in an ecumenical age?

THE EUCHARISTIC HYMNS

With their heightened attention to the Lord's Supper as a preeminent means of grace, it is not surprising that perhaps the most subtle, complex, and penetrating eucharistic theology of the eighteenth century is embodied in Charles Wesley's 166 *Hymns on the Lord's Supper* (1745). Indeed, it has been argued that none of Charles Wesley's other hymns compare in quality and theological depth to those included in this selection. Here we see the Supper described as the "unbloody sacrifice" and an "infallible pledge," the bread and wine "effectual tokens." The benefits of the atonement are both revealed and made effectual in the Supper, and the celebration is a festival of joy in which the presence of Christ is experienced in the hearts of believers. The most popular of all the Wesley hymn collections (it went through nine editions in John Wesley's lifetime), these hymns were intended, as we have seen, to be sung by members of the Methodist societies as communion was being distributed. Given the large numbers of communicants at the Wesleys' Eucharists, this could be quite a lengthy process, and it seems probably that the knowledge of the content of these hymns by ordinary Methodists was high.

As one commentator notes, John Wesley saw the *Hymns on the Lord's Supper* as significant statements of Methodist doctrine; he not only refers to them frequently in his other writing, but he also went back to amend them on matters of doctrine which he had clarified since their composition. The organization of the collection of hymns follows the ordering of categories in the 1673 treatise *The Christian Sacrament and Sacrifice* by Daniel Brevint (1616–95). Following Brevint, Wesley describes the Lord's Supper as at once a "sacrament," a "sacrifice," and a "memorial." In its sacramental aspect, it is the vehicle "through which the Holy Spirit offers us the body and blood of Christ and the benefits of salvation which they procure." As a "sacrifice," it is a means "through which by grace we offer ourselves as a living sacrifice to God." As a memorial, the Eucharist is the mode through which the sufferings of Christ on the Cross are represented, and becomes through the gift of the Holy Spirit the "true recorder of His passion."

But Wesley's eucharistic memorial is not a mere exercise in remembering for those who partake, as it was for many others of his age, but rather a means by which Christ's presence is effected. Because of participating in the Lord's Supper,

> We need not now go up to heaven
> To bring the long-sought Saviour down;
> Thou art to all already given,
> Thou dost even now thy banquet crown:
> To every faithful soul appear,
> And show thy real presence here!

In the end, however, the ways and means of Christ's eucharistic presence remain a mystery:

> O the depth of love divine
> The unfathomable grace!
> Who shall say how bread and wine
> God into us conveys!
> How the bread his flesh imparts,
> How the wine transmits his blood.

Everywhere, Charles Wesley's own firm sense of the eschatological joy experienced by those who participate in the Supper pervades these hymns, even the most penitential of them. As believers join in the Lord's Supper:

> The fruits of the wine   (The joy it implies),
> Again we shall join   To drink in the skies,
> Exalt in His favour,   Our triumph renew;
> And I, in the Saviour,   Will drink it with you!

This sense of eschatological expectancy, which is intended as the attitude of all Methodist Christians, is found everywhere throughout this collection, and especially in the section entitled "The Sacrament as a Pledge of Heaven" (i.e. Hymns 93–115). The Eucharist is the foretaste of the "marriage Supper of the Lamb," the "heavenly banquet," and through it we are "seal'd up in Thy glorious peace."

BAPTISM IN EIGHTEENTH-CENTURY METHODISM

While John Wesley was mostly concerned with the renewal of faith in those who had already been baptized as babies, he did on many occasions in his ministry baptize adults who had been converted by Methodist preaching, as well as infants born to parents who were members of Methodist societies.

The matter of Wesley's views on baptismal regeneration (that is, whether or not the act of baptism itself is a means and assurance of new birth) has been intensely debated, with some arguing that Wesley only retained infant baptism because of his attachment to the Established Church of England, and others insisting that Wesley's affirmation of infant baptism embodied fully his convictions on the matter of prevenient grace and sacramental potency. As in so many things about Mr. Wesley's theology, the truth probably lies somewhere in between these two. In his *Thoughts on Infant Baptism*, and in his revision of the Book of Common Prayer rites of baptism for the Methodists in America, Wesley clearly indicates that baptism is one of the means of grace for believers. But, at the same time, baptism is also a divine–human transaction in which the faithfulness of God and the faithfulness of the baptized meet and a pardoning relationship is established. While baptism conveyed the regenerating indwelling of the Spirit, the full effects of this regenerative indwelling unfolded gradually as the person appropriated it responsibly.

Wesley's ambivalence on this matter of baptismal regeneration can be seen in his revision of the BCP baptismal rite for the SS, especially at the point at which the BCP includes a prayer that the baptized person "*being* born again" (emphasis added) may be an heir of salvation. Wesley makes a significant change to this prayer, which in the SS reads "that he *may* be born again" and be made an heir of salvation (emphasis added). But several other phrases which speak of the regenerating power of baptism are retained: prayers over the baptismal water ask that it may be sanctified "to the mystical washing away of sins," and in an introductory prayer the minister asks God to grant to the newly baptized "remission of sins by spiritual regeneration." Adding to the ambiguity about Wesley's views on baptismal regeneration are those several places in the baptismal rites at which the word "regenerate" (for example, in the prayer after baptism which prays that the newly baptized, "being regenerate," might be a partaker of Christ's resurrection) is simply omitted.

Baptism never occupied the attention of John and Charles Wesley to the same degree as the Lord's Supper. This is perhaps because they clearly saw baptism as the beginning of a life-long process of growth toward Christ-likeness rather than an end in and of itself through which people were undeniably "saved." John Wesley had, of course, been maligned and dis-credited during his sojourn in Georgia for his scrupulous imposition of the minutest of the BCP baptismal rubrics and his desire to return to some ante-Nicene practices (such as the submersion of infants). He had also insisted on re-baptizing Dissenters before they were admitted to communion, which landed him in trouble not only with the candidates themselves but also with the bishop of London. He always maintained, however, that the authority to baptize was given only to the ordained, and throughout his life he fought every attempt to allow his traveling preachers to administer the sacrament of baptism.

REACTIONS AGAINST METHODIST WORSHIP

Hostile reactions to Methodist worship have been very common, exacerbated by the natural heightening of emotion that accompanies differences in religious sensibilities. In the early days of the movement mob hostility was excited by Methodist worship, and both preachers and congregations were routinely subjected to violence and degradation. The Exeter *Morning Post* reported in 1745 that:

The Methodists had a meetinghouse behind the Guildhall, and on May 6th the mob gathered at the door, and pelted those who entered with potatoes, mud, and dung. On coming out, we were all beaten, without exception . . . Some of the other women were lamed, others stripped naked and rolled most indecently in the gutter, their faces being smeared with lampblack, flour, and dirt. The disgraceful mob consisted of some thousands of cowardly blackguards, and the disturbance was continued till midnight.

Even the spellbinding preacher George Whitefield reported that on one occasion in London he had realized that he was in "great jeopardy": "for the pulpit being high and the supports not well fixed in the ground, it tottered every time I moved, and the numbers of enemies strove to push my friends against the supports in order to throw me down." He commends especially the "several little boys and girls who were fond of sitting round me on the pulpit while I preached and handing to me people's notes," who never gave up "though they were often pelted with eggs, dirt, &c thrown at me."

Sometimes this hostility was aroused within families, when parents or spouses refused to allow their Methodist kin to attend services of worship. Mary Gore, for example, was converted by Primitive Methodist preaching in 1827 at the age of thirty-seven. Her husband had remained deeply opposed to Methodism, however, and often refused to let his wife back into the house after she had been to the chapel. On those occasions she had to "seek shelter elsewhere or spend the nights sleeping in the open air." She persisted in her perverse church going, and one day her husband threatened to cut her legs off with an ax if she went to the Methodist Sunday service

13. William Hogarth, "Enthusiasm Delineat'd" (*c.* 1760), a satirical engraving in which
the fervor of Methodist worship is disparaged.

again. Mary Gore is reported to have replied defiantly: "Then I will go
upon my stumps!"

Although the most virulent attacks on Methodist worship came from
the outside, members of Methodist societies also felt free to criticize the
worship they experienced. Many times this was due to what was perceived
as the lack of proper fervor during services. When the Methodist society at
Hockley met on October 16, 1797 for the quarterly love-feast, one woman
is reported to have stood up and said, "Lord have mercy upon you, for you
are the deadest souls I ever met with in all my life."

But by far the most persistent cause of reaction against Methodism was
its excess of fervor, and the pervasive "enthusiasm" that marked Methodist
services of worship. The emotional release occasioned by Methodist

preaching and other forms of worship (the love-feast, for example) was offensive both to the refined sensibilities of "respectable people" and to theologians who sincerely believed that the truest form of religion would necessarily be the most rational and restrained. In William Hogarth's satirical engraving "Enthusiasm Delineat'd" (*c.* 1760), a preacher (modeled, it is said, after George Whitefield) excites those who have gathered to hear, while a "congregational thermometer" registers "Methodist Brain"; in the foreground, a woman succumbs to a fit of religious hysteria and a dog howls while hubbub reigns all around. The Methodist practice of hymn singing came under particular scrutiny from outsiders, in part because it was seen to be music of the "common sort," not entirely suitable for the worship of Almighty God. In England, Methodist singing was often the object of ridicule by members of the Established Church. When visiting one of his own parish churches, one nineteenth-century Anglican bishop was appalled to find the congregation engaged in what he described as "that snuffling Methodistical practice of hymn-singing." But perhaps the main concern about hymnody was that it led participants in Wesleyan meetings to spiritual excitement and religious "enthusiasm."

Many outsiders, however, have been deeply appreciative of Methodist worship, and especially its heartfelt character. In 1910 the writer Charles Morely thought it good to attend and report on a variety of worship services in London. He was impressed with what happened at an ordinary Sunday service in Wesley's Chapel in City Road, which he compared to the worship he had observed in Anglican parish churches in London:

The glories of the Bible pale in the Churches . . . often muttered in humming singsong to a listless, dozing congregation; but now [in Wesley's Chapel] I hear the rolling sentences proclaimed by the minister with just emphasis, warm colour, and profound emotion, and the wise words fall upon the ears as if it came from the prophet himself and go ringing to the utmost corner with startling effect . . . The people listened as though they were weighing the words, and more than one of my neighbours I saw nodding his head as he might approve an orator, even repeating the words to himself in low undertones.

THE COVENANT SERVICE AND THE LOVE-FEAST

While Methodism adapted for their own use certain forms of worship common to all Christians, other services were distinctive to Methodism. One of these characteristic forms of Methodism was the Covenant Service, usually observed annually at the turning of the New Year. The Covenant Service became the occasion for especially vitriolic criticism from outsiders as a cause of what they perceived to be the misplaced religiosity of the Methodist movement. In 1803, one observer declared that:

> Positively and knowingly we assert, that the increase of madness, melancholy madness, religious madness, the worst form of the worst calamity which flesh is heir to, has been proportional to, and occasioned by the growth of Methodism . . . Such are the effects of their denunciations of damnation, and of that tremendous blasphemy, their yearly Covenant with Almighty God.

Susanna Wesley had emphasized to all her children the need to renew the covenant with God periodically, and the devotional practice of covenanting was practiced in the Epworth rectory household. Covenant language appears frequently in Charles Wesley's hymns and poems, and John Wesley responded readily to the Moravian practice of passing the "Cup of Covenant" that he saw on his visit to Herrnhut in 1738. Wesley seems to have begun experiments with a Methodist form of Covenant Service in the period between Christmas and New Year, 1747–8, but it was not until 1755 that a full Covenant Service was devised. In his *Journal* for August 6 of that year, Wesley remarks that:

> I mentioned to the congregation another means of increasing serious religion which had been frequently practiced by our forefathers and attended with eminent blessing, namely, the joining in a covenant to serve God with all our heart and with all our soul. I explained this for several mornings following, and on Friday many of us kept a fast unto the Lord, beseeching Him to give us wisdom and strength to promise unto the Lord our God and keep it.

By 1780, the Methodist Society in London was celebrating a Covenant Renewal each year on December 31. Even John Wesley was astonished at the power of this service, where many people received a "sense of the pardoning love of God" and "the power to love him with all their heart." Charles Wesley added a number of hymns for the occasion of Covenant Renewal, including "Come, let us use the grace divine," which continues to be included in Methodist hymnals around the world and is sung even in those congregations in which the service itself has been abandoned. This hymn calls the people to renew their commitment "for God to live or die" and invites each Person of the Trinity in turn to dwell in the hearts of the gathered believers.

The Covenant Service as Wesley devised it consisted of a long exhortation on the meaning of Covenant Renewal, in which worshipers are enjoined to "choose between Christ and the devil" and to prepare themselves in prayer and resolve, followed by a Covenant Prayer in which covenant promises

14. Cup for use in the love-feast, late eighteenth century.

are made and acceptance of the covenant by God is requested ("O Dreadful Jehovah, become my Covenant Friend . . ."). The hymn written by Charles Wesley for the service, "Come, let us use the grace divine," and a solemn benediction were likely always included as a conclusion. Later the service was elaborated with additional prayers (including the Lord's Prayer), psalms, hymns, and the Eucharist. It was expected that the Covenant Service would be preceded by prayer and fasting, and that it would be held on January 1 or on the first Sunday of the New Year.

The full Covenant Service first appears in a Methodist service-book in 1882, and in British Methodism (and in many of its Methodist offspring in other parts of the world) it continues to be included in official service-books. A form of the Covenant Service was included in the Methodist Church in the USA's *Book of Worship for Church and Home with Orders for the Administration of the Sacraments and Other Rites and Ceremonies According to the Use of the Methodist Church* (1944). Patterned as it was on the rite in the 1936 *Book of Offices*, Methodists brought the Covenant Service with them into the 1947 Church of South India union in which Methodists, Presbyterians, and Anglicans joined to form a new ecumenical body. In the Church of South India's service-book, *The Book of Common Worship* published in 1963, a form of the Covenant Service was included in response to the stated desire of former Methodists to have something from their own liturgical tradition represented in the rites. It too was based on the service contained in the British Methodist Church's *Book of Offices*.

Many other denominations have seen the value in having some form of Covenant Renewal as a part of their liturgical arsenal for use on special occasions in the life of the church, including the dedication of new or renovated church buildings. The consecration of Coventry Cathedral in 1962, for example, used a form of the congregational "service for Affirming Vows," clearly modeled on the Methodist Covenant Service. Others have used it as a form of worship for concluding retreats and other special gatherings, or on the occasion of celebrating mergers of churches or congregations.

Another service peculiar to Methodism, and which, like the Covenant Service, did not arise out of the Prayer Book tradition, was the love-feast. Part of Wesley's attempt to pattern Methodist worship after the worship of primitive Christianity, the love-feast looked back to the *agape* meal of the early church, in which the community ate and drank together as a sign of filial love and as a preparation for "eating and drinking in the Kingdom of God." Other religious groups had experimented with the practice (for similar reasons and with similar meanings), but it was the Moravians who had had the most influence on Wesley's decision to adopt it within the Methodist societies. Originally it was restricted to members of the small and selective groups called bands, but soon the benefits of the practice were spread throughout Methodism.

The love-feast generally consisted of hymns and prayers that prepared for the meal (which according to Wesley's instructions was "a little plain cake and water"). The "bread" was distributed by the stewards and was eaten, and a collection for the poor was taken up. Then the so-called "loving cup" was handed around and all drank water from it. The presider gave an address that elicited testimonies and spontaneous singing from the congregation. The love-feast closed with a hymn and a benediction. Several hymns found an invariable place in the love-feast, among them hymns written especially for the occasion by Charles Wesley.

> Come, and let us sweetly join
> Christ to praise in hymns divine!
> Give us all with one accord
> Glory to our common Lord;
> Hands and hearts and voices raise,
> Sing as in the ancient days,
> Antedate the joys above,
> Celebrate the feast of love.

We see several themes highlighted here that were central to the love-feast: the sense of common purpose, the joy of praising God, the link between this service and the early church, and the feast as an anticipation of the heavenly banquet.

The love-feast was transmitted to the American colonies early in the 1770s, and was popular in classes and bands, in circuits, and as an emotional climax to quarterly meetings and Conferences. It followed much the same form as it had in the British Isles. The love-feast persisted in both the MEC and the MECS after the split in 1858, and was also continued in the African-American denominations that grew up throughout the nineteenth century. In Methodist churches around the world, both those arising from the United States and those from the British traditions of Methodism, the love-feast continues to appear as a service in the most recent revisions of service-books, and very often it has been carried by Methodists into ecumenical mergers. In fact, it is in ecumenical settings that the love-feast has had its most potent usefulness: when Christians are prohibited from sharing in the Lord's Supper, the love-feast has been celebrated as an acceptable alternative that speaks of the deep desire for unity in Table fellowship.

NINETEENTH-CENTURY METHODIST WORSHIP

At the death of John Wesley in 1791, several controversies related to the form and substance of Methodist worship had to be settled, and decisions made in these matters indelibly marked the future of Methodist worship. At the same time, various social and theological factors peculiar to the immediate post-Wesley era would also have profound effects on the direction Methodist worship would take over the next hundred years. Indeed, much of what transpired in the nineteenth century would exert a more profound and lasting impact on Methodist worship as it is seen today around the globe than anything that the Wesleys did or said. In some particulars the trajectory from eighteenth-century Wesleyan Methodism was clearly carried forward; in other ways it was broken entirely. The result is the kind of liturgical diversity that was described at the beginning of this chapter, as well as the bifurcation of Methodist worship into distinctly American and British branches.

We have seen the major disputes among those who were responsible for carrying the Methodist movement forward after Wesley's death surrounding the matter of the administration of the Lord's Supper in the Methodist societies. Wesley himself had authorized only those who had been ordained in the Church of England to celebrate the Lord's Supper. The earliest Conferences after Wesley's death were equally unwilling to move hastily, and at the 1791 Conference the preachers were instructed "You shall not administer the Sacrament in the ensuing year."

The Wesleyan preachers generally showed restraint in this dispute. The wife of John Pawson (1737–1806), then a Methodist itinerant preacher in Scotland, wrote in 1792: "Today my husband gave the sacrament in his own house; a custom he has ever continued since we went into Scotland. But if giving the sacrament in our chapels will occasion any division, I know he will prefer the union of the body, and administer it nowhere in public."

The "Plan of Pacification" in 1795 approved the celebration of the Lord's Supper "wherever a majority of the Trustees, Stewards and Leaders desired it" and conducted either "according to the form of the Established Church" or "according to Wesley's Abridgement." If there were to be hymns, exhortations, and extempore prayer, they were to be included at the discretion of the presiding minister. The Plan of Pacification also outlined a form for baptism, guidelines for holding services during church hours, and Christian burial. In all of these cases, however, the only persons who could preside at the Supper were those authorized by the Conference.

It was clear that this problem was not going to disappear, and indeed as the next few years went by it only worsened. Adam Clarke was among the staunchest supporters of the right of Methodist societies to conduct the Lord's Supper in their chapels. He describes the essence of the problem:

In many instances there were members of our Societies who from the earliest times earnestly wished for the Sacrament of the Lord's Supper, and often considerable parts of Societies, who claimed as a Privilege and Right to have all the ordinances of God administered to them by the men who were the instruments of their conversion.

Clarke goes on to say that denying people the sacrament was denying them access to the means of grace, especially since increasing numbers were now being refused communion in their churches on account of their Methodist affiliation:

we obliged them to go to strange pastures where they were not properly fed . . . that because these ordinances were not administered among us, many (I believe, the greater number) of our Societies did not receive the Lord's Supper *at all* and it began to be lost sight of through the Connexion, notwithstanding our frequent Exhortations to them, to frequent the Church and Sacraments.

Clarke was clearly also interested in taking Methodist worship in a new direction for a new century, away from John Wesley's devout attachment to the liturgical ways and means of the Church of England. Clarke's learned and lengthy "sermon on the Lord's Supper" contains no reference to the practices or the teaching of Wesley and the early Methodists, and there is a paucity of citations to the works of the Wesleys in his other writings, even when there were many apposite references that would have served his purpose well.

The two sources of worship material mentioned in the minutes of the 1791 Conference, the Book of Common Prayer and Wesley's *Abridgement* of that book originally produced for the Methodists in North America, were also the objects of considerable debate. Since there was a fair amount of material in both these service-books that Methodists never used, the British Methodist Conference of 1835 authorized the publication of a smaller manual entitled *The Order of Administration of the Sacraments and other Services*. For the next forty years, many editions of these two books, *The Sunday Service* and *The Order of Administration*, each with its own variations, were issued by the Methodist Publishing House. The 1878 Conference ordered a complete revision and the publication of an entirely new liturgy. Accordingly, in 1882 the *Book of Public Prayers and Services* appeared, and this book was used by Wesleyan Methodism in the British Isles until Methodist Union.

For the most part, these services bore little resemblance to the rites in the BCP that Wesley had so loved. Where Wesley had desired "constant Communion," his nineteenth-century heirs made the Lord's Supper into an occasional service, usually appended to the evening preaching service. Much of the desire to distance Methodist worship from its Prayer Book roots was a fear of what were perceived to be the ritual extravagances of the Oxford Movement which, since the 1840s, had had increasing influence on the ecclesial lives of many Anglicans. As one Methodist commented, the Prayer Book was "the seed-plot of all Romanizing errors which now distract and menace the Church of England." In the United States, as we have seen, the *Sunday Service* that Wesley had provided for the Methodists there was almost immediately abandoned, with the exception of the sacramental rites which remained appended to successive *Books of Discipline*. These dual approaches to worship were transmitted by the missionaries as they established Methodist places of worship around the world.

REVIVALISM

As we have seen, the question of the place of large revival meetings in Methodism gave birth to a number of Methodist sectarian groups in the eighteenth century. But throughout the nineteenth century revivalism had spread, both up and down the increasingly industrializing center of England and Scotland, and onto the American frontier with the westward expansion, affecting both sectarian and mainstream Methodists alike. Contemporary descriptions of nineteenth-century Methodist "camp meeting" revivals reveal a religious phenomenon that was a creative combination of heightened emotional and spiritual experience and sociability, all aimed at the conversion of sinners and the rededication of the faithful. Swedish novelist Frederika Bremer, who traveled throughout the United States in 1849–50, offers one such description. Having visited Quakers, Shakers, Unitarians, and various other religious groups, she is taken to a racially integrated Methodist revival outside of Macon, Georgia, where three to four thousand people had gathered for a three-day "protracted meeting." She remarks especially on the singing of hymns and the fervor of the preachers:

The later it grew in the night, the more earnest grew the appeals; and the short hymns, fervent as the flames, ascended like these with passionate ardor. Again and again they arose, like melodiously flaming sighs, from thousands of harmonious voices. The preachers increased their fervor; two stood with their faces toward the camp of the blacks, two toward that of the whites, extending their hands and calling on the sinners to come, come, all of them, *now* at this time, at this moment, which was perhaps the last that remained to them in which to approach the Savior, to escape eternal damnation!

The enthusiasm of those gathered for these meetings is often remarked upon. Bremer observes that, during the addresses,

Men roared and bawled out; women squealed like pigs about to be killed; many, having fallen into convulsions, leaped and struck about them so that they had to be held down. Here and there it looked like a regular fight, and some of the participants laughed. Many a cry of anguish could be heard, but no words excepting, "Oh, I am a sinner!" and "Jesus! Jesus!" and during this excitement the singing continued loud and beautiful.

But this kind of emotional enthusiasm is not new to the nineteenth-century American frontier. Those who witnessed the preaching of the earliest Methodists describe similar scenes. Wesley himself tells of the effect of his preaching on a gathering in 1743:

Men, women, and children wept and groaned and trembled exceedingly. Many could not contain themselves in those bounds but cried with a loud and bitter cry. It was the same in the morning, while I was showing the happiness of those "whose iniquities are forgiven, and whose sins are covered" [Romans 1:7].

Revivals of this kind, both rural camp meetings and church-based "missions," continued on throughout the next century, and are found even today in many parts of Methodism. The appeal of revivalism's heartfelt piety, and the attraction of worship in the revival mode were particularly strong among those who were downtrodden and disenfranchised: "The theology was battle raising, the hymns were martial, the preaching was led by men who saw the world as a fight. Hardship, struggle, exhaustion, blisters, were mere by-products of a world in sin: Christ was the Way out and the Way forward." A particular order of worship accompanied this revivalist style, an order of worship that can still be seen in many Methodist churches today. It begins with what have been termed "the Preliminaries": singing, prayers, and other acts of worship designed to open the heart to the need for conversion. This is in preparation for the sermon, which was followed by the receiving of the harvest of converts.

In the United States especially, revivalism had important effects on other rites of the church, and especially on baptism. Throughout the nineteenth century various issues surrounding baptism were seriously and hotly debated, but the most problematical of these concerned rebaptism. Should those who had been baptized as infants but who had had a dramatic experience of conversion later in life (at a revival perhaps) be baptized again? Should those who had been baptized by sprinkling or pouring but who now believed immersion to be the only valid mode of initiation be rebaptized by immersion? Most Methodist theologians argued that since God never abrogated a covenant made and sealed with the proper intentionality, rebaptism was never an option, unless the original baptism had been defective by not having been made in the name of the Trinity. But with increasing numbers of heartfelt requests for rebaptism being made by those entering the Methodist Church, considerable pressure was put on pastors to rebaptize. In the last years of the 1860s, statements forbidding the practice of rebaptism were included in the *Disciplines* of the MEC, the MPC, and the AMEC in an effort to put the brakes on the trend toward rebaptism on request. But within thirty years the consensus had shifted, and this restriction was dropped from the MEC *Discipline*.

With the desire by many within American Methodism for baptism on mature profession of faith, the need began to arise for some service marking the birth of a baby, and experiments with rites of "infant dedication" were proposed. The Evangelical United Brethren routinely used such a rite, which it had inherited from the United Brethren in the merger of 1946. In the creation of the UMC in 1968 all rites from the constituent denominations were deemed to have authority in the new body; the service of infant dedication was included in these, but was omitted from the 1992 UMC *Book of Worship*. But the inclination, on the part of pastors and people alike, toward both rebaptism and the restriction of baptism to adults on mature profession of faith persists as one legacy of revivalism that the founders of Methodism would heartily dispute.

"MAHOGANY METHODISM"

A second force was working on Methodism, however, that became equally important in the shaping of the Methodist liturgical future. This was the growing desire for sophistication among some Methodists, and the growing sense that Methodism needed to take its place among the more "respectable" religious bodies. In the big cities of the world, along the east coast of the United States, and in places where the dominant religious culture was of an elitist character, socially upwardly mobile Methodists were demanding style and elegance in their buildings, their worship, and their choral music, and erudition in their preaching. The "esthetic" became a very important category in the judgment of liturgical appropriateness, with "worship the Lord in the beauty of holiness" often transformed into "worship the Lord in the holiness of beauty." The need to create a sense of transcendence manifested itself in the choice of hymns, choral music, architecture, vestments, furnishings, and, perhaps most importantly, orders of worship. Prayers and hymns culled from the great treasury of the Christian tradition, and choral and instrumental music from the European masters, were now the hallmarks of what came to be called "mahogany Methodism," so named because of the desire of many Methodists to furnish their churches in high style rather than in the "plain and unadorned" style advocated by Wesley and his immediate successors.

These two powerful but opposing trends working on Methodism during the nineteenth century, revivalism and gentrification, had pulled both British and American traditions of Methodist worship in divergent directions. On the one hand, a rise in social status, prosperity, and financial stability led many Methodists to desire refinement and elegance in both their worship and in the space in which it occurred. On the other hand, revivalism was spreading Methodism to more impoverished and non-elite constituencies. The first of these "two Methodisms" was comfortable with ritual, read prayers, theological hymns, robed choirs, and formal architectural idioms (neo-Gothic, neo-Georgian, neo-Romanesque). The second was comfortable with informal orders of worship, extempore prayer, devotional hymns, and plain, vernacular church buildings. While preaching was important to both groups, elite orders of worship tended to but-tress the sermon with liturgical prayers, litanies, and choral and organ music; non-elite orders of worship tended to buttress the sermon with revival-style hymns, testimonies, and altar-calls. The Methodism most heavily influenced by revivalism and the Methodism most influenced by upward social mobility both moved into the next century with power and authority.

But throughout the nineteenth century, as Methodism moved around the globe with the rise and success of the missionary movement, several serious issues arose with regard to worship. Both revivalist Methodism and mahogany Methodism took their distinctive attitudes toward worship with them as they evangelized among people around the world. The conflicts which had arisen over the most effective and scripturally sound forms of worship, and which had resulted in divisions in the Methodist family in England and North America, were often simply transplanted to the Methodist mission fields in the nineteenth century, where they made little sense and often hindered the spread of the Gospel. At the same time, of course, elements embedded within the Methodist theology and practice of worship resonated strongly within indigenous communities, contributing to the success of the Methodist witness to the Christian faith around the globe.

METHODIST CHURCH ARCHITECTURE

John Wesley was clearly concerned that the buildings used by the Methodist people be suited to the demands of Christian worship as he envisioned it. In the 1770 *Large Minutes*, he had outlined the principles of Methodist architecture: the buildings should be plain and unadorned, the seating should be simple, and box pews should be avoided at all cost. Both lighting and ventilation should be adequate so that people could comfortably attend to the progress of the service. He also described the ideal shape of the Methodist chapel. In 1761 in his *Journal* (and later in the *Large Minutes*), Wesley commended an octagonal space, with seating both on the floor and in galleries above so that everyone might see and hear the proceedings. In order that the whole congregation should be as close as possible to the leaders of the service, none of these buildings was to be very large. Of course the pragmatic demands of "spreading scriptural holiness" meant that any building (or no building at all) could be used as a worship space; a building that furthered the evangelistic aims of the Methodist movement was the ideal.

Several of these "Wesley octagons" were erected in various parts of England, the first in Rotherham in 1761 and another in Yarm in 1764 (the latter is the oldest octagonal Methodist chapel still standing). In America a number of purpose-built Methodist churches were erected almost as soon as Methodist societies were organized, and although most American Methodists preferred simple and unadorned buildings for worship, beyond this Wesley's architectural instructions were largely ignored. (There were one or two octagons in the USA, but they never proved popular.) Through the first half of the nineteenth century successive *Disciplines* of the Methodist Episcopal Church dictated that buildings for worship be "plain and decent" (this style lasted longer among Methodist subgroups), but as Methodists became more affluent this rule was less often followed, and finally it was dropped from the *Discipline* altogether. Gradually in America buildings for worship began to be referred to as "churches" (rather than "meeting houses" or "preaching houses").

Beginning in the late nineteenth century, the revival of various architectural styles (Georgian, Romanesque, Egyptian, and so on) began to have a significant impact on ecclesiastical architecture. Perhaps the most significant of these, the Gothic revival, which had transformed the look of Anglican churches on both sides of the Atlantic and around the globe from the 1850s onward, profoundly affected Methodism as well. British Methodist missionary C. W. Posnett, for example, built a fine neo-Gothic Methodist church in Medak, India, and in many cities around the world the principal Methodist church in the city center is regularly built in Gothic style, as a statement that Methodism has taken its place alongside other mainline denominations. As the twentieth century progressed, a wide variety of architectural styles, from Romanesque to modern to local vernacular forms, were employed in the design of Methodist church buildings. Some of these architectural idioms have been more suitable to the support of Methodist worship than others. The "fanned auditorium," with the choir spread behind a central pulpit, has come in for particular criticism; one commentator just after the turn of the twentieth century remarked that the church building "had lost much of that which was really churchly and became a hall" in which the congregations were "mere accessories."

Technological innovations in the building and furnishing of Methodist worship spaces also had an influence on the worship conducted within them. In 1803, for example, the incandescent gas mantle was employed, and evening services became both feasible and fashionable. More recently the provision of large projection screens has allowed some Methodist churches to abandon the use of hymnals and service-books altogether. As Methodism

moved into the wider world, questions of the indigenization of church architecture were often raised. In many places, especially in parts of Central and
Latin America and the Far East, the erection of purpose-built Protestant
churches was made illegal or was strongly discouraged, and so Methodists
met in private houses; but in other locations Methodists have used indigenous architectural idioms in building and furnishing the setting for the
community's worship.

MUSIC FOR WORSHIP

With Charles Wesley producing upwards of 9,000 hymns for the Methodist
societies, and John Wesley convinced that language of "utmost simplicity,
plainness, suited to every capacity" should be set to music, it is not surprising that Methodists soon became known as a people who sang their
faith. Wesley's publishing enterprises provided both British and American
Methodists with a number of hymnals, the most significant of which was
A Collection of Psalms and Hymns, which first appeared in 1741 and was
augmented for the American audience and sent along with the SS in 1784.
In 1780 the large *CHPM* was issued; described by John Wesley as "a little
body of experimental and practical divinity," this hymnal formed the basis
for various Methodist hymnals which followed, in all parts of the world.

American Methodists have from the beginning been much more willing
to accept Wesley's advice on music than his advice on worship. John Wesley
had been emphatic that communal hymn singing was designed to build
common bonds among members of the congregation and invite the participation of all. "How shall we reform our singing?" the first American
Discipline asked; and the answer followed with the requirement: "that all
our preachers who have any knowledge in the notes, improve it by learning to sing true themselves, and keeping close to Mr. Wesley's tunes and
hymns." The importance of singing in American Methodist congregations
can be seen in the popularity of the official hymnals: by 1805, thirty-five
different editions of the hymnal had been published. Yet, during these same
years, Methodist singing on both sides of the Atlantic was also moving in
directions away from "Mr. Wesley's tunes and hymns." The kinds of music
which were proving successful in Methodist camp meetings, with simple
and emotionally charged words set not to Wesley's tunes but to popular and
folk melodies, would shape the future of Methodist hymnody the world
over.

Camp-meeting revival music was remarkable for many reasons, and was
often especially noted by observers in their descriptions of revival meetings.

This is what the editor of a Schuylkill County, Pennsylvania, newspaper found at a Methodist camp meeting in 1828:

When this [preaching] has continued a sufficient length of time, the officiating preacher commences singing in a loud voice, some well-known hymn or chorus, in which the members one after another join, until the whole are upon their feet again. The hymn is generally a song of exultation and triumph, calculated to excite the passions, which is continued for a considerable length of time, accompanied with jumping and clapping of hands, in which the ministers partake, and sometimes to heighten the scene, join in by blowing a horn.

The response of the congregation seemed particularly worthy of note in this account:

The degree of sincerity and enthusiasm exhibited during these periods of their worship, is beyond description; each individual sings or rather shouts with all his might, clapping hands or jumping until he falls down exhausted. A singularity remarkable in the devotions of these people is, every person seems at liberty to express his satisfaction in any way he thinks proper.

This description alludes to the method of hymn singing called "lining out." Lining out began in the seventeenth century and was never particularly distinctive to Methodism. But it did fit well with the Methodist desire for inclusiveness in worship, since it allowed even illiterate people to sing with enthusiasm and to learn the words of hymns. In this way of singing hymns, a song leader sang a line of a hymn and then the congregation would repeat it until the hymn was finished. This method of hymn singing persisted well into the nineteenth century in both Britain and America, and in some rural and African-American Methodist churches lining out is still regularly practiced. Lining out has been criticized for producing a dirge-like quality in the singing, but some Methodists remain deeply attached to the custom.

The place of Methodist hymnody in the spiritual lives of ordinary people cannot be overestimated. We saw this in the case of Primitive Methodism, when we told of the death of the miner Robert Grieves. Methodists have always been deeply attached to their hymnals, as both aids to worship and aids to private devotion, and the debates over hymnal revision have been intense and often divisive. (The 1853 British Wesleyan Methodist Conference nearly split the connexion over the introduction of a new hymn-book, laity accusing the clergy of failing to consult them.)

As we have seen, the character of a certain segment of Methodism changed in the later nineteenth century with the increasing prosperity Methodists were enjoying, and the character of Methodist church music changed with it. Revivals remained popular, and revival hymns regularly appeared in a succession of Methodist hymnals of the period. But even revival hymnody had lost its edge, and had become cosy and sentimental. With increasing upward mobility, other forms of music also began to be included in the Methodist worship service: anthems from the European tradition of church music (often sung by robed choirs) and instrumental pieces from the classical organ and orchestral repertoire found their place in Methodist Sunday worship. Indeed, these forms of music became one of the most often cited signs of Methodist elitism whenever any form of merger, local, regional, or national, was being considered.

Because of their pragmatic outlook in all things, including worship, Methodists were able to shape their liturgical music to the customs and traditions of the various indigenous populations who responded to Methodist preaching. In some cases this was accomplished by the integration of local styles of music within the service of worship. In India, for example, various significant attempts were made to rewrite church music in classical Karnatic style, such as that used in the ragas, with the tune of each sung prayer reflecting the mood of the petition. But these were extremely difficult to sing and to perform. In 1996 Israel Selvanayagam, who taught Church of South India preachers at Tamilnadu Theological Seminary in Madurai before moving to Wesley College, Bristol, attempted a musical style for the liturgy that was more inclusive and for which high levels of literacy were not demanded. In parts of Africa and Asia, drums and other native musical instruments have been included as integral parts of worship.

Methodist hymns, in their ability to strike a creative balance between the devotional and the dogmatic, have been singularly important to Methodist conversion, spiritual nurture, and theological development. These aspects of the Methodist hymn tradition are embodied in all the hymnals produced by Methodists across the centuries and around the globe. Hymns have provided warmth and theological insight, communal experience and joy to generations of Methodists, and it is difficult to imagine any form of Methodist worship that does not include singing.

WORSHIP IN SECTARIAN METHODISM

Worship in sectarian Methodism has been described as "serious, austere, intolerant, and deadly earnest." The chapels, one observer commented, "were the places of the religious revival meetings with their impassioned overflow of powerful feeling; and they were the religious resting places for the overburdened, tired and often-desperate working classes." The smaller Methodist bodies of the eighteenth and nineteenth centuries, in both

England and the United States, had much in common in their attitude to, and manner of conducting, services of Christian worship. This, in general, arose from the absence of a set liturgy and the accepted custom that, while the minister normally conducted the service, laymen could and often did so too. In England, the Methodist New Connexion, of all the smaller non-Wesleyan bodies, displayed the closest family resemblance to the parent denomination. One of their first pronouncements was, "members of the old Connexion will be admitted to our Love-Feasts and sacraments." This common bond meant that, when reunion among these bodies was finally achieved, worship would not be a matter of heated controversy.

The United Methodist Free churches in the British Isles were the most "congregational" of all the Methodist subdenominations. Each congregation, or occasionally each quarterly meeting, directed its own affairs and there was little connexional control over worship. In the majority of United Methodist Free Church congregations the preacher was allowed to conduct the service as he thought fit, but the main components were extempore prayer, hymn singing, and an address. Each church or circuit had the right to choose its own officers, and they in turn had the obligation of providing for the regular observance of the Lord's Supper. In the United Methodist Free churches, the sacraments were to be "administered by preachers, itinerant or local," and ministers have generally seen the oversight of communion to be an important part of their pastoral responsibility. But laypeople were not absolutely barred from presiding at communion when the necessity arose, and although it is difficult to imagine a layperson ever doing so when a minister was present, undoubtedly it happened at certain times. On communion days, the stewards or other appointed persons distributed the elements to the people in their pews.

Primitive Methodism arose out of the experience of camp meetings, and its fellowship at first found expression in the love-feast, rather than in the sacrament of the Lord's Supper. So, while the first camp meeting was held in 1807, the first reference to the Lord's Supper in the Primitive Methodist minutes does not appear until fourteen years later in 1821. Where Wesley had been adamant that no one but ordained ministers be allowed to preside at communion in the Methodist societies, the Primitive Methodists allowed laypeople to conduct the service. Primitive Methodism was always concerned to widen, rather than to narrow, the availability of the sacrament, and when the question was asked, "To whom shall the sacrament be administered?" the answer was, "To all our societies which request it." Mainstream Methodists also tended to use the forms of service provided by John Wesley and the Conference, but Primitives resisted this constraint on their freedom in prayer, and seldom, if ever, used a set liturgy.

In the United States, divisions over worship were perhaps more serious, tied as they were to both race and class. The fact that Methodist reunion has never been fully achieved is often lamented, as is the fact that these divisions in American Methodism were spread widely across the various mission fields. The rift between those Methodists who wished their worship to express their prosperity and those Methodists who continued to worship in a revivalist style (even after "revivalism" per se had ceased to be a significant factor) was also more pronounced than it was in the British Isles, and affected all the Methodist subgroups as well as the parent body.

WORSHIP IN AFRICAN-AMERICAN AND AFRO-CARIBBEAN METHODISM

Debates on the "Africanness" of African-American worship have been among the most interesting current controversies in the field of liturgical studies. Certainly elements of traditional African ritual can be detected in Methodist worship wherever Methodism was embraced by members of the African diaspora. The "call and response," the emphasis on the gifts of the Spirit, the "Aunt Jane" tradition, in which an acknowledged elder (usually, but not invariably, a senior woman) regulated the spiritual "temperature" of the service, are all normal features of worship in African, African-American, and many Afro-Caribbean Methodist churches.

But when Richard Allen walked out of St. George's Church in Philadelphia, his principal aim was that people of African descent be treated with the same respect as their white co-religionists. He himself wrote a hymn describing the pain of this congregational discrimination:

> What poor despised company
> Of travellers are these,
> That's walking yonder narrow way,
> Along that rugged maze?

> Why they are of a royal line,
> They're children of a King;
> Heirs of immortal crown divine,
> And loud for joy they sing.

> Why some of them seem poor distress'd
> And lacking daily bread;
> Heirs of immortal wealth possess'd
> With hidden Manna fed.

Throughout the eighteenth and nineteenth centuries, African Americans and Afro-Caribbeans had been drawn in large numbers by Methodist preachers. Those held in the bonds of slavery were sometimes required by their owners to attend Anglo churches, and were relegated to seating in the rear, in a gallery, or sometimes outside the building entirely. In other cases, slaves were able to form their own congregations, or met for worship in "brush arbors" and other secret locations. It was in these latter venues that distinctive forms of African-American and Afro-Caribbean Methodist worship developed. As we have seen, the issue of slavery would divide American Methodism along racial lines, and this division has never been wholly healed, with worship services in most of Methodism largely monocultural and monoracial.

Much of the characteristic tone of Methodist worship among those scattered by the African diaspora has been set by music.

For people who were illiterate or semiliterate, appealing, singable music played an integral part in structuring the world. [It was] a way of giving coherence and meaning to experience. Unconfined by time or space, the spiritual served as a powerful and spontaneous bond of communal identity, imparting hope to the despairing and dignity to the oppressed.

One description of a worship service at the Annual Conference of the Methodist Protestant Church (Colored) in November 1929 gives the flavor of worship in the African-American tradition within Methodism:

7:20 o'clock, Bro. E. L. Green led devotions. Lined Hymns 307 and 312. Bros. J. W. Wheat and J. C. Mangram led in prayer. Rev's C. Mangram and E. L. Hickson ascended the rostrum. Rev. C. Mangrum lined Hymn 307. Rev. E. L. Hickson arose and selected the text – Daniel 1st chapter and 8th verse. With much power he demonstrated the work intrusted [sic] to him. Rev. C. Mangrum closed, lining Hymn 312. The President led in prayer. The stewards came and collected $2.05.

Several things are worth noting here: the importance of singing and the practice of "lining" the hymns, the identification of power in preaching with the simultaneous acknowledgment that that power was being held "in trust" for the sake of the people, and the significance of prayer, including prayer led by laypeople.

Throughout the twentieth century, and especially in the period of the American civil rights movement, Methodist worship became the setting for expressing the longing for social justice in hymns, prayers, and other acts of worship. The *Disciplines* of the AME, the AMEZ, and the CME churches include regulations for the conduct of Christian worship. Music in African-American Methodism has had a profound effect on the music of the United Methodist Church as a whole.

The 1976 United Methodist hymnal includes a number of hymns from the black spiritual and gospel music traditions, which had found their way into African-American Methodist worship in the 1920s and 1930s, as well as James Weldon Johnson's hymn "Lord of the Weary Years," usually referred to as the black national anthem.

THE IMPACT OF METHODIST UNION IN BRITAIN

In the twentieth century, many of the Wesleyan denominations which had divided from one another in the eighteenth and nineteenth centuries began to repent of their estrangement, and conversations about reunion turned into proposals for reunion and then into actual institutional mergers. Worship was often the telltale sign of the kind of class divisions that existed within the Methodist churches, and as such presented a serious problem for denominations desiring to merge, and a problem that was particularly difficult to discuss openly. One English woman recalled the situation after reunion, when the local Wesleyan and Primitive Methodist congregations came together for worship in one building: "The Wesleyans looked down upon us ordinary Methodist mortals and the feeling on the other side was that the Wesleyans were a bunch of snobs."

In 1907 when the Methodist New Connexion, the United Methodist Free churches, and the Bible Christians united to form the United Methodist Church, the matter of forms of worship for the new denomination was raised. One observer was clear that the success of the union depended in part on the fact that "they had much in common in their attitude to the sacrament of the Lord's Supper, so there were no difficult problems to solve. They all preferred a non-liturgical pattern of celebration and they all agreed that the Lord's Supper was 'a divine badge of membership.' " For all these denominations, the Lord's Supper tended to be celebrated once a month in town churches and once a quarter in rural churches. Other worship questions were equally easy to solve, since all these denominations valued extempore prayer, fervent sermons, and hymn singing as the normative pattern for worship.

The administration of the sacraments presented more serious problems to the negotiators of Methodist Union in Great Britain in 1932. The Wesleyans were adamant that the normal practice in the united church should be that ordained clergy would be the ordinary ministers of the sacramental services. At the same time, the smaller Methodist denominations wished provision to be made for those churches that could show that they were "deprived of a reasonably frequent and regular administration [of the sacraments] through lack of ministers." They requested that in such circumstances lay people should be allowed to preside. A compromise between the two parties was reached in the final determination that, in such a case, "the Circuit concerned may apply to the Conference for the authorization of persons other than ministers to minister the Sacrament." No directions are given on precisely how the service should be conducted.

Methodist union in Great Britain resulted in the publication of the *Book of Offices* in 1936, which contained orders of service for holy communion, the first being a traditional Wesleyan service and the second a new compilation intended for the use of societies that were unaccustomed to a liturgy. Many promoted the *Book of Offices* as essential to the success of Methodist Union, highlighting its balance of order and freedom. One supporter argued that:

Its Communion Office, as all the offices in the Book, has the full approval of Conference, yet Ministers are at liberty to conduct the service in any form acceptable to the Methodist people and not untrue to Methodist tradition. The ordination vows of a Methodist minister hold him to be "a faithful dispenser of the Word of God and of His Holy Sacraments," and when he takes those vows, he does so with the intention of fulfilling them according to the book from which his ordination service is taken.

Material from *The Book of Offices* was used by the Methodist Church in the United States in framing the 1945 *Book of Worship*, and other Methodist churches also found it useful in their own processes of liturgical revision.

In 1939 the three main Methodist bodies in the United States merged, and various orders of service were produced for the new United Methodist Church. In 1945 the UMC *Book of Worship* was published, the first official (although declared to be for "voluntary" and "optional" use) service-book for American Methodists since John Wesley's *Sunday Service* in 1784. (Orders for Sunday worship and for the sacramental services had indeed been appended to the various editions of the *Discipline*, but these were for the use of ministers rather than for congregations.) This book shared in both the "esthetic" tradition and the revivalist tradition. It included an order of worship patterned after Wesley, and an argument for a "four-fold movement" of worship (adoration, confession, affirmation of faith, and dedication of life). In the early 1960s, when a new service-book was being compiled, there was a revived interest in Wesley's theological and liturgical work, and the "trial use" services leading up to the 1965 *Book of Worship* displayed that interest in many details. But by the time the *Book of Worship* was published, most of the Wesleyan material had been lost.

THE MODERN PERIOD OF SERVICE-BOOK REVISION

Beginning in the early 1970s, many Methodist churches throughout the world undertook revision of service materials. This widespread enthusiasm for liturgical revision was due, at least in part, to Methodist attention to the process of reform of the rites in the Roman Catholic Church that had issued from the deliberations of the Second Vatican Council (1962–5). These Roman Catholic rites had reflected not only the revolution in Christian theology and biblical scholarship that had taken place in the decades leading up to the Council, but also the substantial research into ancient Christian texts and practices within what has come to be called the twentieth-century "liturgical movement." The first official version containing revised services appeared in 1975, when the Methodist Church in the British Isles published a new *Methodist Service Book* (*MSB*). In the United States a series of "Supplemental Liturgical Resources" began to appear in 1972, preparatory to a set of new services, which were included in the *United Methodist Hymnal* (1989) and then (in a revised form) in a separate service-book published in 1992.

In addition to the Roman Catholic Church, other Christian denominations, including Lutherans, Anglicans, and Presbyterians, were also working on revisions of their own service-books, and Methodist participation in the World Council of Churches' Faith and Order meetings, and in ecumenical conversations in groups like the Joint Liturgical Group in England, and the Consultation on Common Texts and the Consultation on Christian Unity in the United States, was important to the framing of Methodist service materials. In addition, the discussions on worship that accompanied the various unions in which Methodists were participants (e.g. the United Church of Canada, the Uniting Church of Australia) were noted as they progressed. Most Methodist churches throughout the world have produced new service materials in this time of exceptional fecundity in liturgical renewal.

Methodist reception of a number of ecumenical principles is embodied in the services produced in the modern period. Among these principles was the centrality of the Eucharist to Christian faith and life; the Eucharist was, as the Vatican Council documents had put it, the "source and summit" of Christian experience. The *MSB* embodied the desire of many to celebrate the Lord's Supper more frequently, and two services of Word and

Sacrament a month (one morning, one evening) became normal in many British churches. In addition, a challenge was made to the revival pattern of worship services that had prevailed in large tracts of Methodism since the late nineteenth century. In the new orders of worship, the service was often divided into the "Ministry of the Word" and the "Response to the Word." This moved the sermon from the end to the middle of the rite, with various forms of response possible: the Eucharist, baptism, confirmation, and reception of new members, various forms of prayer (prayers of thanksgiving, confession, petition, or intercession), even the possibility of a wedding. The use of an ecumenical lectionary, with lessons from the Old Testament, the Epistles, and the Gospels, as well as a psalm appointed for each occasion, became the norm, and lectionary preaching has replaced topical preaching in much of Methodism. Along with this came the wider adoption of the Christian year, with the introduction of a number of occasions and services new to many Methodists: Advent, Ash Wednesday, the Easter Vigil, and All Saints' Day (a festival for which John Wesley had held particular affection). In the last quarter of the twentieth century, the use of gender-inclusive liturgical language affected many of the Methodist churches, with the United Methodist Church leading the way with several influential publications and conferences.

THE MODERN SACRAMENTAL REVIVAL

In the modern period, many individuals and groups have sought to restore to Methodism the kind of sacramental worship and piety that the Wesleys had sought for the early Methodist societies and which were seen to be the ethos of the early church. Two groups stand out in this regard, one established in the Methodist Church in Great Britain and the other in the United Methodist Church in the United States. Both of these groups were formed in reaction to the preaching-centered style of worship that was so prevalent on both sides of the Atlantic, and both sought to return the sacraments to the center of Methodist faith and practice.

The Methodist Sacramental Fellowship (MSF) was founded in 1935 by British Methodists who were influenced by both the Parish Communion movement in the Church of England and the wider ecumenical movement that would later be embodied in the formation of the World Council of Churches in 1948. The MSF's stated aims were to:

1. reaffirm the Catholic faith based upon the apostolic testimony of Holy Scripture, witnessed to in the Nicene Creed, and professed by the church down the ages;

2. restore to Methodism the sacramental worship of the Universal Church and in particular the centrality of the Eucharist – as set forth in the lifelong teaching and practice of the Wesleys;
3. work and pray for the restoration of Catholic unity in Christ's church.

Each member of the MSF also pledges to say the daily office (according to the rites provided by the Fellowship) each day, to receive holy communion regularly, and to promote the reunion of divided Christianity. The MSF has for many years sponsored a lecture on some liturgical subject at each Annual Conference of the British Methodist Church.

In the United States, the counterpart of the MSF is the Order of Saint Luke (OSL), described as "the Religious Order in the United Methodist Church dedicated to Sacramental and Liturgical Scholarship, Education, and Practice." Founded in 1946, the OSL considers itself as a dispersed community of persons who live under a common discipline. The OSL has a strong publishing ministry designed to "put into the hands of students and practitioners resources which have theological, historical, ecumenical, and practical integrity." Published works of liturgical scholarship that have gone out of print (for example J. Ernest Rattenbury's edition of and commentary on *The Eucharistic Hymns of John and Charles Wesley* [1948/1990]), continue to be produced under the auspices of the OSL.

Even though the return of holy communion to the main weekly Sunday service has been on the agenda of the liturgical movement and the various Methodist sacramental renewal organizations for many years, there are few signs that they will succeed. In most Methodist congregations the Lord's Supper is an occasional service, and the sermon remains the centerpiece of Christian worship. In the contemporary service-books, however, many services (the ordination of ministers, the public recognition of local preachers, the reception of new members, the dedication of Sunday school teachers, and the Covenant Service, for example), are intended to reach their climax with the Lord's Supper. And there is some inclination on the part of ministers to include the Lord's Supper as a normal part of funerals and weddings, with the rubrics in both these cases stipulating: "Here may follow the holy communion."

CONCLUSION

No analysis of Methodist orders of service, hymnals, and church architecture, useful as it may be, can give us an accurate sense of the "feel" of Methodist services of worship. Whether formal or informal, rooted in the revival tradition or the Prayer Book tradition, all Methodist worship aims at a kind of hospitality that is noteworthy. As one British Methodist Church leader opined in 1902:

If we invite, we must welcome. We set ourselves to welcome everybody, make them feel at home, and secure their interest from the start. Fifty workers distribute hymn sheets, conduct people to their seats, smile and shake hands. There is not a dull moment from start to finish. Before a man knows it, he is caught in the swing of things and forgets he is a stranger.

In addition, beyond the normal Sunday service and the sacramental services, many forms of Methodist worship are indistinguishable from Christian services in other denominations. Methodist weddings and funerals, for example, although they have their own history and trajectory, are hardly "Methodist" in any distinctive sense. Methodist pragmatism, which clearly extended to worship, has also allowed the congregational common prayer of Methodists around the globe to adapt itself to local circumstances. In many of these cases, Methodist worship has so fully adapted to the forms of religiosity prevailing in the wider culture that little that is peculiarly "Methodist" remains. Worship in Methodist families shares in much of the style and some of the substance of Methodist public worship, and the reciprocal relationship between private, devotional prayer and prayer in common has been noted by many observers. Over and over we find Methodists learning their prayers in church, and then carrying them into the home, the temperance meeting, and their evangelistic activity. In this way even the distinction between what goes on in church, and what goes on in other settings where prayers are said, is sometimes difficult to make.

Some scholars have wished to describe Methodist worship as a distinct and autonomous liturgical tradition, standing alongside, for example, the Orthodox, the Lutheran, and the Anglican traditions. While this may have some historical validity, it does not describe the current situation "on the ground," since Methodist worship is so often indistinguishable from other forms of Protestant worship, and has in many cases abandoned its Wesleyan roots in favor of a kind of pragmatic inculturation to local circumstances. Indeed, it is the "chameleon-like" character of Methodist worship that has allowed it to enter into so many ecumenical mergers with so few problems in the area of worship, and to adapt to the wide variety of circumstances encountered among other cultures and in different societies.

CHAPTER 9

Methodist social ethics

As we have seen, Methodist theology and spirituality have been marked from the very beginning by a certain essential pragmatism, leading Methodists in every generation toward a deep engagement with the world, including the world of political and social action. This action, however, has been embodied in a wide variety of shapes and forms. Many Methodists have taken important leadership roles in public life: there have been Methodist presidents and prime ministers, legislators, and leaders of political parties and trades union movements. Other Methodists have simply worked behind the scenes, campaigning diligently for persons and causes in which they deeply believed. And if the forms of service embraced by Methodists have been diverse, their political principles have been equally so, ranging from the far left to the far right.

A look at the modern period of global politics reveals the wide variety of patterns of Methodist social involvement. On the left of the political spectrum, Donald Soper, who became Lord Soper in 1965, and Leslie Griffiths, who became a member of the British House of Lords in 2004, have been committed to the agenda of British socialism, and especially pacifism. Other Methodists, such as Harry F. Ward, Frank Mason North, and Bishop Bromley Oxnam of the American Methodist Church, have operated even further to the left and have been accused by their opponents of being communists. Some Methodists, however, have located themselves firmly on the political right wing: George W. Bush of the United States, who came to Methodism in mid-life, and Margaret Thatcher, the daughter of a Methodist local preacher, found conservatism the most congenial way of embodying their desire to serve their respective countries. In changing times, Methodists have sometimes shifted their political strategies if not their political leanings, so in the old South Africa we find Nelson Mandela the revolutionary and in the new South Africa we find Nelson Mandela the mediator. Advocacy for impoverished and marginalized people has occupied the lives of great numbers of Methodists, including liberation theologian

José Míguez Bonino of Argentina, and Methodist political activism has also in many cases taken the form of peacemaking. The bitter ethnic conflict in Macedonia, for example, called for the gifts of a Methodist, Boris Trajkovski, who took the post of President of this new Republic. Tireless in his efforts to prevent a civil war in his own country, Trajkovski died in 2004 in an airplane crash in Bosnia on his way to yet another meeting to reconcile the different factions of the former Yugoslavia. Attitudes to peace and war have also varied widely. When the UMC House of Bishops called for disarmament in 1986, Paul Ramsey, a leading Methodist ethicist, immediately restated the just war theory.

In this chapter we will consider the various strands of Methodist social thinking that have produced such different stances and different forms of political and social activism.

THE WESLEYAN BACKGROUND

The origins of Wesleyan Methodism lay in a diligent search for practical holiness within the framework of the societies, classes, and bands. We have already looked at the ethical behavior expected of the individual Methodist as set out in the *General Rules*, with its prohibitions against drunkenness, trafficking in spirituous liquors, fighting, quarreling, brawling, lawsuits between Christians, returning evil for evil, tax avoidance, and usury. But in addition to this emphasis on the formation of a personal Christian ethic, there is also within the Methodist tradition a deep concern for the wider society, and a persistent desire for implementing beneficial structural changes in the way in which human beings organize their common life. In a series of tracts and pamphlets with titles such as *Thoughts on the Present Scarcity of Provisions* (1773) and *Thoughts upon Slavery* (1784), Wesley demonstrated a strong "this-worldliness" in his theology. But Wesley's political and economic thought ranged well beyond reflection on particular eighteenth-century social ills.

At first, the "worldliness" of Methodism may seem surprising. John Wesley spent much of his life emphasizing the importance of setting the mind and heart upon holy things, and on striving for perfection, and Charles Wesley's hymns often focus on the world beyond, and on the soul's ultimate destiny in heaven.

But the quest for holiness and for the saving of one's soul has to be set within the wider context of eighteenth-century post-millennialism which asserted that, when the world was ready to receive him, Jesus would come in power to inaugurate a glorious thousand-year reign. In this view, the task of the Christian is to transform the world so that it might be ready for the coming of the Christ. In its optimistic vision of the saints of God preparing the way for a kingdom of justice and mercy, post-millennialism differed from the later, largely nineteenth-century, pre-millennialism, which claimed that Jesus' reign would be a terrible judgment on sinners and a sinful world, and that in order to avoid this judgment the saints would be extracted ("raptured") from the world before Jesus came. For pre-millennialists, to be "saved" is to be taken out of this world. For post-millennialists, including Wesleyan Methodists, to be saved is to participate in the world's redemptive restoration.

For some of Wesley's near contemporaries, the earthly restoration envisioned by the post-millennialists had already begun as a result of the church's missionary activity. Isaac Watts (1674–1748) had proclaimed that:

> People and realms of every tongue
> Dwell on his love with sweetest song;

and that:

> Blessings abound where're he reigns;
> The prisoner leaps to lose his chains;
> The weary find eternal rest;
> And all the sons of want are blessed.

In the year after Watts' death, Charles Wesley celebrated the immanent presence of Christ and the "this-worldly" salvation offered in the Gospel message using biblical images similar to those Watts had employed. Hymn 38 in the *CHPM* declares that the blind and the deaf and the dumb are being healed and "Gospel salvation" is being preached to the poor (all signs of the presence of the Messiah according to Matthew 11:4–5). For Charles Wesley it is this world and this present age where Christ is at work:

> To us and to them,   Is published the word;
> Then let us proclaim   Our life-giving Lord
> Who now is reviving   His work in our days,
> And mightily striving   To save us by grace.
>
> O Jesus, ride on,   Till all are subdued;
> Thy mercy make known,   And sprinkle thy blood,
> Display thy salvation,   And teach the new song
> To every nation,   And people, and tongue!

A similar vision of a world ruled and redeemed by Christ animated John Wesley as well. In his sermon on *Scriptural Christianity* he described his vision of the millennial reign of God on earth, using a prolonged sequence of biblical quotations and allusions

Suppose now the fullness of time to be come, and the prophecies to be accomplished. What a prospect is this! . . . Wars are ceased from the earth . . . no brother rising up against brother; no country or city divided against itself, and tearing out its own bowels. Here is no oppression to make (even) "the wise man mad"; no extortion to "grind the face of the poor"; no robbery or wrong; no rapine or injustice; for all are "content with such things as they possess." Thus "righteousness and peace have kissed each other" (Psalm 85:10); they have "taken root and filled the land;" "righteousness flourishing out of the earth," and "peace looking down from heaven."

Wesley was clear that when all this comes to pass, it will have significant social as well as spiritual consequences: because people will be of one heart and soul, no one will say that anything she possesses is her own. In that day there will be "none among them that lacketh; for every man loveth his neighbour as himself." And all walk by one rule: "Whatever ye would that men should do unto you, even so do unto them."

Charles Wesley reinforced his brother's teaching continually in his hymns and poems. So a poem entitled "The Kingdom of Christ" describes the dawn of the millennium:

> The saints shall flourish in his days,
> Deck'd in the robes of joy and praise;
> Peace, like a river, from his throne
> Shall flow to nations yet unknown.

Consequently, then, the task of Christians was to engage in all forms of missionary activity, pressing onward

> Till all the earth, renew'd
> In righteousness divine.
> With all the hosts of God
> In one great chorus join.

With the coming of Christ, men and women would be able to look into each other's hearts, said John Wesley, "and see that only love and God are there." Because Methodists were to become people who longed for the coming of Christ, and who (in Charles's words) prayed urgently: "Thy quiet and peaceable reign; In mercy establish below," there would be no element of "quietism" in individual ethics, nor any possibility of sequestering themselves from social action.

In order to reach this goal, both Wesleys summoned human beings to be agents for moral and ethical change in wider society. "We Methodists," said John Wesley, "attempt as much as we can, to make mankind happy." Sometimes, to be sure, he seems to imply that action in the world is merely palliative. So in their work among the poor, Wesley says, Methodists must strive "to lessen their sorrows, and to teach them, in whatsoever state they are, therewith to be content." Some historians have looked upon this, and other similar remarks, as clear evidence that Karl Marx was right when he described religion as the "opium of the people," designed to foster "the spiritual incorporation of workers into expanding industrial capitalism."

John Wesley lived long before the great social and economic theorists of the nineteenth century, and his writings about social ethics perhaps display a rather naive sense of the relationship between economic cause and effect. But Wesley's sincere desire "to make mankind happy" and his sharp perceptions of the ills of his own eighteenth-century world did lead him to ponder deeply on issues of social ethics. Many of the issues that occupied his mind and heart continue to challenge Methodists today, even though they may analyze their social and economic situation rather differently. What is quite certain is that contemporary Methodism derives much inspiration from John Wesley's willingness to engage theologically, biblically, and practically such questions as the causes of poverty and slavery, and the status of women, as well as the most appropriate methods of dealing with all the various forms of social deprivation.

JOHN WESLEY AND THE POOR

Few reformers of the church have ever addressed the needs of the poor so wholeheartedly as John Wesley. And his concern never took the form of superficial charity. "I love the poor," he wrote in his *Journal*. "In many of them I find pure genuine grace, unmixed with paint, folly and affectation." His own practice of visiting, providing for, and tending to the needs of those on the underside of society speaks volumes, as does his sensitivity to the causes for poverty:

On Friday and Saturday, I visited as many more sick as I could. I found some in their cells underground, others in their garrets, half starved both with cold and hunger, added to weakness and pain. But I found not one of them unemployed who was able to crawl about the room. So wicked, so devilishly false is that common objection, "They are poor only because they are idle." If you saw these things with your own eyes, could you lay out money in ornaments and superfluities?

John Wesley had, in the language of contemporary liberation theology, a "preferential option for the poor." It was to the poor that the promises of

God were made and to the poor that Wesley's own preaching was primarily directed. "It is well a few of the rich and noble are called," he wrote. "Oh, that God would increase their number! But I should rejoice (were it the will of God) if it were done by the ministry of others. If I must choose, I should still (as I have done hitherto) preach the gospel to the poor."

For his part Charles Wesley set these sentiments in verse in his hymns:

> Thy mind throughout my life be shown.
> While listening to the sufferer's cry.
> The widow's and the orphan's groan
> On mercy's wings I swiftly fly
> The poor and helpless to relieve
> My life, my all for them to give.

As Methodism spread, Methodists were taught not only to use the "instituted" means of grace as they pressed toward holiness, that is, the Lord's Supper, prayers, Bible reading, fasting and "Christian conference" or fellowship, but also to use what Wesley called the "prudential" means of grace. Among these latter was "visiting the poor" in which Methodists would discover "grace." Recent scholarship has shown that Charles Wesley also expressed his brother's commitment to "works of mercy," which he considered to be as certainly means of grace as were the "works of piety" (p. 150). In other words, to be merciful was not merely a matter of the "imitation of Christ," but truly established an arena for divine encounter. So Charles Wesley saw Methodists as called to live out the faith and love they experienced as "vessels, instruments of grace."

Rule 17 of the *General Rules of the United Societies* echoes this commitment to the poor as a supreme work of mercy. Methodists are there enjoined to provide for the physical needs of their neighbors "by giving food to the hungry, by clothing the naked, by visiting or helping them that are sick or in prison." Obedience to this rule resulted in many practical schemes in early Methodism to defeat poverty, ranging from the establishment of dispensaries for the sick to loan societies for people who had been victimized by moneylenders who demanded extortionate interest. Wesley himself set up these kinds of loan societies, one based at the Foundery and another at the New Room, with financial transactions handled by administrators from the United Societies. The medical dispensaries often proved too expensive to operate (although on many occasions physicians volunteered their services to further Wesley's work in this area), but Wesley did publish a popular little medical guide, his *Primitive Physick: an Easy and Natural Method of Curing Most Diseases*, which went through thirty-two editions before 1828. Some of Wesley's recommendations seem bizarre to contemporary sensibilities, but *Primitive Physick* did at least offer some advice on proper nutrition, hygiene, the treatment of illnesses, and the care of the sick for those who would otherwise have had no guidance at all.

But despite the Wesley brothers' protestations against an interest in the wealthy, both John and Charles had wideranging contacts with the elite of London, Dublin, and elsewhere. They express genuine concern about the readiness of the rich to isolate themselves from the world's harsher social realities:

One reason the rich in general have so little sympathy for the poor is because they so seldom visit them. Hence it is that, according to the common observation one part of the world does not know what the other suffers. Many of them do not know because they do not care to know: they keep out of the way of knowing it – and plead their voluntary ignorance as an excuse for their hardness of heart.

But whether they knew it or not, Wesley argued, the prosperous actually *needed* the poor, who had much to teach them. To one of his followers who was, in the eighteenth-century phrase, a "gentlewomen," John Wesley gave the following advice: "I want you to converse more, abundantly more, with the poorest of people, who if they have no taste, have souls, which you may forward in their way to heaven. And they have (many of them) faith, and the love of God, in greater measure than any persons I know."

POLITICAL ACTION TO CHANGE THE CONDITION OF THE POOR

While John Wesley's concern for the physical wellbeing of the poor led him to admonish the rich to be generous out of their plenty, he also saw the necessity of altering the prevalent economic circumstances in order to eradicate the root causes of poverty. This meant that Methodists were called to engage in political action. Most decades of the eighteenth century were marked by inflationary rises in prices and chronic shortages of staple foodstuffs; the rich were not only prospering at the expense of the poor but were also causing that poverty by their self-indulgent habits and customs. It was Wesley's opinion that, whenever the rich made unnecessary expenditures on ostentatious banquets and balls, on lavish furniture and ornamentation, and on extravagant diversions, they not only robbed the poor, but robbed God as well. But Wesley also recognized that before any change could take place, the conscience of the rich would have to be awakened. Wesley tried to accomplish this in his tract *Thoughts on the Present Scarcity of Provisions* (1773):

I ask, first, Why are thousands of people starving, perishing for want, in every part of the nation? This fact I know; I have seen it with my eyes, in every corner of the land. I have known those who could only afford to eat a little coarse food once every other day. I have known one in London (and one that a few years before had all the conveniences of life) picking up from the dunghill stinking sprats, and carrying them home for herself and her children. I have known another gathering the bones which the dogs had left in the streets, and making broth of them to prolong a wretched life! I have heard a third artlessly declare, "Indeed I was very faint, and so weak I could hardly walk, until my dog, finding nothing at home, went out and brought a good sort of bone, which I took out of his mouth, and made a pure dinner!" Such is the case at this day of multitudes of people, in a land flowing, as it were, with milk and honey! Abounding with all the necessaries, the conveniences, the superfluities of life!

Wesley's analysis was straightforward. The cost of food was so great that people had no money to buy manufactured goods. This put small business owners out of work and caused widespread unemployment, and greater numbers of men and women became unable to afford food. Why was bread so inflated in its price? Bread was expensive because wheat was expensive. And why was wheat so costly? Because, Wesley answered, almost half of the wheat produced in Britain in each year went to the distilling industry. Oats too was exorbitantly expensive because there were four times as many coach and post-chaise horses as there had been, which had pushed up the price of oats. In addition, the demand for, and the profit to be made from, highly bred horses had shifted production away from the sheep and cattle needed to feed the industrial towns. Landowners had also discovered that using their land for cash crops would yield larger profits than could be had from renting out their lands to smallholders: those who kept a few pigs and poultry and sent pork and bacon, fowls and eggs to the towns. This Wesley called the "monopolizing of the farms: perhaps as mischievous a monopoly as was ever introduced into these kingdoms."

The remedy for this disastrous situation of inadequate provisions, Wesley proposed, was structural political change. First, the government should prohibit the distilling of liquor, which would immediately drive down the price of wheat. Similarly, a reduction in the demand for horses would result in a parallel reduction in the price of oats. Here taxation was the key: additional taxes should be levied on carriages and a tax of ten pounds imposed on each horse exported to the continent of Europe. The state would also have to put a ceiling on land rental. Above all the routine imposition of high taxes had to be reduced by cutting the national debt in half. It was obvious to Wesley that poverty had to be recognized to be a social and economic problem with which government ought to be immediately concerned as it set its macroeconomic policies.

It is hard to avoid the conclusion that Wesley's economic ethics contradict the spirit of capitalism, and any glorification of capitalism is contrary to Wesley's vision. His insistence that with property ownership came a radical social obligation, and his insistence in *Thoughts on the Present Scarcity of Provisions* that the state should intervene in economic processes, have consistently been major themes in Methodist social ethics since his time. The numbers of Methodists who would happily identify themselves as socialists attest to the persistence of Wesley's socioeconomic vision into the present day.

JOHN WESLEY AND THE RIGHTS OF WOMEN

It is not surprising that John and Charles Wesley would make a singular contribution to championing the rights of women in the context of a deeply patriarchal society. Under the tutelage of a formidable mother they could deeply appreciate gifts of intellect and spirituality in women, and the contributions women had to offer to the spiritual nurture of others. From early in its history, the Methodist movement involved women at all levels of its activity. They exhorted and prayed, led classes and bands, visited the sick and provided funds. Some were appointed to oversee charitable or educational institutions. Women like Grace Murray (later Mrs Bennet), Sarah Taft, Hannah Ball, Sarah Crosby, and Elizabeth Ritchie were even authorized, with the strong approval of John Wesley, to "travel the connexion" as itinerant preachers. He seemed entirely willing to lay aside St. Paul's statement "I permit not a woman to speak in the congregations" so that these women (who, he argued, had an "extraordinary call from God") might engage in the preaching ministry.

But Wesley also turned his attention to the more general state of women in eighteenth-century society. In his sermon *On the Visiting of the Sick* he attacks the requirement of submissiveness that was so often imposed upon his sisters in the faith:

It has long passed for a maxim with many that "women are only to be seen but not heard." And accordingly many of them are brought up in such a manner as if they were only designed for agreeable playthings! But is this doing honour to the sex? Or it is a real kindness to them? No, it is the deepest unkindness; it is horrid cruelty; it is mere Turkish barbarity. And I know not how any woman of sense and spirit can submit to it.

Consequently he urged "the natural right" of women to resist this kind of oppression: "Let all of you that have it in your power assert the right which the God of nature has given you. You as well as them are rational creatures. Yield not to that vile bondage any longer. You as well as men were made in the image of God: you are equally candidates for immortality. You too are called of God."

In Wesley's view, women must take full responsibility for themselves, becoming conscious, active agents for social change, and demanding equality, and he recognized this many years before either Jane Austen or Mary Wollstonecraft had ever set pen to paper. Two prominent Methodist ethicists have recently seen this as "a powerful liberationist statement," that was "radical when it was issued in 1786, because it still sounds radical today." Wesley also made a number of small liturgical changes that reinforced his ideas about the equality of men and women, including the removal of the word "obey" from the revision of the marriage rite that he sent to the Methodists in North America in 1784.

Consequently Methodist women have been always challenged to find their place in the life of their ecclesial institutions, and all major Methodist churches now ordain women, increasingly calling them to serve in the major leadership roles. But this progress toward full recognition of women's call to ordained ministry did not come easily. Even with Wesley's strong affirmation that a full range of ministries was open to women, after his death the increasing "respectability" of Methodism tended to reinforce the idea that the proper sphere of women was domestic rather than public. We can see the difficulties of the road back to full equality in the case of the MEC in the United States.

In March of 1880, the alumni association of Boston University School of Theology passed the following resolution:

Resolved: That the Alumni of the Theological School of Boston University memorialize the General Conference to ordain those women who have felt called to the Gospel ministry and who have taken thorough preparation in our colleges and theological schools, and who have shown by gifts, grace, and usefulness, that they have the essential qualifications for the Methodist ministry.

This motion was occasioned by the desire of one of their own graduates to be ordained. Anna Oliver had received a Bachelor of Sacred Theology degree at Boston University School of Theology in 1876, and had served two churches (one in Passaic, New Jersey, and one in Brooklyn, New York) with evident success. But when she was examined by the New England Annual Conference, Bishop Edward G. Andrews refused to present her to the General Conference for ordination, alleging that it was not lawful for him to do so, since, in his judgment "the law of the Church does not authorize the ordination of women."

Oliver was not presented, but those who proposed her candidacy decided on an alternative course of action: they would seek to have all distinctions on the basis of gender removed from the *Discipline* statutes on ordination. In support of this action, Oliver prepared a pamphlet in which she outlined the case for the ordination of women, which she herself distributed at the General Conference of the Methodist Episcopal Church in Cincinnati in May 1880. Her argument rested on several foundations: the natural gifts of women for pastoring, the sacramental needs of the mission field (where often the only Christians allowed access to indigenous women were other women), and the demands of charity and the Golden Rule. She concludes with the plea that Conference asks itself: "What would John Wesley do?" But the Conference not only rejected the motion regarding women's ordination in general, it also revoked the licenses to preach of all those women who currently held them. (Oliver was not the only woman presented for ordination at the New England Annual Conference in 1880. When Anna Howard Shaw, who had received her theological degree from Boston University in 1878, was told that there was no place for women in the ordained ministry of the Methodist Episcopal Church she left the denomination and was ordained in the Methodist Protestant Church later that same year.)

In the following meetings of General Conference, laywomen were chosen as delegates but until 1906 they were not allowed to be seated. At the same time, many within the Methodist Episcopal Church began work toward the political enfranchisement for women which culminated in the passage of the nineteenth Amendment to the United States' Constitution giving women the vote. The increasing equality of opportunity for women in the social and political realm raised the pressure on the church to address the issue of the ordination of women. But there remained substantial opposition. In 1924, after much bitter debate on the matter of ordination and Conference membership for women, a compromise proposal was advanced, whereby women would be allowed to be ordained locally but not admitted to Conference membership.

In the meantime, another obstacle was put in the way of full clergy rights for women. Talks surrounding the merger of the MEC and the MECS were at a delicate stage, and church leaders became concerned that the question of women's ordination would derail the entire process. As a result, women were not given clergy status in the charter of the new denomination, and when a motion was made to the first Annual Conference of the Methodist Church in 1939 that women be ordained and admitted to Conference membership, it was soundly defeated on the grounds that the new denomination already faced sufficient problems. It would take another seventeen years for women to be granted unrestricted clergy standing with the simple amendment to the *Discipline*: "All foregoing paragraphs, chapters and sections of Part III [of the *Discipline*] shall apply to women as well as to men."

With local variations, this story was played out throughout the Methodist family of churches during the nineteenth and twentieth centuries. As we can see, roles for women in Methodism have not only been defined by theological and biblical factors, but also by prevailing cultural norms, by the larger course of political enfranchisement, by internal church politics, and by access to training. While almost all Methodist churches around the world now ordain women, this does not mean that gender discrimination no longer exists within Methodism, and many pastoral charges are effectively closed to women because of opposition within individual congregations. In places where the system of itinerancy and connexional appointments remains strong, however, bishops and Conferences have met these challenges with creative and sensitive pastoral appointments.

But there remain too many places in the world where women are routinely exploited and oppressed, as well as situations where women internalize the inferior status attributed to them by the wider society. In many such cases, political and social documents issued by the various Methodist churches speak to the condition of women, and address many of the same issues that Wesley forcefully raised for his eighteenth-century followers. But new issues are always rising to the surface. Domestic violence, a living wage for women workers, equal access to educational opportunities, and equal treatment under the law are all questions that animate the work of Methodist Conferences around the world, and they have abundant resources in the theological and biblical work of the Wesleys to aid them in this task.

JOHN WESLEY AND WAR AND PEACE

John Wesley's idealized Christianity corresponded neither to the political realities of a fallen world nor to the institutional realities of a fallen church. In his sermon *The Mystery of Iniquity*, he attributes the history of the corruption of the church to the activity of Constantine the Great (d. 337), who tied the Christian Church to the secular empire in the closest possible way:

Persecution never did, never could give any lasting wound to genuine Christianity. But the greatest it ever received, the grand blow which struck the very root of that humble gentle patient love, which is the fulfilling of the Christian law, the whole essence of true religion, was struck in the fourth century by Constantine the Great, when he called himself a Christian, and poured in a flood of riches, honours, and power upon the Christians, more especially upon the clergy.

Wesley drew a direct line between the secularizing influence of Constantine and what he considered to be the acute scarcity of true Christians in the world around him. As he remarked, "the few Christians that are upon the earth are only to be found where you never look for them." As John Wesley contemplated the fallen condition of the world, he was most distressed by the persistent existence of war, and he thought deeply about the causes and the remedies for this situation.

Wesley had a clear sense of the "complicated misery" that war always represents: "Hark, the cannons roar! A patchy cloud covers the face of the earth. Noise, confusion terror, reign over all! Dying groans are on every side. The bodies of men are pierced, torn, hewed in pieces; their blood is poured upon the earth like water." He was equally convinced of the irrationality of using war as a means of settling disputes. In a graphically imagined scene, he pictures two armies in battle, with the soldiers on each side bayoneting their opponents "through the head or body, to stab them, or split their skulls, and send most of their souls into everlasting fire, as fast as they possibly can": "Why so? What harm have they done to them? But a man who is King of France has a quarrel with another man, who is King of England. So these Frenchmen are to kill as many of these Englishmen as they can to prove the King of France is in the right."

Yet Wesley was not essentially a radical pacifist, nor did he ever suggest that pacifism was the only way to be a Methodist. His first Conference in 1744 asked the following:

Q. Is it lawful to bear arms?
A. We incline to think it is: 1. because there is no command against it in the New Testament, 2. because Cornelius, a soldier, is commended there.

It is interesting to note that there is a tentativeness about the words "incline to think," which may suggest that opinions were divided in the Conference. We do know that John Nelson (1707–74), one of Mr. Wesley's preachers, took the pacifist position. Early in his life Nelson had been caught by a press-gang, and his testimony on that occasion was clear and forceful:

When brought before the court, John Nelson refused to serve: "I shall not fight; for I cannot bow my knee before the Lord to pray for a man, and get up and kill him when I have done" . . . When a uniform was forced upon, he responded: "Why do you gird me with these warlike habiliments? For I am a man adverse to war, and shall not fight, but under the Prince of Peace, the Captain of my salvation; and the weapons he gives me are not carnal like these."

There were, however, many equally devout Methodists who did wear the king's uniform, and we have seen them founding Methodist societies wherever the king's armies went.

If Wesley himself cannot be described as a pacifist, this does not mean that he was not an advocate of peacemaking, and of the diligent search for alternative modes of solving human disputes. The key to Wesley's attitude toward war and peace is contained in the words quoted above from the sermon on *The Mystery of Iniquity*: "the few Christians that are upon the earth." For Wesley, to be a "Christian" in this sense is to be committed to restoring the image of God in self and in neighbor, and this restoration creates sons and daughters of peace. In his third sermon on *The Sermon on Mount*, Wesley describes what he means by the term "peacemakers":

In its literal meaning it implies those lovers of God and man who utterly detest and abhor all strife and debate, all variance and contention; and accordingly labour with all their might either to prevent this fire of hell from being kindled, or when it is kindled from breaking out, or when it is broke out from spreading any farther.

Their aims and methods are distinctive:

They endeavour to calm the stormy spirits of men, to quiet their turbulent passions, to soften the minds of contending parties, and if possible to reconcile them to each other. They use all innocent arts, and employ all their strength, all their talents which God has given them, as well as to preserve peace where it is as to restore it where it is not.

If the Gospel of Jesus was ever to transform political ethics, Wesley's people were compelled to become peacemakers like this. But Wesley's teaching was not radically pacifist, since he remained wedded to the possibility of a "just war." (There are many instances where he allows violence in self-defense, for example.) The important thing, however, was that God intends peace and justice to prevail and there would come a moment in the political affairs of humankind when grace might break through, when God's salvation would be allowed to change human life. The task of the Christian is to stand ready for such moments to occur. Wesley certainly looked for a time when "wars are ceased from the earth." Under the prevalent veil of iniquity, as he saw it, the time of peace might only be an eschatological dream, but perhaps, if Christians were not so few, and those that there were learnt the arts of peacemaking, this dream might become reality.

In the twentieth century, when the full horror of mass warfare became only too apparent, questions of pacifism and peacemaking moved to center-stage in Methodist thought and action. Many Methodists, in every part of the world, committed themselves to the search for alternatives to the violence of war. As a result, wherever picketers have surrounded military bases, wherever people have boycotted those profiting from the arms race, wherever such groups as Amnesty International have operated, Methodists have been there, carrying forward Wesley's vision of a world transformed by the Prince of Peace. At the same time, Methodist theologians like Stanley Hauerwas explicate the radical pacifist position, claiming that supporting the taking-up of arms for any reason places one outside of the Methodist framework.

JOHN WESLEY AND SLAVERY

Just six days before his death John Wesley wrote to William Wilberforce (1759–1833), the leading British advocate of the abolition of slavery, that "he should temper his steel" as God's weapon against "that execrable villainy, which is the scandal of religion, of England, and of human nature." Wesley's aversion to slavery had deep roots in his American experience in the 1730s. As well as being exposed to many obvious cases of inhumane treatment of slaves in Georgia, he had traveled to Charleston in the neighboring colony of South Carolina where he had seen a slave market where families were broken up and the individual members sold. From that moment he regarded slavery as "that execrable sum of villainies." Forty years later in 1775 Wesley's opinions had not changed, and he published his *Thoughts upon Slavery* where, simply and unequivocally, he stated the principle: "liberty is the right of every human creature as soon as he breathes the air and no human law can deprive him of that right which he derives from the law of nature."

Wesley also recognized the wider economic ills that resulted from the slave trade. He firmly believed that this "horrid trade" was the origin of the treachery and warfare that was spreading across Africa. Describing the results of one battle to procure slaves so bloody that "four thousand five hundred men were slain upon the spot," Wesley added sardonically, "Thus Christians preach the Gospel to the Heathen." Addressing the plantation owners and their slave masters in the *Thoughts upon Slavery*, Wesley wrote: "now it is your money that pays the merchant, and through him the captains and the African butchers. You therefore are guilty, yea, principally guilty, of all these frauds, robberies and murders." This attitude to slavery was quite different from that of George Whitefield, who had bought seventy-five slaves for the plantation in Savannah in order to maintain his Orphan House there. "I trust many of them will be brought to Jesus," Whitefield said, claiming that the practice of the Old Testament patriarchs legitimated the owning of slaves. The ethical gap between these two men, both claiming the name Methodist, foreshadows the great division of American Methodism after Wesley's death.

An early American Conference in 1780 entirely endorsed John Wesley's stand against slavery, asking, in the traditional Conference style:

Q. Do we pass disapprobation on all our friends who keep slaves and advise their freedom?
A. Yes.

More practically the further question was put:

Q. Ought not this Conference to require those travelling preachers who keep slaves to give promises to set them free?
A. Yes.

So, while Methodist laypeople were merely (if strongly) advised to free their slaves, Methodist preachers were obliged to comply absolutely. The Christmas Conference in 1784 was crystal clear on this matter, and the first *Rules* of the MEC affirmed that "slavery is contrary to the golden rule of God." In that year all Methodists, lay persons as well as clergy, were required to draw up "within a year" an instrument emancipating their slaves. The preachers were to exclude from their congregations those who would not do so; and no slaveholders would thereafter be admitted to membership. The only exceptions to this requirement were made for those who lived in the states where the law did not permit emancipation. Both Francis Asbury and Thomas Coke were adamant about enforcing this decision. Asbury asked rhetorically, "If the Gospel will authorize slavery what will it not authorize?"

But the Baltimore Conference's decision on slaveholding unleashed swift and negative reactions from Methodist people, and within six months efforts to enforce the Conference resolutions were abandoned. Many preachers continued to speak out courageously in support of the Conference stand against slavery, but four years later the next Conference found itself forced to forsake implementation of the minute on slavery "till the deliberations of a future Conference." "We had to compromise or lose the South," wrote one early nineteenth-century bishop.

This is not to say that many white Methodists were not moved by the plight of their African brothers and sisters. On the first Friday of March 1796, the "general traveling ministry" of the MEC declared a "solemn day of fasting, humiliation, supplication and prayer." Among the "manifold sins and iniquities" that members of Methodist societies were called to address in their prayers were the "enslavement" groups of people within the free United States, in order that soon "Africans and Indians may help to fill the pure church of God." On the first Thursday of October in that same year, a day of "holy gratitude and thanksgiving" was called inviting the Methodist people to give thanks to God for the "African liberty," which was represented in the First Emancipation which had, beginning in 1780, resulted in the freeing of slaves from Delaware to New England. In some cases American Methodists put their money where their prayers were and raised funds for the purchase of individual slaves who were members of Methodist societies. Such was the case of John Charleston, a black Methodist from Virginia, who was freed after traveling preacher Stith Mead organized a fund-raising effort for the purpose. Ordained a deacon in 1809, Charleston traveled the circuit with Mead for a number of years in the 1820s, and would regularly "walk thirty miles a day and preach three times."

Slaveholding Methodists (who were to be found in the North as well as the South) used several main lines of argument in support of their position. Some rooted the institution of slavery in their reading of the Bible. In the New Testament, it was argued "it is nowhere forbidden," and furthermore "in the perfect society of the primitive Christian community, slaves were held." It was further pointed out that St. Paul expressly enjoined slaves to be submissive to their masters. George Whitefield's argument that the Old Testament patriarchs held slaves was endlessly repeated, and it was reinforced by the proposition that blacks could be enslaved as part of the divine economy because they were the descendants of Ham. (This argument was also used later, even by Methodists, to justify apartheid in South Africa.) Others took a more practical approach, contending that "the Negro was better off and better cared for as a slave than if he were free." (This idea was given a further nuance by comparing the situation of the slaves with the condition of free white laborers in the Southern states.)

How deeply and sincerely these convictions were held by Southern Methodists can be illustrated by the case of William Winans (1788–1857), a presiding elder from the state of Mississippi. He was asked by his Southern colleagues to be one of the spokesmen for the right of Methodists to keep slaves, and passionately debated these issues on the floor of the Conference in the years leading up to 1844. In 1835, Winans assured a Northerner that the only possible object of frenzied Yankee agitation for abolition was "to rouse the Slaves to an attempt to effect their own deliverance from bondage." This, he projected, meant "insurrection, bloodshed, anarchy, and disaster, not only for the South, but also for the North." Furthermore, Winans asked, what good would result to the slaves, if Christians were to refuse to be slaveholders? He answered his own question: none whatsoever. Perhaps one slave in five hundred would be manumitted, leaving the remainder in the possession of non-Christian owners. This course of action would "interdict all intercourse between their slaves and religious men" and would commit slaves to the dominance of irreligious masters.

Like many of his slaveholding colleagues, Winans was convinced that the most ethical choice for Methodists in the matter of slavery lay in supporting the work of the Colonization Society, which had been founded in 1817 in order to raise funds for returning Africans to Africa, chiefly to Liberia. "But Alas!" Winans expostulated, the abolitionists were blind to "its divinely-directed design for a peaceful and orderly removal of former slaves to Liberia." Of the abolitionists in general Winans wrote: "I do not impugn their motives, I infer insanity." The abolitionists, he continued, "came forward as friends of the slave par excellence," when in actuality their activities "overcast the prospects with tenfold darkness" by adding "chains, and bolts, and burdens to the miserable objects of their pestiferous kindness." For Winans both the slaves and the slaves' friends in the South were "thwarted, outraged and grieved by the mischievous philanthropy" of the Northerners, who were putting at risk the safety of whites and blacks in the slaveholding states. Consequently, Winans warned as early as 1838 of the potential for a civil war. Stating that unless Congress "put a strong and emphatic negative upon the Abolition practices of some of its members," the time was not far away when Americans would be a "divided people, exposed to all the horrors of neighbor-warfare, rendered more horrible by the feeling of fraternal hatred."

These deeply felt ethical differences ultimately divided the MEC. By 1844 Southern Methodists had reached the end of their patience and declared that "the continued agitation on the subject of slavery rendered the jurisdiction of the General Conference over their Conferences inconsistent with the success of ministry in the slaveholding states." The division resulting from the creation of the MECS in 1845 was to last until 1939, and in some ways is still not fully healed.

ETHICAL ATTITUDES DIVIDING AMERICAN METHODISTS

An early manifestation of the ethical differences that were to play themselves out in the years of separation may be seen in the strongly expressed view of the Southern Methodist bishops in 1866, that "a large proportion, if not a majority, of Northern Methodists have become incurably radical. They teach for doctrine the commandments of men. They preach another Gospel. They have incorporated social dogmas and political tests into their Church creeds."

The MECS was to continue a pattern of holding to the old ways and resisting change until the beginning of the twentieth century, convinced that they were maintaining the purer Gospel. We shall see that although it did adhere to the Social Creed of the Federal Council of Churches, the MECS was reluctant to develop organizational structures for tackling social concerns. But over against the deeply embedded racism represented by the Ku Klux Klan, the southern bishops did speak out in favor of justice and equality under the law and against the involvement of Methodists in Klan activities. The social and economic problems resulting from segregation continued, however, and few educational opportunities were available for the African-American population, helping to create a permanent underclass in the South. In 1870, five years after the end of the Civil War, the failure of the MECS to address these troubling matters led to the formation of the Colored Methodist Church (which was to change its name to the Christian Methodist Episcopal Church in 1954). Even though some African-American congregations stayed within the MECS structure, after the split it was left a largely white, heavily segregated church. Even as late as 1939, when the MEC and the MECS reunited, one of the most vexing issues Methodists faced was the problem of continuing racial segregation in Methodist church life. Bishop John M. Moore, the leading Southern Methodist in the negotiations toward union, admitted candidly:

Separation of the races in the South had become a well-established custom. The Southern people were fully convinced that this state of things was best for both races, and best for Southern civilization, and that it should continue. Any movement or trend that might change this condition was disturbing and was regarded with suspicion and opposition.

As a response to predominantly Southern demands, the concept of the racially based Central Jurisdiction was born, into which all African-American Annual Conferences were placed while white Conferences were administered in regional jurisdictions. This plan produced considerable anguish among the African Americans in both North and South, as well as among whites committed to genuine Methodist equality. Controversy about the Central Jurisdiction persisted until the early 1970s when it was dissolved.

A different example of the cleavage between North and South that still continues, it has been suggested, is the difference in the degree of enthusiasm displayed by the Northern and the Southern Methodists for the work of the World Council of Churches and the World Methodist Council. The WCC has been seen by many Southerners to be too committed to social change (and thus to "social dogmas and political tests"). Particularly controversial was the WCC's adoption of the Programme to Combat Racism (PCR) in 1969, and the WCC's ongoing commitment to political action toward a just, sustainable future for the world. By contrast, Southern Methodists are by and large more comfortable with the WMC and its extensive commitment to evangelistic programs.

There are many other places around the world where the racial question has divided Methodists. South African Methodism was long tormented by the apartheid (literally, "apartness") policies of the republic that forced blacks, whites, colored, and Indians to live in separate communities. Tragically the "apartheid" policies became for some white Methodists an "apartness" mentality, and it has only been in the last few decades that black Methodists have been appointed to leadership positions in the South African Conference. Yet the trajectory of human rights that began with John Wesley led to sustained efforts by many South African Methodists to overcome governmental policies. Like other black Methodists, Nelson Mandela's ideals of Christian freedom can be traced back to those preached by John Wesley himself. The idea that, as Wesley had put it, "liberty is the right of every human creature" sustained him and others in the long years of struggle before he became President of the Republic of South Africa.

NINETEENTH-CENTURY SOCIAL ETHICS

We have seen the ways in which the two major traditions of Methodism, British and American, became engulfed in the massive social and economic shifts that were taking place on both sides of the Atlantic. In the period when revolutions in agriculture and the migration to the industrial areas were unraveling the bonds of family and feudal allegiances, the Methodists offered a new way for people to integrate their lives and to acquire new identities and social networks. People on both sides of the Atlantic received an invitation, from preachers of the same social groups as themselves, to join a movement promising them a new and genuine human dignity. The movement also invited such newly uprooted men and women to acquire new social standing as class leaders, exhorters, local preachers, and perhaps even as itinerant preachers or circuit riders. Such men and women became powerful symbols that there was no longer an impenetrable wall between gentry and commoner.

This was most marked in the new United States, where Methodism precisely caught the spirit of the Jeffersonian republic and embodied its democratic ideals. But the message was certainly not lost on the British working classes. The nearly ubiquitous presence of the Methodist preachers and the large company of class leaders and exhorters showed great numbers of men and women the possibilities that were opening to them as self-determining individuals, capable of making their own ethical choices. How many people were actually affected by this new sense of autonomy is difficult to estimate, for while the numbers of actual members of the Methodist movement grew steadily in both Britain and America (and in other parts of the world), a much greater circle of people responded to the new movement in other ways, inspired to become involved in community education and new forms of political and social agitation. Such people were caught up in a form of "secularized Methodism," and their energy and idealism were to shape the new patterns of democracy that emerged in the nineteenth century.

AN EARLY AND LASTING ETHICAL DECISION

The social ethics of Methodism in the early American republic were embodied in the *General Rules*, which were adopted as a part of the first *Discipline* of the MEC and reprinted in every succeeding edition for both the MEC and the MECS, as well as for the AME and the AMEZ. One concern of the *Rules*, "against drunkenness, buying or selling of spirituous liquors," turned out also to be a defining issue for the American Methodists, in both North and South, and in both white and African-American churches. The transplantation of this concern about alcohol by Methodist missionaries as they moved out across the globe led to a deep-rooted opposition to the use of alcoholic beverages all across the Methodist family of churches worldwide. As early as the 1780s, American Methodists were wrestling with the social and economic problem of alcohol trafficking. One result of this was the rule that a Methodist minister, bishop, elder, or deacon had to forfeit his ministerial standing if convicted of "making, selling, or drinking spirituous liquors." (For lay members this rule was advisory but not mandatory.) Even though the various Conferences remained firm on this matter, the issue of the use and sale of alcohol was debated at almost every General Conference for many years, largely because alcohol played an important part in the social life of the wider communities within which Methodists were embedded.

By the 1840s temperance societies were established in response to the increasingly disastrous impact of drunkenness on family life in the new cities. Campaigning against alcohol gave Methodist women like Frances Elizabeth Willard (1839–96) a natural outlet for their talents and energies, and they enlisted many other women in what some have seen as one of the first feminist struggles. Almost immediately, the issue moved on from the curbing of drunkenness to the promotion of total abstinence, and the public signing in church services of "the teetotal pledge" became a crucial moment in the spiritual life of the individual, sometimes rivalling baptism as the high-water mark of religious experience. At the same time, the annual "temperance sermon" became part of the Methodist calendar. In their preaching, temperance advocates pointed to the effects of alcohol on the human body and mind, as well as to the spiritual, social, and economic consequences of heavy drinking on the social fabric. But a small beginning was also made in recognizing that alcoholism was a disease, and soon heavy drinkers became objects of compassion rather than contempt. Contemporary Methodist concerns about drug and substance abuse have deep roots in the nineteenth-century concern for the reformation of morals, as well as in the desire to see that all people reached the fullness of the potential implanted in them by God.

American Methodist churches also recognized the political aspects of alcohol trade and consumption. As the various Annual Conferences took up the cause of total abstinence as the best solution to the social problems caused by drinking, they began to exert intense political pressure toward preventing the issuing of liquor licenses and restricting the legal opening hours of saloons. Ultimately, the vision that drove the temperance movement onward was Prohibition, the total outlawing of the sale of spirituous liquor, and in 1869 Methodists flocked to join the National Prohibition Party when it was founded. Prohibition came into law in 1920 after the passing of the Eighteenth Amendment to the United States' Constitution in 1918. To the dismay of temperance reformers, corruption, gangsterism, and vice did not disappear and the Prohibition amendment was repealed in 1933.

But the battle against alcohol was not over. Methodists on both sides of the North–South divide remained equally adamant in their opposition, and statements about alcohol abuse continue to appear in the *Disciplines* of all American Methodist churches. Methodist churches throughout the world have similar statements. But the total abstinence stance has not been without its problems. On one level, refraining from alcohol became a "fixed point of righteousness," and an easily identifiable badge of respectability, enabling men and women to, in the words of a popular bit of doggerel, "compound for the sins they were inclined to, by damning those they had no mind to." The total abstinence movement also diverted Methodists from the wider issues that the Social Gospel movement was trying to tackle, such as the systemic sins of industrial exploitation, child labor, and slum housing.

CHANGES IN THE STRUCTURE OF AMERICAN SOCIETY

As we have seen, by the 1820s American Methodism was set on a path toward becoming a respectable middle-class church. This inexorable process was deeply intertwined with the rapid transformation of the economy, not only with the rise of industrial capitalism, but also with the growth of market economies, and in particular the labor market. Increasingly Methodists, like other citizens, began to own private property and businesses both large and small. They were able to calculate accurately profits and losses, overhead and implied costs. They accumulated capital in cash and material assets, used the banking system (and in particular interest on loans), and employed other human beings as hired help. Methodists, like members of many other American Protestant denominations, became seamlessly part of the new economic system. Indeed, they thrived in it. Their habits of self-discipline and self-denial led to an accumulation of wealth that their thrifty religious disposition prevented them from spending on luxury. With large sums of money to invest they bought into the cycles of accumulation and reinvestment and left the ranks of the poor in large numbers.

Some Methodist preachers denounced these nouveau riche capitalists and their social climbing; anxiety about wealth had always been part of the Methodist temperament. As early as the turn of the nineteenth century, in offering an explanation as to why camp meetings were not acceptable to the Methodist authorities, Lorenzo Dow claimed that opposition to camp meetings was not a matter of theology but of sociology: the unwillingness of "men of self-importance" to lower themselves and mix with ordinary people. Addressing such Methodists, he chastised them thus:

You may support your distinction and feed your pride, but in a religious point of view all men are on a level, and the good man feels it. The very fact, your aversion to worship your Creator with the poor and despised, proves to me that you have neither part nor lot in the matter; that you know not God nor his worship, and that to follow your advice would be the sure road to perdition. The Lord hath declared his intention and purpose to exalt the humble whilst he will put down high looks.

There are many other examples of such rhetoric, but the battle was lost. White American Methodism was no longer the church of the poor but rather a church that had to be summoned to a mission to serve the poor. There are, of course, exceptions to this rule. We have seen how the radical and Holiness churches rose up to challenge this gentrification of the MEC, and wherever Methodism moved into areas of genuine social and economic deprivation the old Wesleyan suspicion of riches strikes a chord. And to be sure the African-American Methodist churches remained until relatively recently churches of the oppressed, with a hymnody and spirituality to match their aspirations, producing in the late twentieth century powerful theological writings like James H. Cone's *Black Theology of Liberation* (1970) and *God of the Oppressed* (1975).

THE RISE OF THE SOCIAL GOSPEL

Faced with the social disorders of the rapidly growing industrial cities, Methodist pastors and theologians in the North were led to participate in what came to be called the Social Gospel movement. The Social Gospel was a pan-denominational enterprise, guided by Congregationalist Washington Gladden (1836–1918) and Baptist Walter Rauschenbusch (1861–1918), committed to establishing programs of social welfare under the overarching slogan of the "Fatherhood of God and the Brotherhood of Man." Many of these efforts were aimed at changing the working conditions of the poor by giving a voice to working people and ensuring that they received their fair share of the new national prosperity. Methodist participation in the Social Gospel movement had institutional as well as theological consequences. For example, the MEC revived the office of deaconess as a part of this effort, in order to aid women and children caught up in the insatiable demands for cheap labor of the big cities. In Methodist circles some of the enthusiasm for the Social Gospel was rooted in a mutation of the post-millennialist vision that we saw inspired John and Charles Wesley, asking again the question, "When will the New Age be inaugurated?" Many would have answered with the Wesleys that Christ would come as soon as "there is none among them that lacketh; for every man loveth his neighbour as himself."

This biblical vision of all people walking by the rule of love so that "the kingdom of this world shall become the kingdom of our God" (Revelation 11:12) was widely felt to be compatible with the prevailing nineteenth-century faith in inevitable progress. It was certainly the faith that undergirded the work of Harry F. Ward (1873–1966), a Methodist pastor and street preacher in the slums of Chicago, who was the designated successor of Walter Rauschenbusch. Ward, who later became Professor of Ethics at the Methodist seminary in Boston and at Union Seminary, New York, affirmed that:

His Kingdom is to come on earth by intensive conquest – by the power of a love, mighty to save the whole of life, a transforming leaven able to reach the heart of society as well as of men, to capture its motives and motor powers. This was the purpose of Jesus, and his followers must consciously undertake the task of realizing his vision.

The idea of the coming of the reign of God on earth also preoccupied John R. Mott (1865–1955) as he grew up in an Iowa Methodist church. Capturing the spirit of this vision he wrote a book for students whose title became a potent missionary slogan: *The Evangelization of the World in this Generation.* The sense of a world transformed is very powerful throughout Mott's later writings and in his important work in the twentieth-century ecumenical movement. Another key figure for American Methodism was Frank Mason North (1850–1935), a pastor in New York, who put the message of social transformation into the hymn "Where cross the crowded ways of life," verses of which are still sung by Methodists on both sides of the Atlantic and in other continents.

> In haunts of wretchedness and need
> On shadowed thresholds dark with fears
> From paths where hide the lures of greed.
> We catch the vision of thy tears.
>
> O Master, from the mountain side,
> Make haste to heal these hearts of pain;
> Among these restless throngs abide,
> O tread the city's streets again.

Methodist social and educational work was primarily directed to this worldly transformation:

> Till sons of men shall learn thy love,
> And follow where thy feet have trod;
> Till glorious from thy heaven above
> Shall come the city of our God.

By 1908 the concerns represented by Harry F. Ward, John R. Mott, and Frank North were widespread in the MEC and led to the adoption of a "Social Creed" by the General Conference.

The Methodist community had rediscovered its social conscience and in the Social Creed the MEC affirmed that it stood:

For equal rights and complete justice for all men in all stations of life.

For the principle of conciliation and arbitration in industrial dissensions.

For the protection of the worker from dangerous machinery, occupational diseases, injuries, and mortality.

For the abolition of child labor.

For such regulation of the conditions of labor for women as shall safeguard the physical and moral health of the community.

For the suppression of the "sweating system."

For the gradual and reasonable reduction of the hours of labor to the lowest practical point, with work for all: and for that degree of leisure for all which is the condition of the highest human life.

For a release from employment one day in seven.

For a living wage in every industry.

For the highest wage that each industry can afford, and for the most equitable division of the products of industry that can ultimately be devised.

For the recognition of the Golden Rule and the mind of Christ as the supreme law of society and the sure remedy for all social ills.

A few months later, also in 1908, the newly organized Federal Council of Churches of the USA adopted the "Social Creed of the Churches" as its agreed-upon statement of faith. This creed, largely modeled after the Methodist Social Creed, was composed for the FCC by Frank North, who had helped to found this new ecumenical body. At its next Conference, the MECS adopted the MEC "Social Creed" in exactly the same form. The Methodist Protestant Church adopted it in 1916, as did the African-American Methodist denominations. As members of the Federal Council of Churches, the Methodist churches were caught up in the formation of a broadly ecumenical social ethic, with result that there would be hardly any distinctively Methodist positions on many issues.

In 1934 and 1938 the MECS added material to its "Social Creed" in defense of the freedoms of speech, of assembly, and of the press, all of which were adopted by the newly reunited Methodist Church in 1939. As the twentieth century progressed, numerous other affirmations of Christian principles were promulgated, including some that called attention to the need for prison reform, for adequate education, for industrial welfare, and for justice for African Americans. These documents bolstered the social

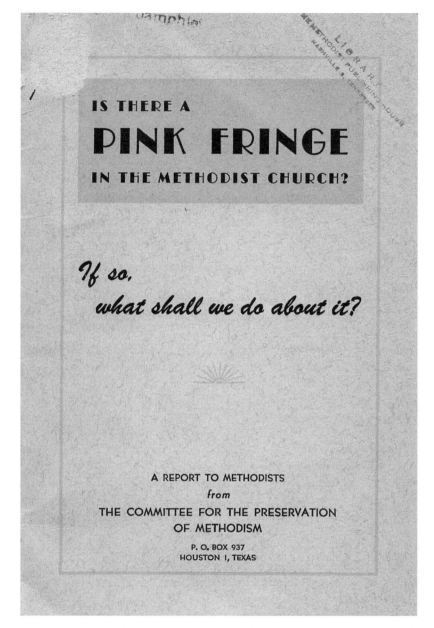

15. 1951 pamphlet attacking the Methodist Federation for Social Action as a communist organization, correlating quotations from official publications with the works of Marx, Lenin, and Stalin.

justice efforts of determined bishops and pastors, many of whom were attacked as communists or as communist-inspired by much more conservative Methodists, as well as the many fundamentalist denominations of the USA. A form of the "Social Creed" continues to be used today and is included in contemporary *Disciplines* and service-books. As both its name and form may suggest, the "Social Creed" is intended for use in services of worship, thus enabling the whole church to affirm a commitment to social justice. One recent commentator has suggested that the "Social Creed" stands as an indication "that many moral issues have the status of the formal doctrines expressed in our more historic confessions."

One North American Methodist political initiative in the twentieth century deserves special mention. This is the Crusade for a New World Order in 1943–4. Initiated and led by bishop G. Bromley Oxnam (1891–1963), it was often popularly referred to as "the Bishops' Crusade" since all the bishops of the Methodist Church participated in it. At a time when the outcome of the Second World War was much in doubt, unleashing rampant jingoism and pseudo-patriotism, the "Crusade" was an attempt to mobilize the total resources of the Methodist Church for peace and world order. This is echoed in a declaration issued by the 1944 General Conference meeting in Kansas: "Christianity cannot be nationalistic: it must be universal in its outlook and appeal. War makes its appeal to force and to hate, Christianity to reason and love . . . The time is at hand, when the Church must arise in its might and demand an international organization which will make another war impossible." These words played a powerful role in creating fertile ground for the establishment of the United Nations after 1945.

Since the uniting of the US Methodist Church with the Evangelical United Brethren to form the UMC in 1968, successive *Books of Discipline* have carried statements expressing the perspectives of the UMC on social issues. A major development was a new statement of "Social Principles" first published in 1972 and further revised in 1976. The "Social Principles" are intended to be "a prayerful and thoughtful effort on the part of General Conference to speak to the human issues of the contemporary world." In the 2002 *Book of Discipline*, the "Social Principles" fill some twenty-eight pages and deal with such subjects as "The Natural World," "The Nurturing Community," "The Social Community," and the "The World Community." These commitments are summed up in a paragraph that is titled "Our Social Creed." The reader is invited to consider the similarities and the differences between this 2002 statement and the 1908 version:

We believe in God, Creator of the world; and in Jesus Christ the Redeemer of Creation. We believe in the Holy Spirit through whom we acknowledge God's gifts, and repent of our sin in misusing these gifts to idolatrous ends.

We affirm the natural world as God's handiwork and dedicate ourselves to its preservation, enhancement and faithful use by humankind.

We joyfully receive for ourselves and others the blessings of community, sexuality, marriage, and the family.

We commit ourselves to the rights of men, women, children, youth, young adults, the aging, and people with disabilities; to the improvement of the quality of life; and to the rights and dignity of racial, ethnic, and religious minorities.

We believe in the right and duty of persons to work for the glory of God and the good of themselves and others in the protection of their welfare in so doing; in the rights to property as a trust from God, collective bargaining, and responsible consumption; and in the relief of economic and social distress.

We dedicate ourselves to peace throughout the world, to the rule of justice and law among the nations, and to individual freedom for all people of the world.

We believe in the present and final triumph of God's Word in human affairs and gladly commit ourselves to manifest the life of the gospel in the world.

The *Book of Discipline* recommends that the whole statement of Social Principles be made available to every member of the United Methodist Church and that "Our Social Creed" be frequently used in Sunday worship. At the same time, a wide variety of new hymns on diverse social justice have appeared in the hymnals of the various Methodist churches in the USA, and are sung by congregations as a part of their corporate affirmation of the importance of the values of peace, equality, and tolerance.

SOCIAL ETHICS IN THE DEVELOPMENT OF BRITISH METHODISM

Similar socioeconomic developments were also shaping Methodist ethics in Britain during the nineteenth and twentieth centuries. Non-Wesleyan forms of Methodism (the Primitive Methodists, the Wesleyan Reform Union, and the Independent Methodists) were vibrant enough among urban artisans to exercise a strong influence on left-wing politics and on the growing trades union movement. And while Jabez Bunting and the Buntingites attempted to impose anti-radicalism on the Wesleyan Methodists, many paid little attention to the admonitions of their leaders. Working-class Methodists were deeply imbued with radical and activist notions and had strong links with the Chartists. But Methodist discipline saved them from becoming a revolutionary people and, like their American cousins, by the mid-nineteenth century they were on their way to becoming well-respected members of a community that was increasingly conforming itself to evangelical and Methodist values. There is much truth in the judgment of a recent writer that even though Methodist roots lay in the crosscurrents of eighteenth-century thought and politics, it was "the nineteenth century which Wesley and Wesleyanism helped to form." By the end of the century there were a number of Wesleyan and Primitive Methodist Members of Parliament who identified with the Liberal Party, combining a kind of Christian imperialism with an essentially paternalist concern for domestic social problems. We have seen how Hugh Price Hughes and others were involved in the Forward Movement to tackle social problems. We also noted that the central concern was for "social purity." Methodist opposition to vice was embodied in the Wesleyan Committee for Social Purity, established in 1886 to deal with the problem of prostitution. Inadequate housing and dangerous, unhealthy industrial conditions were also on the list of evils to be combated through the Forward Movement. Large numbers of Methodists were mobilized to these efforts, inspired by Hughes' call, "Let us not only save people's souls but . . . sanctify their circumstances."

In general, however, plain homespun personal morality was the staple of Methodist preaching. Thus the Wesleyan Methodist theological educator, Benjamin Hellier (1825–80), expounded the doctrine of perfect love, not as a second blessing for the especially holy, but in everyday terms for the ordinary Methodist:

Entire sanctification means the sanctification of everything. The sanctification, for example, of the daily work; that is, doing it to the Lord, and, therefore, doing it as well as we can. If a ploughman be entirely sanctified, he will plough a straight furrow, – or at least try his best to do so. If he be a mason, he will put no bad work into his walls; if a doctor, he will care more about curing his patients, than about getting large fees; if he be a minister of religion, he will serve the people of his charge to the utmost of his ability . . . Entire sanctification means simply this: spending all our time in the Lord's service; making our religion our life, our life our religion.

Hellier puts into words an ethic that was basically individualist, highlighting the virtues of thrift, frugality, and hard work. Such a moral code had an inbuilt disdain for the vices of drinking and gambling and Methodists within the British tradition could be as fierce in denunciation of these twin evils as their American counterparts. In part this was the result of their day-to-day awareness of the personal and family disasters caused by "booze and betting" in industrial towns and cities. Perhaps it was only in the twentieth century that Methodists would fully realize that there were structural evils in society that need fundamental political solutions. One marker of this new awareness was the renaming in 1949 of the Temperance and Social Welfare Department of the British Methodist Church to the Christian Citizenship Department (later the Division of Social Responsibility). Led by social ethicists like Edward Rogers (1909–97) and Kenneth Greet (b. 1918), the Department, and later the Division, produced significant reports and studies on unemployment, war, racism, homelessness, and world poverty. All recent Conferences of the British Methodist Church have been asked to make judgments on contemporary social, economic, and international issues. One historian of British Methodism has commented that the Division of Social Responsibility did "something to destroy the persistent public image, never correct and now wildly inaccurate, of the typical Methodist as a rabid and humourless teetotaller who mistakes abstinence for Christianity."

The British Council of Churches (BCC) was formed in 1942 with the active participation of the British Methodist Church. Particularly in the last quarter of the twentieth century this relationship was so close that Methodist social ethics took on the full flavor of ecumenical social thought. Among other reasons for this was a preponderance of Methodist personnel on the staff of the BCC in the field of social ethics, among them Methodist ministers Harry O. Morton, Brian Duckworth, and Elliott Kendall, and laypeople like Pauline Webb and Roger Williamson. In the last three decades of the twentieth century the BCC challenged the endemic racism of British society, worked to end apartheid in South Africa, and protested the Falklands War, with the full support of the Methodist Conferences.

British Methodist political and social witness has also been led by a significant group of socially concerned ministers: Donald Soper (1903–98), superintendent of the West London Mission, was untiring in his proclamation of a dynamic pacifism; Colin Morris (b. 1929) championed the cause of the "Third World" as it was then called through public broadcasting and a succession of books; and John J. Vincent (b. 1929) called the Methodist people back to mission alongside the poor. The finest Methodist hymn writer in Britain in the twentieth century was Fred Pratt Green (1903–2000), who expressed the social conscience of Methodism in his poetry. The following verses are included in Hymn 804 in *Hymns and Psalms*, the British Methodist hymn-book:

> The Church of Christ in every age
> Beset by change but spirit-led
> Must claim and test its heritage
> And keep rising from the dead.

Across the world, across the street,
The victims of injustice cry
For shelter and for bread to eat,
And never live until they die.

Then let the servant Church arise,
A caring Church that longs to be
A partner in Christ's sacrifice,
And clothed in Christ's humanity.

CONTEMPORARY ISSUES IN METHODIST SOCIAL ETHICS

Very few of the issues that Methodists have concerned themselves with have disappeared. Though African slavery is no longer an issue, there is still much to be done about the exploitation of domestic workers, the forced prostitution of women and children, and the oppression of illegal immigrants. In recent years, traditional Methodist concern about the use of alcohol and tobacco has expanded into concern for drug trafficking and substance abuse. Ecological issues, questions of human sexuality, matters of crime and punishment, racial justice, international reconciliation, peace and peacemaking come regularly to the Annual and General Conferences of Methodists throughout the world and engage the attention of their Boards of Social Responsibility. The internet now gives instant access to the ways in which Methodists are reacting to both the chronic and immediate crises in the world and in individual countries.

But there is one theme that claims the attention of nearly all Methodist social thinkers as the twenty-first century begins. It is hard to avoid the fact that there is an extraordinary economic disparity between wealthy nations and poor nations, and the awareness that 20 percent of the world's total population (those living in highly developed, industrialized nations) consume 80 percent of the world's resources. Progress toward changing this imbalance is thwarted by the amount of indebtedness underdeveloped countries have accrued, ensuring that they can never make progress toward self-sufficiency. Equally challenging is the situation within these very wealthy nations, where there is an enormous gap between the living conditions of the rich and the poor. Even as affluence and productivity continue to rise in the West, huge numbers of people have no access to the benefits of increasing national prosperity. To those nurtured in the Methodism of the Wesley brothers, this is nothing less than an affront to God.

A number of Methodist social theorists are addressing these issues from a variety of political and theological perspectives. One of these is José

Míguez Bonino of the Iglesia Evangelica Metodista Argentina and a former professor in the Protestant School of Theology in Buenos Aires. At the forefront of the liberation theology movement in South America (which continues to be effective today), Bonino often reflects on the ways in which John Wesley might help his contemporary followers to discover how best to serve the poor today. While he is clear that the poor of today's world are in a quite different situation from those of the eighteenth century, Bonino is sure that a dialogue with Wesley will be fruitful, citing the importance of Wesley's treatises *Thoughts upon Slavery* and *Thoughts on the Present Scarcity of Provision*. Writing in 1999, he observes that South America is even further away from being a growing, dynamic, and open political economy than it was at the beginning of the century, and that illiteracy, infantile mortality, drug trafficking, and delinquency project themselves into the foreseeable future.

In this situation, our "thoughts" today have to move in at least three different directions: (a) the analysis and critique of the ideology that justifies the present form of globalization, a task that Wesley could only do, and did, in a symbolic way in his critique of luxury, dissipation and unconcern (with the exception of slavery where he was able to construct a powerful ethical and theological critique); (b) the discussion of possible alternatives in issues like foreign debts, equitable liberation on issues like trade, construction of local coalitions, that have a greater possibility of negotiation on laws of the market, and international legislation for the control of the financial market; and (c) the strengthening of "civil society" and especially of the forms of organization that give to the poor the possibility of participation in power.

Bonino believes that for these tasks Wesley functions not so much as an intellectual or political resource but as "an inspiration, an invitation to put into action in relation to our poor the best analytical tools, the most creative forms of association and action, and the persistent commitment he tried to exercise in his ministry."

In the end, Bonino believes that there is one essential ingredient for addressing social change, an ingredient that is contributed by his Methodist heritage. For Latin America, and quite certainly everywhere else, altering the conditions of society must go hand in hand with changing the self-understanding of members of those societies. In this task, he says, the role of religion is central, functioning as "both comforting and prophetic presence, as both assurance and challenge." His own church, the Iglesia Evangelica Methodista Argentina, defines its mission as "Liberation: this word involves two concepts which are inseparable: personal salvation and the redemption of society."

We end this survey of Methodist social action by pointing to just a few samples of current projects being undertaken by Methodists around the globe. Care for the homeless, the hungry, the inmates of prison, and drug addicts appear on the list of priorities of all Methodist churches in the world: thus the tiny Methodist Church in the Czech and Slovak Republics (representing just 1,500 people) reports its activities as: "prison ministry, shelter for homeless people, work among drug addicts, humanitarian aid among gipsy people, radio and television ministry." The scourge of contemporary Africa is HIV/AIDS, and all the various African Methodist churches are involved in pastoral and educational activity throughout the continent. Peacemaking is high on the agenda for Methodists in Sri Lanka where there is a Peace and Reconciliation Committee that has tried to mediate between the conflicting parties in the civil war and to help them move toward a negotiated settlement to the ethnic crisis in that island. The Irish Methodist Church has been a leading agency in reconciliation in the years of community strife there, and similarly in Liberia and Sierra Leone Methodists have been intensely engaged in peacemaking activities, in the resettlement of refugees, and in the rehabilitation of child soldiers. Using its own idiom, the Iglesia Evangelica en Bolivia (IEMB) reaffirms, "from the perspective of our historic Wesleyan heritage," "Its evangelical vocation of proclamation and criticism and its commitment to the poorest and marginalized in society," asking at the same time "for the solidarity and participation of our sister Methodist churches who are on the same road of common ministry: the building of the Kingdom of God along with its justice."

The evidence from around the world suggests that this plea from Bolivia will not go unheard. Methodists remain deeply engaged with issues of peace and justice, and broadly apprehend a journey toward salvation that is expressed in terms of a renewed and restored life in this world.

CHAPTER 10

Methodism's ecumenical and interfaith commitments

ECUMENICAL ACTIVITY

In the middle of the twentieth century, Archbishop William Temple described the modern ecumenical movement as "the great new fact of our era," and for the past one hundred years at least Methodists have committed themselves as full and lively participants to the important work of Christian reunion. The contemporary quest for unity among the various Christian denominations can trace its origins to the kinds of Western missionary activity that we saw in chapter 4, and to the recognition that it was counterproductive at best, and dangerous at worst, to have churches engaged in competitive and overlapping work in the mission territories. In Africa and Asia especially, visible and practical unity was crucial. With this in mind, the World Missionary Conference in Edinburgh was called in 1910 to evaluate the missionary situation, and most historians view this as marking the first step in a process that eventually brought to birth the World Council of Churches (WCC) in 1948. A major force behind the Edinburgh Conference (indeed it would never have taken place without his forceful persuasion) was the general secretary of the World's Student Christian Federation (WSCF), John R. Mott (1865–1955), a Methodist layman from Iowa. Mott presided over the Edinburgh Conference, and over its Continuation Committee, and later played major roles in the formation of the International Missionary Council (IMC), the Faith and Order Conference, and the Life and Work Movement. In 1948, at the age of eighty-three, Mott preached at the opening service of the WCC, and was elected a life-long honorary president by its membership. John R. Mott was undoubtedly the most widely traveled and universally trusted Christian leader of his time, and in recognition of this he was awarded the Nobel Peace Prize in 1946.

Methodists were actively involved at every stage of the progress toward the formation of the WCC. Present at the first Faith and Order Conference meeting in Oxford in 1937 was British Methodist theologian Robert

Newton Flew (1886–1962). Flew presided over the intense doctrinal discussions of how the churches might achieve unity in "faith and order" both in 1937 and at a later meeting in Lund in Sweden in 1951, where those assembled laid down the central ecumenical principle that churches "should not do separately what they can do together." The official volume that was produced out of the Lund gathering was called *The Nature of the Church*, and Newton Flew became something of a legendary figure for writing a brilliantly impartial account of the Roman Catholic view of ecclesiology. This was necessary since at that time there was no Roman Catholic participation in the WCC. The Vatican was very resistant to ecumenical activity, believing that the only possible and godly end to ecumenism was that all churches would "return to the Roman Catholic fold." This changed with the Second Vatican Council, but even today Roman Catholics remain "observers" rather than members of the WCC assemblies and committees.

Another American Methodist ecumenist working at the international level was Albert C. Outler (1908–89), for many years professor at Perkins School of Theology, Dallas, Texas. At the WCC Faith and Order Conference which met in Montreal in 1963, Outler helped to shape the document entitled "Scripture, Tradition, and Traditions," which would be the foundation of two of the most significant pieces of Faith and Order work: "Baptism, Eucharist, and Ministry" (BEM) and "Confessing the Faith Today." Between 1962 and 1965, Outler served as a Protestant observer at the Second Vatican Council and his detailed descriptions of the Council helped Methodists to understand their Roman Catholic brothers and sisters better than they ever had before. The UMC, like all other Methodist churches throughout the world, is fully engaged with the WCC and with the National Council of Churches of the USA, committing a succession of able and talented ecumenical leaders. Geoffrey Wainwright (b. 1939), a British Methodist minister and, since 1979, a theological teacher in the USA, has been a participant in the work of the WCC for forty years, playing a major role in the ecumenical agreements associated with the BEM study, and a ubiquitous presence in Methodist dialogues with various partner churches, as we shall soon see.

The history of Methodist dedication to overseas missions has resulted in an international group of Methodist leaders in the work of ecumenical and missiological reflection. Much of this work has been done within the framework of the World Council of Churches where Methodists have served in various capacities. Daniel Thambyrajah Niles (1908–70) from Sri Lanka was president of the WCC, and over a twenty-year period, from 1972 to 1992, a succession of general secretaries of the WCC were Methodists.

Philip Potter (b. 1921) from the island of Dominica in the Caribbean served from 1972 to 1984; Emilio Castro (b. 1927) served from 1985 to 1992; and Kenyan Methodist minister Samuel Kobia (b. 1947) was elected general secretary in 2003. Many observers have noted that of a total of six WCC general secretaries since the founding of the organization, three have been Methodists. In addition, a British Methodist laywoman, Pauline Webb, has given strong leadership in the WCC, particularly in the Programme to Combat Racism and as an historian of the role of women in the ecumenical movement. On the more local level, Methodists have also taken important leadership roles in their national, regional, and community-wide Councils of Churches, and have taught university, seminary, and graduate students the principles and practice of ecumenical work. Some may think this a disproportionate contribution to ecumenical work from a world communion of only just over 75 million adherents but, as we shall see, there are important underlying reasons for this deep and widespread Methodist quest for Christian unity.

Methodist ecumenical activity begins in a conflict between theory and practice, a conflict not wholly resolved even today. The very first *CHPM* in 1747 contained a hymn composed by Charles Wesley that begins "Come all who truly bear / The Name of Christ your Lord." This hymn, designated for use in the Lord's Supper, ends with this verse:

> Part of his church below,
> We thus our right maintain;
> Our living membership we show,
> And in the fold remain
> The sheep of Israel's fold,
> In England's pastures fed;
> And fellowship with all we hold.
> Who hold it with our Head.

The defensive tone of these words reveals that early Methodists felt that they had to maintain their "right" to be regarded as a part of the Christian community in England. Already the signs of an impending break with the Established Church were beginning to trouble John Wesley and his preachers. In 1744 the Conference discussed the possibility of separating from the Church of England, recording its thinking in its characteristic "question-and-answer" form:

Q. 8. How far is it our duty to obey the bishops?
A. In all things indifferent. And on this ground of obeying them, we should observe the canons so far as we can with safe conscience.

Q. 9. Do we separate from the Church?

A. We conceive not. We hold communion therewith for conscience sake, by constantly attending the word preached, and the sacraments administered therein.

Q. 10 What then do they mean who say, "You separate from the Church"?

A. We cannot certainly tell. Perhaps they have no determinate meaning unless by the Church they mean themselves, *i.e.* that part of the clergy who accuse us of preaching false doctrine. And it is sure we do herein separate from them by maintaining the doctrine which they deny.

Q. 11. But do you not weaken the Church?

A. Do not they say who ask this mean by the Church themselves? We do not purposely weaken any man's hands, but accidentally we may thus far: they who come to know the truth by us will esteem such as deny it less than they did before. But the Church in the proper sense, the congregation of English believers, we do not weaken at all.

Although never an advocate of ecclesiastical radicalism, Wesley did invariably consider obedience to ecclesiastical authority to be ultimately governed by individual conscience, and once again his Conference asserts that obedience to the bishops of the Church of England is a matter of indifference. The rules of the church are to be obeyed, but only "as far as we can with safe conscience"; Methodist doctrine was to be maintained whatever it cost.

Having established these principles of Methodist self-identity, the 1744 *Minutes* proceed, somewhat poignantly given the subsequent history of the movement, to question 12, "Do you not entail a schism upon the Church? That is, is it not probable that your hearers after your death will be scattered into all sects and parties, or that they will form themselves into a distinct sect?" The form of the answer shows us that John Wesley himself drafted this minute. He insists, "We are persuaded that the body of our hearers will after our death remain in the Church unless they be thrust out." Until that time, the task of the Methodists was to "leaven the whole Church." Meanwhile he says: "We do, and will do, all that we can to prevent those consequences which are supposed likely to happen after our death." But, manifestly, the corporate mind of the early Methodists was made up: "We cannot with good conscience neglect the present opportunity of saving souls while we live for fear of consequences which may possibly or probably happen after our death."

Both the Wesley brothers maintained this as their position to the end of their lives. In his *Farther Thoughts on Separation from the Church*, John Wesley explained his actions like this:

When the people joined together, simply to help each other to heaven, increased by hundreds and thousands; still they had no more thought of leaving the Church than of leaving the kingdom. Nay, I continually and earnestly cautioned them against it; reminding them that we were a part of the Church of England, whom God had raised up, not only to save our own souls, but to enliven our neighbours, those of the Church in particular. And at the first meeting of all our Preachers in Conference, in June, 1744, I exhorted them to keep to the Church; observing, that this was our peculiar glory, – not to form any new sect, but, abiding in our own.

But the Wesleys' allegiance to the church contains its own irony, for that church was itself a breakaway from the original Catholic Church whose bishop was the Pope, which was, in turn, divided from the Orthodox churches of the East. Article 19 of the Thirty-Nine Articles of the Church of England (1552) is clear that "The Churches of Jerusalem, Alexandria, and Antioch are in error as much as the Church of Rome. They have erred not only in their teaching and manner of ceremonies, but also in matters of faith." In their own version of the Articles of Religion, American Methodists make the same point: "The Romish doctrine concerning purgatory, pardon, worshiping, and adoration, as well of images as of relics, and also invocation of saints, is a fond thing, vainly invented, and grounded upon no warrant of Scripture, but repugnant to the Word of God." In striving to keep within the boundaries of the Church of England, then, the Wesleyan movement perpetuated a breach with both the Roman Catholic and Orthodox churches. But, unusually for Church of England clergymen, John and Charles Wesley were among the first to begin to break down these walls of separation. This they did in two ways: the first was in regard to Roman Catholicism.

The impulse toward better relations with Roman Catholics arose out of the Wesleys' long ministry in Ireland. In England, organized Catholicism did not have a public face until Catholic emancipation came in 1828, but in eighteenth-century Ireland Protestants and Roman Catholics lived side by side. This was a very different context for the Methodist preachers; here sometimes they looked like Roman Catholics to the Protestants and sometimes they looked like Protestants to the Roman Catholics. In other instances, however, as Charles Wesley reported of his experience in Cork in 1748, "The Presbyterians say that I am a Presbyterian; the church-goers that I am a minister of theirs; and the Catholics that they are sure I am a good Catholic in my heart." This is not to say that all of their ecumenical encounters with Roman Catholics were happy ones; on several occasions hostile Catholic priests stirred mobs up against them.

Against this background Wesley wrote two influential works, both in 1749: the *Letter to a Roman Catholic* and the sermon on the *Catholic Spirit*. Both of these emphasized the need to focus on the essentials of the Gospel and to be more tolerant of diversity in matters of opinion. Another two related sermons were also composed at about this time, one on *The Nature of Enthusiasm* and another entitled *A Caution against Bigotry*. These three sermons appear in the third volume of *Sermons on Several Occasions*, published in 1750, and have been part of the Wesleyan Doctrinal Standards ever since. They are therefore required reading for candidates for the Methodist ministry.

The *Letter to a Roman Catholic* is both courteous and irenic in tone. The mistrust that exists between Roman Catholics and Protestants, which is mutual, Wesley wrote, made both sides "less willing to help one another and more ready to hurt each other." Wesley's way forward was to elucidate the principles of his own Christian faith (broadly following the Nicene Creed), and then to ask "Now, is there anything wrong with this? Is there any one point which you do not believe as well as we?" Wesley immediately admitted that a Roman Catholic might think that he ought to believe more than that which is contained in the historic creeds, but he refused to enter into that dispute. He was convinced that the early creedal formulas are sufficiently complete to sustain a Christian community in which "we ought to love one another": "We ought, without this endless jangling about opinions, to provoke one another to love and to good works. Let the points on which we differ stand aside: here are enough wherein we agree, enough to be the ground of every Christian temper and of every Christian action."

Such thinking would soon become the basis of a sermon for his own people, and in 1749 he preached the *Catholic Spirit* sermon in both Newcastle and Bristol. There he asked the Methodist people why Christians are so slow to obey the New Testament commands to love one another (John 13:34–5; 1 John 3:11; 1 John 4:11):

All men approve of this, but do all men practise it? Daily experience shows the contrary. Where are even the Christians who "love one another as he hath given us commandment"? How many hindrances lie in the way? The two grand, general hindrances are, first, that they can't all think alike; and, in consequence of this, secondly, they cannot all walk alike.

So the issues that divide Christians turn almost exclusively upon differing opinions and modes of worship, and soon Wesley would have to expand upon the distinction between true faith and the various conceptualizations of faith that he had identified in *The Character of a Methodist*. In this document he had been clear: "All opinions which do not strike at the root of Christianity, we think and let think." In *A Plain Account of the People Called Methodists* he had gone even further, saying that "orthodoxy, or right opinions, is at best a slender part of religion, if it can be allowed to be any part at all." In the sermon on the *Catholic Spirit*, Wesley now asserted that differences of opinion were the inevitable consequence of "the present weakness and shortness of human understanding," and "that different men will be of different minds in religion as well as in everyday life." This limitation in understanding means that all human beings need to reckon with the likelihood of being mistaken:

although every man necessarily believes that every particular opinion which he holds is true (for to believe any opinion is not true is the same thing as not to hold it), yet can no man be assured that all his own opinions taken together are true. Nay, every thinking man is assured that they are not, seeing *humanum est errare et nescire* – to be ignorant of many things, and to be mistaken in some is the necessary condition of humanity. This therefore, he is sensible is his own case. He knows in general he is mistaken; though in what particulars he mistakes he does not, perhaps cannot, know.

Consequently, he tells his hearers in the most often quoted words of the sermon: "If thy heart is right with my heart give me thine hand," cannot mean "be of my opinion". No more, he said, could it mean "embrace my modes of worship" or, alternatively, "I will embrace yours." "This also is a thing which does not depend on either your choice or mine. We must both act as each is fully persuaded in his own mind. Hold you fast that which you believe is most acceptable to God and I will do the same."

Addressing Protestant Dissenters, the Congregationalists, Presbyterians, Quakers, and Baptists, Wesley said:

I believe the episcopal form of church government to be scriptural and apostolical. If you think the Presbyterian or independent is better, think so still and act accordingly. I believe infants ought to be baptized, and that this may be done either by dipping or sprinkling. If you are otherwise persuaded, be so still, and follow your own persuasion. It appears to me that forms of prayer are of excellent use, particularly in the great congregation. If you judge extemporary prayer to be of more use act suitably to your own judgement. My sentiment is that I ought not to forbid water, wherein persons may be baptized, and that I ought to eat bread and drink wine, as a memorial of my dying Master. However, if you are not convinced of this, act according to the light you have. I have no desire to dispute with you one moment upon any of the preceding heads. Let all these smaller points stand aside. Let them never come into sight.

All this, according to John Wesley, teaches us what a "catholic spirit" was and what it was not. But it is also clear that the catholic spirit of which he speaks is not "speculative latitudinarianism." Neither is it an indifference to all opinions. Such an attitude, he said, would be the "spawn of hell, not the offspring of heaven." On the contrary, the Christian, in Wesley's view, had to be "united in the tenderest and closest ties to one particular congregation." Only with this foundation would it be possible to build bridges of understanding and embrace with "strong and cordial affection neighbors and strangers, friends and enemies.

Wesley's sermon on *Catholic Spirit* and the *Letter to a Roman Catholic* form essential ingredients in the process of healing currently taking place between Roman Catholics and Methodists. Indeed, in 1969 the *Letter to a Roman Catholic* was republished in Dublin by a Roman Catholic press. Charles Wesley contributed in his own way to this gently irenic process by writing ecumenically sensitive verse like "Christ from whom all blessings flow," which we have already quoted, in which occur the lines "Love like death hath all destroyed / Rendered all distinctions void / Names and sects and parties fall / Thou, O Christ art all in all," which have inspired generations of Methodist people and their fellow pilgrims in the ecumenical movement.

With such spirituality permeating their faith and nurture, the consciences of Methodists have been sensitive to the tragic consequences of divisions within their own Wesleyan family as well as within the Christian Church as a whole. We have seen that this sensitivity did not always result in actions toward unity, and in the nineteenth century, that period of rapid growth and social upheaval, there was more divisiveness than there was healing. Nevertheless the yearning for reconciliation was subtly present. Even in times of the greatest interdenominational tension, individual voices insisted that there was a better way, and pressure grew in the nineteenth century to gather the various divided parts of Methodism together. The General Conference of the MEC adopted a resolution in 1876 proposing an "Oecumenical Conference of Methodism" composed of Methodist organizations that "accept the Arminian theology, and maintain usages which distinguish them to some extent from every other denomination of Christians." This proposal was communicated to the Wesleyan Methodists under the general slogan "Methodists are one people." The British Conference demurred at that description, writing in its official reply:

The plan assumes that there is such a substantial community among various bodies descended from the English Methodism of John Wesley, that all may be regarded as one people, distinguished into sections, which vary from each other only in matters quite subordinate and almost insignificant. We are bound to say that to us there seems a certain unreality about this view . . . No such virtual identity is found among the different ecclesiastical bodies enumerated in your communication. They do not acknowledge the same standard of doctrine, and characteristic differences are found in their exposition even of the doctrines which are nominally held in common.

But such objections did not deter the American Methodists, and the next General Conference of the MECS approved the proposal and instructed the bishops to appoint a committee to organize the meeting, making the conciliar gathering of Methodists under one umbrella a largely American initiative from the beginning. (Indeed, the ethos of Methodist world ecumenism has largely been determined by the numerically and financially strong American churches.) The first meeting of the Ecumenical Methodist Conference took place at Wesley's Chapel, London, in 1881, and the Conference subsequently met at ten-year intervals until 1931. From the records of these gatherings, however, it is clear that they were largely opportunities to express Methodist triumphalism.

Because of the Second World War, no Conference was possible in 1941, but meetings were resumed in 1947. In 1951, the Ecumenical Methodist Conference changed its name to the World Methodist Council (WMC). Ten years was deemed to be too long a period of time between meetings, and from 1951 the WMC began to assemble every five years in the various centers of global Methodism: Oslo, London, Denver, Hawaii, Singapore, Dublin, Nairobi, Rio de Janeiro, and Brighton, England. By the time of the Brighton meeting in 2001, people from 108 countries were in attendance, representing seventy-three member churches reporting 35 million members and a wider Methodist community of over 70 million people. The nineteenth meeting of the WMC is due to take place in Seoul in 2006. The WMC has its headquarters at the Methodist Conference Center in Lake Junaluska, North Carolina.

While the Council has no executive power over its members, it has done vigorous work in the promotion of mission and evangelism in the local contexts of its member churches and in the exchange of pastors and experiences among different congregations across national frontiers. It encourages reflection on theology through the Oxford (England) Institutes of Methodist Theology and facilitates various processes of ecumenical dialogue. Sometimes it acts as a mediator when Methodist groups fall out with one another, as sometimes happens when Methodists from one part of the world suddenly arrive in another country and begin mission work where there are already well-established Methodist churches. The WMC is engaged in a process of study to produce guidelines to reduce tension in such situations. The WMC also represents the Wesleyan/Methodist traditions in consultations with other world Christian organizations such as the Lutheran World Federation and the World Alliance of Reformed Churches.

For some participants, the WMC is the terminus of the ecumenical journey, and they have neither the energy nor the enthusiasm for active involvement in bodies like the World Council of Churches or in national and local Councils of Churches. But for most contemporary Methodists the search for organic unity among Christian denominations continues. In the twentieth century the search for visible unity became more urgent when Methodist theologians on both sides of the Atlantic came increasingly to the sobering conclusion that Methodists were not equipped with an ecclesiology, or doctrine of the church, adequate to sustain their communion in separation from the rest of Christianity. The British Methodist theologian Gordon Rupp (1910–86) expressed this concern in 1951 when he wrote about the seeds of difficulty that lie deep within the origins of Methodism:

Not only the occasion, but also the results of separation from the Church of England have to be considered. When we have defended the sincerity of John Wesley and when we have repudiated the discussion in Anglo-Catholic terms, we have still to face the question whether there has not been in consequence a moving away from the deep elements in historical Christian continuity, which gave original Methodism a depth and stability not always evident in later days.

On the other side of the Atlantic, Albert Outler was suggesting that Methodism might have to learn to see itself as "an evangelical order of witness and worship, discipline and nurture" set firmly within "an encompassing environment of catholicity." Methodism, scholars such as Rupp and Outler believed, urgently needed the reunion of the churches.

Most Methodist churches throughout the world are fully committed to losing themselves in a larger Christian unity. Thus, as part of its 1968 constitution, the UMC affirmed that "the Lord of the Church is calling Christians everywhere to strive toward unity," and is engaged with other American churches in the current search for unity entitled "Churches United in Christ" (CUIC). Like most other Methodist churches throughout the world the UMC fully supports the WCC, and like other US Methodist churches commits a succession of its able men and women to leadership in the National Council of Churches.

Since 1952 the British Methodists have had an ecumenical mandate in place embodied in a Conference Declaration that says:

As long as Christians of one communion part company with Christians of another communion at the table of the Lord, it is impossible that the world will believe that they hold the secret of a fellowship which overlaps religious, cultural, economic and racial differences. The quest of Christian unity assumes an urgency that cannot be exaggerated, when the disabling consequences of our divisions are seen against the background of a generation which so often either repudiates Christian values or dissociates them from the Christian faith.

An unmistakable note of anxiety is sounded in these words. After the Second World War it was increasingly apparent that Britain was becoming a de-Christianized society with both the Church of England and the Methodist Church (as well as other denominations) experiencing a severe numerical decline that has lasted until the present day. From one point of view, British ecumenism might be interpreted simply as Christian denominations huddling together for warmth against the icy blasts of modernity. More positively, however, there are large numbers of British Methodists who live with a genuine sense of diminishment that they are not part of the national church, and who work toward reunion alongside many Anglicans who wish that the eighteenth-century separation had never taken place.

Methodist conversations with the Church of England toward reunion began formally in 1955 and it was soon clear that the Methodist and Anglican negotiators were committed to the visible, institutional unity of the two churches. In the words of the *Interim Report* of 1967, the goal was "one servant church, to teach the people of our nation with one Christian doctrine, and with one voice to present to the world our crucified and risen Saviour." The Methodist negotiating team made many concessions to accommodate the Anglican point of view on matters of practical significance. These concerned particularly the issues around episcopacy and priesthood. A deliberate ambiguity was built into proposals for what might happen in a "Service of Reconciliation," during which bishops in the "apostolic succession" would lay hands on Methodist ministers. Catholic Anglicans could believe that Methodist ministers were being ordained for the first time, but the Methodist ministers and many Anglicans (both evangelicals and liberals) would be able to resist the notion that reordination was taking place. On both the Anglican and Methodist sides there was much discontent about this studied ambiguity, with a spate of tracts issuing from both parties. A movement called the Voice of Methodism pressed the case against the unity scheme, and some well-known Methodist theologians of the period spoke strenuously against what seemed to them to be an evasion of the central issues, insisting that episcopacy in the Anglo-Catholic sense was unscriptural and unprovable. Other voices believed the scheme to be irrelevant to the needs of mission, and yet others saw it as the blunting of Methodism's radical edge. When the votes were taken in the Church of England's General Synod in May 1972, the bishops voted 34 in favor and 6 against. The clergy voted 52 in favor and 80 against, and the laity 147 in favor and 87 against. The motion was lost.

For many Methodist ecumenists in Britain the failure of this unity scheme was extremely disheartening, and it drained their energy for the movement toward organic unity. Some effort was made to restart the process in a Covenant Scheme that did not require Methodists to adopt episcopacy, but in 1982 this too failed. But many ecumenical unions did take place at the local level in the 1970s, often under the umbrella term Local Ecumenical Project (LEP), and these have continued ever since. There always remained, however, those within both British Methodism and the Church of England who refused to be discouraged about the prospects for Anglican-Methodist unity, and who struggled on at a national level to bring the two churches together. In 1999 they proposed to their member churches the concept of an Anglican–Methodist Covenant.

On November 1, 2003 this effort came to fruition as the president of the British Methodist Conference and the Archbishop of Canterbury signed a Covenant for Unity. There is no commitment to institutional unity in this scheme, for the Covenant simply affirms that "both our churches confess in word and life the apostolic faith revealed in the Holy Scriptures." It includes mutual affirmation of the other church's ministries as means of grace, and that there exists a basis for agreement on the principles of episcopal oversight. The hope is that both churches will increase opportunities for sharing a common life including participation in each other's Eucharists. In the service of thanksgiving that followed the signing of the Covenant, the Anglican members of the congregation recited these words:

Our brothers and sisters of the Methodist Church, we thank God for you. In the name of Christ, we your sisters and brothers of the Church of England dedicate ourselves to share our life with you. Guided by the Holy Spirit, we look forward in the years ahead in the common life of worship and mission, and of ministry and service.

Methodists replied using, with the appropriate alterations, the same form of words. In his sermon the Archbishop of Canterbury reflected on the two centuries of division, acknowledging the "insensitivity and missionary sluggishness of the Church of England," but suggested that this was not to be considered to have been wasted time. He asked, "don't we have to say that both of our church communities have been given gifts and learned lessons that we might not have learned or received had this never happened?" and then answered his own question: "We have all, in the intervening years discovered things about Christ and his Kingdom that we are now eager to share with one another, as brothers and sisters working together, working to overcome the distant legacy of arrogance and resentment." Whether this Covenant will result in a United Church in the British Isles remains to be seen. But the hopefulness with which each of the parties to the 2003

Anglican–Methodist Covenant is approaching the future, and the growing sense of the huge potential within the new situation for strengthening the Christian witness in Britain, appear to be bringing fresh energy to both churches.

But the wider hope for Christian reunion remains unfulfilled and, through the Ecumenical and Dialogue Committee of the WMC, Methodist churches are engaged internationally in many strands of relationship building with the great communions of world Christianity. The most ancient of these are the Orthodox churches, and the influence of Greek patristic writers on the Wesleys established deep affinities between the theology of those Eastern Rite churches and Methodist theology. (These links have been explored in a number of major studies.) In 1990 the Ecumenical Patriarch Dimitrios I agreed, in principle, to a dialogue between Methodism and the Orthodox churches, and his successor Bartholomew I has sponsored the work of a Preparation Committee to meet three times in the first decade of the new millennium. This was but the first step in a lengthy journey, and the WMC affirmed in Brighton in 2001 its openness to future conversations.

From the Methodist point of view, in the modern period relations with the Roman Catholic Church have been both cordial and hopeful. Neither side has experienced the bitterness of direct schism from the other that is sometimes present in Anglican–Methodist conversations. Roman Catholics are in agreement with the Wesleyan emphasis on prevenient grace and the synergy of divine and human action in the process of salvation. As the first dialogue meeting between the WMC and the Pontifical Council for Promoting Christian Unity noted, there is a "central place held in both traditions of the ideal of personal sanctification, [and] growth in personal holiness through daily life in Christ." Historically much of this cordiality in Catholic–Methodist relations can be attributed to the pioneering work of Albert Outler who, as we have seen, served as a Protestant observer at the Second Vatican Council. Within the UMC, he helped forward the relationship with Roman Catholics by inspiring a successful "resolution of intent" at the 1970 General Conference. Outler cleared the way for a full-fledged Methodist–Roman Catholic dialogue by arguing that UMC doctrinal standards (such as Article 14 quoted on p. 247) should be interpreted "in consonance with our best ecumenical insights and judgment." There are, of course, places around the world where the relationship between the Roman Catholic Church and the national Methodist Church remains tense, and it was a Methodist bishop from Mexico who suggested at the WMC that the Ecumenical and Dialogue Committee should not be too sanguine about harmony where it does not exist. Nevertheless, the WMC remains committed to further explorations of Catholic–Methodist rapprochement.

The quest for renewed relationships with the Reformed churches (i.e. Presbyterians, Congregationalists, Disciples of Christ) has a deeply embedded ambiguity within it for Methodists. At the level of church administration there is normally no difficulty: churches in Reformed and Methodist traditions are already in a position mutually to recognize membership and ministry. From 1925, when the Methodists in Canada joined with Presbyterians and Congregationalists to form the United Church of Canada, there have been many instances of this kind of federal and organic union involving Methodists and Reformed churches, as happened in India, Zambia (the United Church, 1970), Australia (the Uniting Church, 1977), and Italy (1979). There is, however, the persistent theological problem of Calvinism against which the Wesleys inveighed long and hard. The characteristic response to this issue among those involved in the dialogue is to recall John Wesley's ascription of all the good in men and women to the free grace of God alone, and then to suggest that *both* traditions have tended to be too certain in their claim to knowledge of the ways and means of God. A humble reticence about such matters as election and predestination seems to be required on the part of both traditions.

Relations with the Lutheran churches have been the concern of Methodists both in the United States and in continental Europe. In the United States this results from an awareness of the considerable German heritage within the UMC, and in Europe the dominance of Lutheran state churches in Germany and the Scandinavian countries has made dialogue imperative. The Lutheran World Federation (LWF) and the WMC conducted bilateral conversations between 1977 and 1985, and concluded that there was sufficient agreement between Lutheranism and Methodism to allow several positive recommendations. These included "full fellowship of word and sacrament," and "common work in every place to manifest unity in witness and service." These recommendations have been particularly important for the UMC in Germany, where historically the Lutheran Church has had grave difficulties about intercommunion with Methodists. More recently the LWF and the Pontifical Council for Promoting Christian Unity have achieved a Joint Declaration on the Doctrine of Justification (December 1999). The Brighton meeting of the WMC in 2001 noted that the form of this agreement appeared to be compatible with Methodist Doctrinal Standards and that it looked forward to ways in which Methodist churches might become associated with what it called this "significant step towards fuller unity in the faith."

Along with high-level ecumenical conversations goes an unceasing commitment to local unity among Christians. The Methodist churches of Latin America are particularly notable for this kind of cooperation. For example, the Iglesia Evangelica Methodista in Argentina, a church with only 20,000 members, is active in thirty-three ecumenical projects; the Uruguayan Methodist Church, an even smaller community, provides leadership in such projects as the "Hospital Evangelico" and the formation of the YMCA, as well as allowing one of its ministers, Emilio Castro, to serve as general secretary of the WCC. Theological education remains an important sphere of ecumenical cooperation in which Methodists are heavily involved, as can be seen, for example, in St. Paul's College, Limaru, in Kenya; the United Theological College of Malaysia in Kuala Lumpur; the Ecumenical Theological College in Pilimatalawa in Sri Lanka, and the Pacific Theological College in Suva, Fiji.

In such ways the trajectories started by the theology of the Wesleys still impel Methodists to search for the unity among Christians that the fourth Gospel speaks of: "that they all may be one" in John 17:21.

METHODISM AND OTHER RELIGIOUS TRADITIONS

If Methodists have made disproportionate contributions in the search for Christian unity, the same can be said for Methodist leadership in the wider Christian search for interreligious understanding in the twentieth century. At each level of the churches' life, men and women nurtured in the traditions of Methodism have pioneered new understandings of the religious life of, and new relations with, people of non-Christian commitments. Methodists are everywhere to be found in national and international interreligious dialogues, in national and local interfaith councils, and in the scholarly work that supports these activities.

Very often Methodists have seemed to perceive the presence of God in places where others operating out of the European and North American cultural tradition see only heathenism and paganism. This can certainly be seen in the life and work of Edwin W. Smith (1876–1957). In 1936, Smith, a British Primitive Methodist missionary in Northern Rhodesia (today, Zambia), added to a long list of publications about African religion a volume called *African Belief and Christian Faith*. The title itself caused a contemporary European intellectual, who persisted in thinking of Africa as the "Dark Continent," to exclaim "How can untutored Africans conceive of God?" But Edwin Smith had insisted as early as the 1920s not only that Africans possess a profound understanding of God and God's purposes, but also that, as a result of their insights, they had much to contribute to Christian life and thought. Edwin Smith's influence crossed a number of academic frontiers, and he served as president of the Royal Anthropological Institute from 1933 to 1935, the only missionary and the only Methodist ever to have held this position. His achievement inspired the work of Geoffrey Parrinder (b. 1910), the immensely influential London University Professor of Comparative Religion, who laid the foundations of the current burgeoning of studies in African religion. In turn, Parrinder's attention to the religious lives of African people inspired the work of African Methodists like Bolaji Idowu and Egemba Igwe, both of Nigeria.

Like Edwin Smith, Parrinder served as a missionary in Africa, and elsewhere in the world many other Methodist missionaries pioneered the study of the great traditions of the people they were ostensibly sent to convert. In China, W. E. Soothill, a missionary of the UMFC, and Homer Dubs of the MECS, both so thoroughly learned the language and entered the Chinese thought-world that each became the Professor of Chinese in the University of Oxford. Contemporary Methodist exponents of Christian–Confucian understanding include Robert Neville of Boston University School of Theology and Peter Lee of Hong Kong.

In India, E. Stanley Jones (1884–1973) became a close friend of Gandhi and other leading figures in Indian politics and intellectual life, and was celebrated for his work in the "Round Table Conferences" and other early pioneering efforts in interfaith dialogue. His popular books on missionary work offered readers a more sensitive view of the religious life of the peoples who were the object of the Western evangelistic enterprise. More recently, scholars like David C. Scott of the UMC and Eric Lott and Roy Pape of the British Methodist Church have inspired a new generation of Indian theologians who are now taking a leading part in interfaith dialogue. Another important figure in Britain, particularly in Sikh–Christian understanding, is Inderjit Bhogal, who was president of the Methodist Conference in 2000.

Because of the history of political difficulties which the British and Americans had experienced in eastern Asia, an understanding of the issues of interfaith relations in the Buddhist context came later to Methodists than it did, for example, to Roman Catholics. But North American Methodist scholars like John B. Cobb, Jr., David Chapell, and Roy C. Amore and, in Britain, Elizabeth Harris have opened many avenues of mutual understanding. In a similar way, Methodists from both North America and Britain have also worked to build bridges with Muslims. Among them can be counted the American Murray Titus whose writings in the 1930s showed new directions through which such relations could come to fruition. In our own day the UMC scholar R. Marston Speight, and the English Methodist Martin Forward, now teaching in Chicago, have been key figures in increasing Christian–Muslim understanding. The urgency of this task is growing as the world comes to terms with the various political, social, and religious forces at work in the Muslim world after 9/11.

The history of Christian–Jewish rapprochement in the twentieth century is filled with Methodist names on both sides of the Atlantic. The British Council of Christians and Jews (CCJ) had as its founding general secretary in 1942 English Methodist minister William W. Simpson. Another Methodist minister, Peter Jennings, was secretary of the CCJ in the 1980s. In the United States leading post-Holocaust theologians like Franklin H. Littell and Roy and Alice Eckhart have been Methodists.

It is, however, within the circles of the WCC that we find the strongest and most persistent Methodist influence, chiefly within the Dialogue Sub Unit and more recently the Office of Interreligious Relations. Methodists who have worked in these circles include John Taylor and Kenneth Cracknell from England, Allen Brockway from the UMC, Wesley Ariarajah of the Sri Lankan Methodist Church, and the UMC laywoman and Harvard professor, Diana Eck. All of these acknowledge their debt to perhaps the greatest theorist of interfaith understanding of the last century, Wilfred Cantwell Smith (1916–2000). Smith was an ordained minister of the United Church of Canada, but owed his nurture in Christian faith to his Methodist mother, and the leading themes of faith and experience that emerge in his writings are distinctively Wesleyan.

Behind each of these figures stands a company of Methodist men and women who work in their local communities on these same issues of interreligious understanding, as well as the various boards and agencies within the Methodist churches around the globe which have given their official approval to interfaith activity. For the past several decades these groups have not only issued statements of support for the work of dialogue, but have provided extensive financial backing for interfaith work.

All this evidence invites the question: what impulses within the Wesleyan tradition have shaped the theology and spirituality of Methodist interreligious understanding? While in any given case these impulses are often complex and ambiguous, it is clear that the enthusiastic participation of Methodists in interfaith work takes its chief inspiration from significant aspects of Wesleyan thought: the repudiation of doctrines of election, the absorption of Enlightenment thinking, the emphasis on pragmatic common sense, the priority given to faith and experience over assent to prepositional doctrines, and above all the constant plea for the preeminence of love in all human relationships.

John Wesley's theology was worked out against the Latinate, Augustinian theologies of both the Catholic Church and the Protestant reformers. On the Catholic side there was the straightforward declaration that "there is no salvation outside the church" (*nulla salus extra ecclesiam*). The Council of Florence (1438–45) had declared that "none of those who are outside the Catholic church – not only pagans, but Jews also, heretics and schismatics – can have part in eternal life, but will go into eternal fire . . . unless they are gathered into that Church before the end of life." On the Protestant Reformation side, there was no salvation outside Christ. Martin Luther stated unequivocally that the "Christian faith is set apart from every other religion and faith of men – it makes all the others false and useless"; and that "all worship and religions outside Christ are the worship of idols," for "whatever is outside faith [*extra fidem*] is idolatry." Similarly, John Calvin asserted that none among the old philosophers ever merited divine favor, even though "the Lord has bestowed on them some slight perception of his Godhead that they might not plead ignorance as an excuse for their impiety." Calvin even thought that God might have occasionally instigated non-Christians to deliver some truths, the confession of which, however, would always be "to their own condemnation." In the hands of the hyper-Calvinists of the seventeenth century, Calvin's line of thinking established the doctrine of double predestination, and the Westminster Confession of Faith (1646) clearly maintains that "those not elected" cannot be saved, even though they may live within the Christian framework.

The Calvinist doctrines of limited atonement and double predestination were repugnant to the Wesleys, who countered them with his sense of the all-pervasiveness of grace. This took a Christological shape in the *Explanatory Notes on the New Testament*. When Wesley comments on the doctrine of the Logos (or "Word") that was with God in the beginning of creation, he insists that Christ enlightens everyone by "what is vulgarly called natural conscience, pointing out at least the general lines of good and evil." "And this light," Wesley continued, "if man did not hinder, would shine more and more to the perfect day." In his *Letter to John Mason* he affirmed that "No man living is without some preventing grace, and every degree of grace is a degree of life." This grace is not restricted to Christians, any more than it is limited to the means or channels of grace determined by the church. God, as he wrote in his sermon *The Means of Grace*, "is able to give the same grace, though there were no means on the face of the earth . . . since he is equally able to work whatsover pleaseth him by any or none at all." In Wesleyan understanding, prevenient grace is replete with divine intentionality. God is at work among all people at all times to save and deliver humankind. Wesley's view of the divine initiative in all spiritual paths understands that Christ is at work through the Holy Spirit in the action of prevenient grace and thus avoids any suggestion of the Pelagian heresy.

As a child of the Enlightenment John Wesley was deeply imbued with the early Romantic or "Rousseauesque" notion of the "noble savage." We can see this in his attitude toward his own mission to Georgia. On his way to the United States he told John Burton that he expected "to learn the true sense of the Gospel by preaching it to the heathen." Rather naively he added that those to whom he would be preaching are "as little children, humble, willing to learn, and eager to do the will of God." But despite all the harsh realities that challenged this simplistic view, some of Wesley's early belief in the innocence and goodness of others remained to the end. Wesley's Enlightenment point of view also enabled him to conceive that true spiritual insights were to be found in the "natural religion" of which he often spoke favorably. Thus in the *Explanatory Notes* on Acts 17:28, he comments specifically on the Hymn of Cleanthes to Jupiter or the Supreme Being (in this passage Paul is quoting the words from this or a similar poem: "in Him we live and move and have our being"). Wesley argues that this hymn is "one of the purest and finest pieces of natural religion in the whole world of pagan antiquity." He found similar evidence of true natural religion in at least one Islamic source. Wesley expressed his opinion on the religious significance of a Muslim writer in his sermon *On Faith*. Comparing this unknown author to ancient philosophers such as Cleanthes, Wesley declared:

we have great reason to hope, although they lived among heathens, yet were quite of another spirit; being taught of God, by his inward voice, all the essentials of true religion. Yea, and so was that Mohametan, and Arabian, who, a century or two ago, wrote the Life of Hai Ebn Yokton. The story seems to be feigned; but it contains all the principles of pure religion and undefiled.

What Wesley had read was a work of Islamic fiction, about a man who had been marooned on an island and left to fend for himself. In the process he worked out the essentials of Islam. (This work provided the inspiration for Daniel Defoe's *Robinson Crusoe*.) But the point that Wesley perceived was that the lone islander had taught himself the rudiments of theology: "the principles of pure religion and undefiled."

Providing a fitting complement to this generous theological under-standing was John Wesley's consistent application of "common sense" in discerning both the goodness outside Christianity and the wrong within it. This pragmatic approach was taken in Wesley's interpretation of the Bible as well as in his routine encounters with people who were other than Christians. There is a biblical example to be found in the *Explanatory Notes*, on Mark 9:39ff., where Wesley comments on the outrage of the disciples because they had found a man casting out demons in the name of Jesus. Wesley observed, "Christ here gives us a lovely example of candour and moderation. He was willing to put the best construction upon doubtful cases and treat as friends those who were not avowed enemies." From this incident Wesley infers that Methodists should not "discourage any man who brings sinners from the power of Satan to God, 'because he followeth not us,' in opinions, modes of worship, or anything else which does not affect the essence of religion."

Two examples of Wesley's ability to see evidence of the "essentials of pure religion" in others came in his encounters with Jewish people. His transatlantic missionary experience had left him lonely and despondent but there were Sephardic Jews in Savannah, and Wesley freely consorted with them. He reported in his *Journal* for April 3, 1737, "I began learning Spanish in order to converse with my Jewish parishioners, some of whom seem nearer to the mind that was in Christ than many of those who call him Lord." Thirty years later he could still be impressed by Jewish faith and practice. "I was desired," he writes in his *Journal* for February 23, 1769, "to hear Mr. Leoui sing at the Jewish synagogue. I never before saw a Jewish congregation behave so decently. Indeed the place itself is so solemn, that it might strike an awe upon those who have any thought of God."

Wesley wrote the sermon on the *Catholic Spirit* in Dublin with the hope that it might contribute to healing the division between people of differing Christian traditions. But the pattern of thought within the sermon can certainly be extended into interfaith understanding. Jehu and Jehonadab, the protagonists in the incident from which Wesley derived his text "If your heart is right with my heart, give thy hand" (2 Kings 10:15), were men of different faith commitments. The oddity of their encounter was not lost on Wesley, who considered it possible that many good men may "now also entertain peculiar opinions; and some of them may be as singular herein as even Jehonadab was." As we have seen, Wesley thought this was the inevitable consequence of "the present weakness and shortness of human understanding that different men will be of different minds in religion as well as in everyday life." Within certain parameters (in his eighteenth-century context, he is unable to push these boundaries beyond Christian forms of faith) there may be profound differences in doctrines, but the central and vital questions are not about right formulations, but about faith in and experience of God:

Dost thou believe his being and his perfections? his eternity, his immensity, wisdom, power, his justice, mercy, and truth? Dost thou believe that he now "upholdeth all things by the word of his power?" . . . Hast thou a divine evidence, a supernatural conviction of the things of God? Dost thou "walk by faith, not by sight" looking not at temporal things?

In the twentieth century Wesley's Methodist followers persisted in asking the same question, "Is your heart right with my heart?," but now they began to ask it of people of other faith traditions. Once they began to look across the borders between religions they found a world full of the kind of sincere faith and experience Wesley had described. Accordingly Methodists have set out on the path of interreligious dialogue with a profound sense of loyalty to their own tradition. As John Wesley had asked of them they have found their "hearts enlarged towards all mankind."

These themes, so central to the extensive Methodist involvement in interfaith dialogue, are all expressions of the universal love that Wesley enjoined on his people: it belongs to the essential character of the Methodist:

And remembering that God is love, he is conformed to the same likeness. He is full of love to his neighbour: of universal love not confined to one sect or party, nor restrained to those who agree with him in his opinions, or in outward modes of worship, or to those who are allied to him by blood or recommended by nearness of place.

In a muddled complicated world that is marked by religious and cultural tribalism such a vision motivates New Zealand Methodists to live creatively in the tension between the Tangata Whenua (the original people) and the Tauiwi (the people who came after), or the Uniting Church of Australia to engage with the ancient cultures of the Aborigines and Islanders. The groundswell among Asian and African, Pacific, and Latin American Methodist people to rediscover their ancient cultural and religious roots springs from the sense that God has been at work among all people from the beginning of creation. Korean theologian Hyun Younghak has stated this view admirably: "I do not believe in an invalid God who was carried piggy-back to Korea by some missionary. God was active in our history long before the missionaries came." Wesleyan theology, in both John Wesley and his recent followers, has much to contribute to this rediscovery.

Epilogue

At the beginning of this book, we encountered a group of worshipers at Wesley's Chapel in City Road, London, and we asked "What draws these people together? What allows them all to describe themselves as Methodists, despite their many differences?" Some of them represented independent Methodist churches, some were members of other denominations that trace their roots back to John and Charles Wesley, others were former Methodists whose churches have been absorbed within ecumenical mergers. They were a remarkably diverse congregation, racially, ethnically, economically, culturally. Part of the task of this book has been to give some account of how this astonishingly wide range of differences came into being. But at the core of our task has been the identification of the kinds of basic religious commitments and attitudes which Methodists share and to examine what the peculiarly Wesleyan way of being Christian entails.

But we are convinced that while these shared commitments and attitudes do indeed allow Methodists to claim a common identity, they also have certain distinctive and significant contributions to make in shaping the future of the global Christian family, its interrelationships, and its connections with the larger world. The religious climate within which contemporary Methodism is situated is a complex and ambiguous one. Clearly, as the twenty-first century begins, the churches find themselves in a kind of ecumenical doldrums: unity schemes have fallen into stagnation and gloomy predictions are made about the future of Christian unity. A mark of this pessimism can be seen in the serious decline in financial support for the World Council of Churches and national ecumenical bodies. At the same time, the "center of gravity" of Christian vitality has shifted from Europe and North America to Africa, Asia, South America and the Pacific region. Christians in many of these regions often struggle against poverty, oppression, and persecution in the context of politically unstable societies, and have little energy left over for what seems to be the comparative luxury of seeking Christian unity. Some older and established churches, experiencing a loss of confidence that parallels chronic losses of membership, are hanging on tenaciously to comforting structures and patterns, unwilling to risk the kinds of changes that ecumenism demands. In 1961, the WCC New Delhi Assembly put the matter sharply: "The achievement of church unity will involve nothing less than a death and rebirth of many forms of church life as we have known them. We believe that nothing less costly can suffice." Many churches would now say that such a cost is simply too high.

At the same time, much if not most of the world's political and social volatility has a significant religious component. The various forms of fundamentalism and radicalism, the disputes between religious groups and subgroups within national borders, and the varied theological interpretations given to historical events contribute to a situation in which "the other" is often demonized and mutual suspicion between and among religious communities reigns. Exacerbating this situation is the ever increasing economic disparity between wealthy nations and developing nations, and between rich and poor within all nations. And so we ask: are there aspects of the Methodist approach to faith and life that might contribute to finding solutions to these seemingly intractable problems?

Throughout their lives, John and Charles Wesley were engaged in a struggle against the notion that God's love was restricted to only a certain portion of humanity, and that some men and women had been predestined to eternal salvation and others to eternal damnation. In hymn after hymn and sermon after sermon, their emphasis lay on God's "everlasting love" embodied in Jesus Christ, and on the "immense, unfathom'd, unconfined" mercy of God. The Wesleys and their preachers were intensely, and perhaps uniquely, aware of the fearsome pastoral consequences of teaching divine reprobation, and the harm that would be done should men and women come to believe that they were eternally damned. The doctrinal implications were equally unsettling. To teach the predestination of some to damnation was a blasphemous affront of the divine name and nature, since the ultimate conclusion to be drawn from placing a limitation on the redemptive love of God is that "God is hate" and that anger belonged to God's essence.

Certainly one of Methodism's singular contributions to the trials of the contemporary church and world is this core doctrine of God's "pure, universal love." This doctrine undoubtedly gives comfort to all those who have been damaged by preaching and spiritual counsel that has led them to believe that they are beyond the love of God. But, even more importantly, it offers a profound challenge to those who believe themselves to be on the "winning side" of the divine economy, those who think that they are special to God. This attitude, which is certainly not unique to Christianity, often leads to arrogance and intolerance toward those who do not belong within their theological framework. The political implications of this exclusivist view are obvious; it is an easy step from proclaiming that God's favor is restricted to the group to which one belongs to declaring that God "hates" other groups. Although voices alleging this kind of divine "hatred" have always been present within religious groups, the interconnectedness of humanity in the twenty-first century makes exclusivist commitments a danger to global survival.

Methodists on both sides of the Atlantic have always been convinced that they have been raised up, in the words of John Wesley, "to spread scriptural holiness through their lands," and a second attitude that Wesleyans carry with them into the world is the strong sense of the unlimited possibilities for the transformation of both individuals and human societies. Unlike those Christians who are convinced that the world is "fallen," that it is irredeemably opposed to the purposes of God, Methodists persist in believing that human systems, institutions, and structures can indeed be vehicles through which God's will is done "on earth as it is in heaven." Because of this kind of pragmatic optimism, Methodists enter every situation deeply committed to the idea that through the cooperative action between the grace of God and the work of human hands the evils of the world can be confronted and overcome. This provides a necessary corrective to all those who are tempted to give up on the world, to leave it to its own devices and to wait to be extracted from it into some kind of otherworldly salvation.

From the very beginning, Methodists have been convinced that obedience to the redemptive and reconciling mission of God takes precedence over all externally imposed demands and limitations. When John Wesley declared that "the world is my parish" and that despite official, ecclesiastical restriction on his movements he was compelled wherever he found himself "to declare unto all who are willing to hear it the glad tidings of salvation," he set the pattern for his followers' approach to the relationship between the church and the world. For Christians tempted to take a triumphalist attitude toward the church, to view the church as the ultimate goal of all God's saving activity, the Wesleyan understanding of all ecclesial structures as servants of the wider purposes of God is a helpful and necessary challenge. The willingness of Methodists to enter into ecumenical mergers for the sake of a common witness to the Gospel, to engage in dialogue across faith boundaries for the sake of doing the common work of love and charity, and to seek out areas of agreement instead of highlighting areas of conflict provides a much needed model for the ways in which people might put aside their divisions for the accomplishment of some higher purpose. If there is ever to be global peace and harmony, these deeply held Wesleyan attitudes must be more widely adopted.

Of course these themes are not unique to Methodism; many Christians recognize and claim these points of view. Conversely, many Methodists and communities of Methodists may have been disconnected from them in the course of their variegated histories. There is no Methodist "superstructure" or "Supreme Governor" to impose these attitudes on all Methodist Christians; nor is there any set of sanctions imposed upon Methodists who might fail to recognize themselves in the description presented in these pages. But generations of Methodists have believed that carrying forward these values is their particular calling, and that by faithfully declaring, in word and in action, the universal love of God, the perfectability of the world, and the subservience of institutional Christianity to the redemptive purposes of God, they are contributing to the health and wellbeing of the world.

Further reading

We offer here a brief guide to further reading. A much fuller resource is available at http://www.brite.tcu.edu/directory/cracknell where there are detailed references to the sources of quotations and ideas set out in the previous pages. In addition to listing the books we have used, we also offer detailed bibliographical guidance to areas and topics we have barely been able to touch upon in this introduction to world Methodism. By using the internet in this way we hope to keep the information up to date.

GENERAL

There are two indispensable recent dictionaries of Methodism. For the British tradition John A. Vickers has edited *A Dictionary of Methodism in Britain and Ireland* (Epworth Press, 2000), and for the USA there is the *Historical Dictionary of Methodism* edited by Charles Yrigoyen, Jr., and Susan E. Warrick (Scarecrow Press, 1996). Older and larger dictionaries are now very much out of date as a guide to the contemporary shape of world Methodism, but *The Encyclopedia of World Methodism*, sponsored by the World Methodist Council and the Commission on Archives and History of the United Methodist Church with Nolan B. Harmon as its general editor, published by Abingdon Press (1974), has much valuable historical material.

There are some notable journals: in the USA the UMC General Board of Higher Education and Ministry publishes the *Quarterly Review: A Journal of Theological Resources for Ministry*; and the General Commission on Archives and History publishes *Methodist History*. All the Methodist traditions have a forum in the *Wesleyan Theological Journal*, the bulletin of the Wesleyan Theological Society. In Britain the *Epworth Review*, published by the Methodist Publishing House, is the main forum for Methodist thinking. There are many other similar resources in Methodist churches through the world that the internet will help identify.

CHAPTER 1: THE BEGINNING OF WORLD METHODISM: JOHN WESLEY AND HIS MOVEMENT

For assistance in getting a sense of John Wesley and his movement there are some first-rate resources. For John Wesley's life Richard P. Heitzenrater offers detailed and accurate information on every aspect of the early development of Methodism in *Wesley and the People Called Methodists* (Abingdon Press, 1995), which is frequently reprinted. The British scholar Henry Rack's *Reasonable Enthusiast: John Wesley and the Rise of Methodism* is now in its third edition, published in the UK by Epworth Press (2002) and in the USA by Trinity Press International (2002). Rack's particular strength is to place Wesley against the social, political, and religious influences of his time. Briefer treatments of Wesley and the rise of Methodism are also available. Two by British scholars can be particularly recommended: John H. S. Kent, *Wesley and the Wesleyans* (Cambridge University Press, 2002), and John Munsey Turner, *John Wesley: The Evangelical Revival and the Rise of Methodism in England* (Epworth Press, 2002). A couple of bigger books also place the Wesleyan revival in the wider context of what was happening throughout Europe: *The Protestant Evangelical Awakening*, by W. R. Ward (Cambridge University Press, 1992) and Ted Campbell, *The Religion of the Heart: A Study of European Religious Life in the Seventeenth and Eighteenth Centuries* (University of South Carolina Press, 1991). In 1964 Albert C. Outler published a lavish selection of Wesley's works, together with a sparkling commentary, in the Oxford University Press Library of Christian Thought series. Entitled *John Wesley*, it has never since been out of print. This volume heralded the indispensable scholarly edition of the works of John Wesley: begun as *The Oxford Edition of the Works of John Wesley* published by the Clarendon Press (1975–83), it continued from 1984 as *The Bicentennial Edition of the Works of John Wesley* published by the Abingdon Press. So far fifteen of the thirty-five projected volumes have been published. They are: volumes I–IV, *Sermons*, edited by Albert C. Outler, and published between 1984 and 1987; volume VII, *A Collection of Hymns for the use of the People called Methodists*, edited by Franz Hildebrandt and Oliver A. Beckerlegge, with assistance from James Dale (1983); volume IX, *Methodist Societies: History, Nature, and Design*, edited by Rupert E. Davies (1989); volume XI, *The Appeals to Men of Reason and Religion, and Certain Related Open Letters*, edited by Gerald Cragg (1975); volumes XVIII–XXIII, *Journal and Diaries*, edited by W. Reginald Ward and Richard P. Heitzenrater (1988–95); and volumes XXV–XXVI, *Letters*, edited by Frank Baker (1980–2). Other writings of John Wesley that have not had the benefit of recent scholarly attention are to be found in *The Works of John Wesley*, edited by Thomas Jackson in fourteen volumes (1829–31) and frequently reprinted. The Jackson volumes were republished by Hendrickson Publishers in 1984. For Charles Wesley a very convenient source is *Charles Wesley: A Reader*, edited by John R. Tyson (Oxford University Press, 1989), and Kenneth G. C. Newport has edited *The Sermons of Charles Wesley* (Oxford University Press, 2001). Also very useful is *Charles Wesley: Poet and Theologian*, edited by S. T. Kimbrough, Jr. (Kingswood Books, 1992). Two excellent biographies take us into the life and thought of John Wesley's most important colleagues: John A. Vickers, *Thomas Coke: Apostle of Methodism* (Epworth Press, 1969) and Laurence W. Wood, *The Meaning of Pentecost in Early Methodism: Rediscovering John Fletcher as John Wesley's Vindicator and Designated Successor* (Scarecrow Press, 2002).

CHAPTER 2: THE BRITISH METHODIST TRADITION AFTER
JOHN WESLEY

The History of Methodism in Great Britain, in four volumes, edited by Rupert E. Davies, A. Raymond George, and E. Gordon Rupp (Epworth Press, 1964–88), is the standard work. The last volume is of special importance, since it contains documents and source material edited by John A. Vickers and an exhaustive bibliography up to 1988 compiled by Clive D. Field. Specialist works on Wesleyan Methodism after John Wesley's death include John C. Bowmer's *Pastor and People: A Study of Church and Ministry in Wesleyan Methodism from the Death of John Wesley (1791) to the Death of Jabez Bunting (1858)* (Epworth Press, 1975), John Kent's *The Age of Disunity* (Epworth Press, 1966), and John Munsey Turner's *Conflict and Reconciliation: Studies in Methodism and Ecumenism in England, 1740–1982* (Epworth Press, 1986). Books on Primitive Methodism include Julia Stewart Werner's *The Primitive Methodist Connexion: Its Background and Early History* (University of Wisconsin Press, 1984). Rewarding books about the social impact of Primitive Methodism include Robert Moore, *Pit-Men, Preachers and Politics: The Effects of Methodism in a Durham Mining Community* (Cambridge University Press, 1974) and R. W. Ambler, *Ranters, Revivalists and Reformers: Primitive Methodism and Rural Society in South Lincolnshire 1817–1875* (Hull University Press, 1989). From the enormous wealth of secondary sources we select just some that point to further reading. There is a cluster of books that deal with the wider questions of Methodism's influence on British society in the nineteenth century. Bernard Semmel translated and edited Elie Halévy's *The Birth of Methodism in England* (University of Chicago Press, 1971), and made his own contribution to the debate in *The Methodist Revolution* (Basic Books, 1973). Detailed studies of Methodism and society are found in two works by David Hempton, *Methodism and Politics in British Society, 1750–1850* (Stanford University Press, 1984) and *The Religion of the People: Methodism and Popular Religion c. 1750–1900* (Routledge, 1996). Three older works by Robert F. Wearmouth, *Methodism and the Working-Class Movements of England, 1800–1850* (Epworth Press, 1947), *Methodism and the Struggle of the Working Classes, 1850–1900* (E. Backus, 1954), and *Methodism and the Trade Unions* (Epworth Press, 1959) remain important. For an overview of the later part of the nineteenth century and the early twentieth century see Dale A. Johnson, *The Changing Shape of English Nonconformity, 1825–1925* (Oxford University Press, 1999). Two recent full-scale biographies that take us into the issues confronting the Wesleyan Methodists at the end of the nineteenth century are Christopher Oldstone-Moore's *Hugh Price Hughes: Founder of a New Methodism, Conscience of a New Nonconformity* (University of Wales Press, 1999), and Alan Turberfield's *John Scott Lidgett: Archbishop of British Methodism* (Epworth Press, 2003).

CHAPTER 3: METHODISM IN NORTH AMERICA

The first resource to cite here is *The Methodists* by James E. Kirby, Russell E. Richey, and Kenneth E. Rowe (Praeger, 1998). These three authors focus on "three ways in which Methodism has continuously constructed and reconstructed itself," dealing particularly with the bishops, the Conferences and the discipleship of American Methodists. There is detailed bibliographical information on pp. 261–71. For an introductory guide see *United Methodism in America: A Compact History*, edited by John G. McEllhenney, with Charles Yrigoyen Jr. and Kenneth Rowe (Abingdon Press, 1992). A larger widely used general history is *The Story of American Methodism: A History of United Methodists and their Relations*, by Frederick A. Norwood (Abingdon Press, 1974), together with *A Sourcebook of American Methodism*, edited by Norwood (Abingdon Press, 1982). *The People(s) called Methodist: Forms and Reforms of their Life*, edited by W. B. Lawrence, D. Campbell, and R. Richey (Abingdon Press, 1998), contains essays on many aspects of American Methodism. The earliest period was extensively studied by Frank Baker, *John Wesley and the Church of England* (Abingdon Press, 1970) and *From Wesley to Asbury: Studies in Early American Methodism* (Duke University Press, 1976) and his work has not been superseded. Russell E. Richey, *Early American Methodism* (Indiana University Press, 1991), has important insights. In recent years a distinguished cluster of scholars have set early American Methodism in its various historical contexts, according it a decisive role in the new republic; see Nathan O. Hatch, *The Democratization of American Christianity* (Yale University Press, 1989), frequently reprinted; Dee A. Andrews, *The Methodists and Revolutionary America, 1760–1800: The Shaping of an Evangelical Culture* (Princeton University Press, 2000); Nathan O. Hatch, and John H. Wigger (eds.), *Methodism and the Shaping of American Culture* (Abingdon Press, 2000); John H. Wigger, *Taking Heaven by Storm: Methodism and the Rise of Popular Christianity in America* (Oxford University Press, 1998); Richard J. Cardwardine, *Evangelicals and Politics in Antebellum America* (Yale University Press, 1993) and the same author's *Transatlantic Revivalism: Popular Evangelicalism in Britain and America 1790–1865* (Greenwood Press, 1977), which links the two Methodist traditions. There are many specialist studies of the Methodist denominations and many of them are listed in the extended references on the website http://www.brite.tcu.edu/directory/cracknell.

CHAPTER 4: WORLD METHODISM AT THE BEGINNING OF THE
TWENTY-FIRST CENTURY

We have used the World Methodist Council's *Handbook of Information, 2002–6*, revised edition published by the WMC, 573 N. Lakeshore Drive, Lake Junaluska, North Carolina, 28745, USA for statistics on the Methodist churches of the world. The reports of the meetings of the WMC are also good sources of information about the state of world Methodism. The latest is entitled *Jesus Christ: God's Way of Salvation*, published by the WMC in 2002. The older mission histories are still a primary source up to the dates in which they were published. There is the four-volume *History of Methodist Missions* by Wade Crawford Barclay, published by the Board of Missions and Church Extension of the Methodist Church (1949–75). For British Methodism there is a summary article on "Methodist Missions" by Allen Birtwhistle in *The History of Methodism in Great Britain*, edited by Rupert E. Davies, A. Raymond George, and E. Gordon Rupp (Epworth Press, 1983), vol. III, pp. 1–116. For the Irish story see Norman W. Taggart, *The Irish in World Methodism*,

1760–1900 (Epworth, 1986). To trace the history of Canadian Methodism see *A History of the Christian Church in Canada*, general editor, John Webster Grant (McGraw-Hill Ryerson, 1966–72), and for a reflection on what has happened since union in 1925 see *The Churches and the Canadian Experience: A Faith and Order Study of the Christian Tradition*, also edited by John Webster Grant (Ryerson Press, 1963). For a recent treatment of Methodism throughout the world, see *The Global Impact of the Wesleyan Traditions and their Related Movements*, edited by Charles Yrigoyen, Jr. (Scarecrow Press, 2002). For a spirited account of the changes taking place in world Christianity, see *The Next Christendom: The Coming of Global Christianity* by Philip Jenkins (Oxford University Press, 2002).

CHAPTER 5: METHODIST THEOLOGY

A very usable recent Methodist "systematic theology" is *Living Grace: An Outline of Methodist Theology* (Abingdon Press, 2001), the English translation of the 1993 German work, *Gelebte Gnade: Grundriss einer Theologie der Evangelisch-methodisten Kirche* by Walter Klaiber and Manfred Marquardt. Important studies to enable the student to go deeper include Randy L. Maddox, *Responsible Grace: John Wesley's Practical Theology* (Kingswood, 1994); Theodore Runyon, *The New Creation: John Wesley's Theology Today* (Abingdon Press, 1998). Pioneering works on the Wesleyan theological renaissance were Colin W. Williams, *John Wesley's Theology for Today* (Abingdon Press and Epworth Press, 1960) and Albert Outler's two stimulating monographs: *Evangelism in the Wesleyan Spirit* and *Theology in the Wesleyan Spirit*, recently republished in one volume as *Evangelism and Theology in the Wesleyan Spirit*, by Discipleship Resources (1996). Also useful is John B. Cobb Jr., *Grace and Responsibility: A Wesleyan Theology for Today* (Abingdon Press, 1995). A sample of the discussions that have been taking place in the Oxford Institutes of Theological Studies is M. Douglas Meeks (ed.), *The Future of the Wesleyan Theological Tradition* (Abingdon Press, 1985). A close study of why there had to be a rediscovery of Wesleyan theology is Robert E. Chiles, *Theological Development in American Methodism, 1790–1935* (University Press of America, 1984). Three books by Thomas Langford are also significant sources for understanding Methodist theology: *Practical Divinity: Theology in the Wesleyan Tradition* (Abingdon Press, 1983), *Wesleyan Theology: A Source Book* (Labyrinth, 1984), and *Doctrine and Theology in the United Methodist Church* (Kingswood Books, 1991). Note also Kenneth Collins, *The Scripture Way of Theology: The Heart of John Wesley's Theology* (Abingdon Press, 1997). From the wider family of Methodism is the Irish Church of the Nazarene theologian Herbert Boyd McGonigle's thorough study *Sufficient Saving Grace: John Wesley's Evangelical Arminianism* (Paternoster Press, 2001) and two books by Donald W. Dayton, *Discovering an Evangelical Heritage* (Harper and Row, 1976) and *The Theological Roots of Pentecostalism* (Scarecrow Press, 1987).

CHAPTER 6: THE COMMON LIFE OF METHODISM

Leslie Church's two books, *The Early Methodist People* (Epworth Press, 1948) and *More About the Early Methodist People* (Epworth Press, 1949), are primary quarries of information about the early days of Methodism. David Lowes Watson is the best guide to the societies, classes, and bands of early Methodism in his *The Early Methodist Class Meeting: Its Origins and Significance* (Discipleship Resources, 1985). The role of the women preachers and class leaders is ably dealt with by Paul Chilcote in *John Wesley and the Women Preachers of Methodism* (Scarecrow Press, 1993) and *She Offered them Christ: The Legacy of Women Preachers in Early Methodism* (Abingdon Press, 1993). For current thinking about the structures of Methodism, see, for North America and the UMC throughout the world, Thomas Edward Frank, *Polity, Practice, and the Mission of The United Methodist Church* (Abingdon Press, 2000), and for the British view, David C. Carter, *Love Bade Me Welcome: A British Methodist Perspective on the Church* (Epworth Press, 2002).

CHAPTER 7: METHODIST SPIRITUALITY

Consult first Gordon S. Wakefield, *Methodist Spirituality* (Epworth Press, 1999), much of which is an updating of an earlier work by the same author, *Methodist Devotion: The Spiritual Life in the Methodist Tradition, 1791–1945* (Epworth Press, 1966). A different treatment of Methodist spirituality is in E. Brooks Holifield, *Health and Medicine in the Methodist Tradition: Journey toward Wholeness* (Crossroad, 1986). An excellent way into the spirituality of the Holiness movement is in *Phoebe Palmer: Selected Writings*, edited by Thomas C. Oden (Paulist Press, 1988) (one of the Sources of American Spirituality Series), and there is a study by Harold E. Raser, *Phoebe Palmer, Her Life and Thought* (Edward Mellen Press, 1987). A helpful book that illuminates Methodist spirituality by comparing it with another tradition is *Orthodox and Wesleyan Spirituality*, edited by S. T. Kimbrough, Jr. and published by the St. Vladimir's Seminary Press (2002). The chapter on Methodism in Frank Senn's *Protestant Spiritual Traditions* (Paulist Press, 1986) is also useful.

CHAPTER 8: METHODIST WORSHIP

This topic is treated not only in more general studies of Methodism on both sides of the Atlantic and worldwide, but also in a variety of special studies. Older books by John S. Bowmer, *The Sacrament of the Lord's Supper in Early Methodism* (Dacre Press, 1951), and *The Lord's Supper in Methodism, 1791–1960* (Epworth Press, 1961), and Trevor Dearing, *Wesleyan and Tractarian Worship* (Epworth Press, 1966), offer insights into the centrality of eucharistic worship in early British Methodism that may be compared with the North American experience described in Karen B. Westerfield Tucker's more recent full study in *American Methodist Worship* (Oxford University Press, 2001). More specialized studies include Frank Baker's *Methodism and the Love-Feast* (Macmillan, 1957); David Tripp's *The Renewal of the Covenant in the Methodist Tradition* (Epworth Press, 1969); and Lester Ruth, *A Little Heaven Below: Worship at Early Methodist Quarterly Meetings* (Kingswood Books, 2000). James F. White's edition of *The Sunday Service for the Methodists in North America* (1784) was published as a special issue of the *Quarterly Review* in 1984 and provides a full text and notes to that central document for understanding the mind of John Wesley in matters of worship. The importance of Methodist hymnody for Methodist worship and theology is discussed by J. Ernest Rattenbury in two books: *The Evangelical Doctrines of Charles Wesley's Hymns* (Epworth Press, 1942) and *The Eucharistic Hymns of John and Charles Wesley* (Epworth Press, 1948). There is a revised edition of the latter published by the Order of St. Luke Publications, Cleveland, Ohio (1990). The special emphases of African-American Methodists are treated by William B. McClain in *Come Sunday: The Liturgy of Zion* (Abingdon Press, 1990). A sense of world Methodist styles of worship can be gained from *The Sunday Service of the Methodists: Twentieth-Century Worship in Worldwide Methodism: Studies in Honor of James F. White* edited by Karen B. Westerfield Tucker (Kingswood Books, 1996).

CHAPTER 9: METHODIST SOCIAL ETHICS

Perhaps the most prominent area in which the Methodist theological renaissance is playing itself out is social ethics. We have fine studies of John Wesley's convictions about social issues in Manfred Marquardt, *John Wesley's Social Ethics: Praxis and Principles* (Abingdon Press, 1992), Theodore Runyon, *The New Creation: John Wesley's Theology Today* (Abingdon Press, 1998), and Theodore R. Weber, *Politics in the Order of Salvation: Transforming Wesleyan Political Ethics* (Kingswood Books, 2001), and many vigorous books challenging contemporary Methodists to take up social ethics in a Wesleyan spirit: Theodore Runyon (ed.), *Sanctification and Liberation: Liberation Theologies in Light of the Wesleyan Tradition* (Abingdon Press, 1981); M. Douglas Meeks, *God the Economist: The Doctrine of God and Political Economy* (Fortress Press, 1989), and, edited by Meeks, *Trinity, Community, and Power: Mapping Trajectories in Wesleyan Theology* (Kingswood Books, 2000); Theodore W. Jennings Jr., *Good News to the Poor: John Wesley's Evangelical Economics* (Abingdon Press, 1990); Richard P. Heitzenrater (ed.), *The Poor and the People called Methodists* (Kingswood Books, 2002); and Joerg Rieger and John Vincent (eds.), *Methodist and Radical: Rejuvenating a Tradition* (Kingswood Books, 2003). An example of a South American Methodist biblical scholar rereading the Bible in this tradition is Elsa Tamez, *The Scandalous Message of James: Faith without Works is Dead* (Crossroad, 2002). Useful historical material on special topics can be found in Warren Thomas Smith, *John Wesley and Slavery* (Abingdon Press, 1986); D. Stephen Long, *Living the Discipline: United Methodist Theological Reflections on War, Civilization and Holiness* (Eerdmans, 1992); and Paul Ramsey, with an epilogue by Stanley Hauerwas, *Speak up for Just War or Pacifism: A Critique of the United Methodist Bishops' Pastoral Letter "In Defence of Creation"* (University of Pennsylvania Press, 1988). For historical material there is Walter G. Muelder, *Methodism and Society in the Twentieth Century*, edited by the Board of Social and Economic Relations of the Methodist Church (Abingdon Press, 1961), with a convenient summary by Georgia Harkness, *The Methodist Church in Social Thought and Action*, edited by the Board of Social and Economic Relations of the Methodist Church (Abingdon Press, 1964). The British Methodist Church has convenient collections in *Declarations on Social Questions* (Epworth Press, 1959); *Declarations and Statements on Social Responsibility* (Methodist Publishing House, 1981);

and *Statements on Social Responsibility 1946–1995* (Methodist Publishing House 1995).

Albert C. Outler's two contributions to ecumenical theology, *The Christian Tradition and the Unity We Seek* (Oxford University Press, 1957) and *That the World May Believe: A Study of Christian Unity* (Board of Missions of the Methodist Church, 1966), make good starting points to go further into Methodist understanding of ecumenical work. *Methodism's Destiny in an Ecumenical Age*, edited by Paul M. Minus, Jr. (Abingdon Press, 1969), also sets out some of the dreams of a new world church after the Second Vatican Council. A volume of essays about Outler's ecumenical drive is *Albert Outler: The Churchman*, edited by Bob W. Parrott (Bristol House, 1995). Geoffrey Wainwright, *Methodists in Dialog* (Kingswood, 1995), presents an honest picture of Methodist activity in the last four decades, as well as sharing his own insights into the growth of understanding between separated traditions. For J. R. Mott's leadership see C. Howard Hopkins, *John R. Mott, 1865–1955: A Biography* (Eerdmans, 1979). For the commitment to new religious understanding there is a cluster of books by Methodist men and women who are deeply involved: John B. Cobb, Jr., *Christ in a Pluralistic Age* (Westminster Press, 1975); Kenneth Cracknell, *Towards a New Relationship: Christians and People of other Faith* (Epworth Press, 1986), Diana L. Eck, *Encountering God: A Spiritual Journey from Bozeman to Banaras* (Beacon Press, 1993), and S. Wesley Ariarajah, *Not Without My Neighbour: Issues in Interfaith Relations* (WCC Publications, 1999). A major influence upon these writers was the "Methodist" from the United Church of Canada, Wilfred Cantwell Smith, and a good way into his work is *Wilfred Cantwell Smith: a Reader*, edited by Kenneth Cracknell (Oneworld, 2001). Pentecostalist theologians aware of their Methodist heritage are also beginning to contribute to this discussion. One such writer is Amos Yong in *Beyond the Impasse: Toward a Pneumatological Theology of Religions* (Paternoster/Baker Academic, 2003).

General index

Index of names